KT-492-828

Ethical
Business

LINDA FERRELL & O.C. FERRELL

London, New York,
Munich, Melbourne, Delhi

Senior Editor Peter Jones
Senior Art Editor Helen Spencer
Production Editor Ben Marcus
Production Controller Hema Gohil
Executive Managing Editor Adèle Hayward
Managing Art Editor Kat Mead
Art Director Peter Luff
Publisher Stephanie Jackson

Produced for Dorling Kindersley Limited by

cobaltid

The Stables, Wood Farm, Deopham Road,
Attleborough, Norfolk NR17 1AJ
www.cobaltid.co.uk

Editors Kati Dye, Maddy King,
Marek Walisiewicz
Designers Paul Reid, Lloyd Tilbury

First published in 2009 by
Dorling Kindersley Limited
80 Strand
London WC2R 0RL
A Penguin Company

2 4 6 8 10 9 7 5 3 1

Copyright © 2009
Dorling Kindersley Limited
All rights reserved

No part of this publication may be reproduced,
stored in a retrieval system, or transmitted in any
form or by any means, electronic, mechanical,
photocopying, recording, or otherwise, without
the prior written permission of the copyright owner.

A CIP catalogue record for this book
is available from the British Library.

ISBN 978-1-4053-3543-0

Colour reproduction by
Colourscan, Singapore
Printed in China by WKT

See our complete catalogue at

www.dk.com

Contents

CHAPTER 3

Implementing an ethics programme

CHAPTER 4

Looking beyond your organization

Introduction

Unlike at any other time in our history, business ethics today have a real impact upon each and every one of us. From times of financial crisis to the daily organizational decision-making that creates our work environments, business ethics matter.

The subject of business ethics has moved from the philosopher's study to the boardroom. Ethics are incorporated into every aspect of business strategy and decision-making, and running an ethical business is no longer the province of a few well-meaning individuals, but the essence of sustainable success.

Ethical Business addresses the complex environment of ethical decision-making in today's organizations, large and small. It makes a sound business case for implementing ethical policies and identifies real-life issues, areas of risk, and choices that every company faces in a time of intense scrutiny by media and stakeholders. It looks at the responsibilities of leaders, managers, and employees to their organization, the environment, and wider society and provides a practical introduction to ethics that will enhance corporate achievement and career advancement.

Chapter 1

Understanding business ethics

Understanding what is right or wrong and acceptable or unacceptable based on organizational and societal expectations constitutes business ethics. It is an area that will shape business activity ever more in the 21st century.

Succeeding through ethics

Ethics is a broad area, encompassing diverse business activities – from maintaining work–life balance to assessing the impacts of globalization. In today's business environment, the active management of ethical risks will steer your organization away from crises and boost financial success.

ASK YOUR EMPLOYER

When looking for a job, make sure to ask during your interview about the company's ethics programme. The response you receive will speak volumes about the culture of the organization.

Managing risks

Business ethics is all about managing risks. For example, if you are a human resource manager, you will be concerned with hiring practices, termination processes, and record keeping. If you work in marketing you will deal with honesty in advertising, integrity in the sales force, and products that function effectively. If your role is in finance, you will be held responsible for providing accurate and truthful information. Without precise risk identification, proper training, strong leadership, and support for ethical conduct, wrongdoing can and will occur in an organization.

Building ethics into the business

Business ethics are distinct from personal ethics. Personal values, such as honesty and fairness, are important in ethical decision-making at work, but they are just one of the elements that guide the actions and strategies of organizations. Business decisions involve complex economic, legal, and social considerations and it takes years of experience in an industry to understand the risks and expected conduct.

Good businesses have robust ethics programmes that run alongside other quality-management systems. They have a set of bedrock principles that guide behaviour, and processes for ensuring that these principles are implemented. For example, one of a company's principles may be never to lie to customers and suppliers; this may be supported with zero tolerance for abuse. At the heart of success is strong leadership of enlightened employees, who have been trained to understand the risks associated with their jobs and how to deal with "grey areas".

PROVIDE STRONG GUIDANCE

Hiring good people puts you on the road to having an ethical organization, but it's not enough on its own. Individuals require strong leadership and encouragement to maintain standards.

GETTING THE BASICS RIGHT

FAST TRACK	OFF TRACK
Focusing on shared ethical principles	Focusing only on individual values
Creating an ethical culture within the organization	Making uncoordinated ethical decisions
Providing strong ethical leadership	Expecting good conduct to spring from the bottom up
Making ethics an ongoing concern within the organization	Addressing issues only as they arise

Setting principles and values

Principles are the foundation of our social existence. They are law-like statements that provide guidance and direction for behaviour, and relate to issues such as fairness, equity, justice, duty, and liberty. Values, on the other hand, are more related to choice. They are enduring beliefs, shared by members of an organization, that establish what is right and wrong.

Understanding principles

Principles are the true north on the ethical business compass – they are self-evident, self-validating, natural laws that do not shift or change. They get in the way of "rule bending" and are key to maintaining an ethical organizational culture. Crucially, they provide guidance for decision-makers who need to address situations that they may not have faced before. Principles help structure relationships, communication, customs, habits, and ultimately the civility that is shown to all stakeholders.

"We will not give or accept bribes to obtain or retain business."

PRINCIPLES
- universal and absolute
- specific boundaries that must be respected
- used to develop rules
- valued across cultures

"We will conduct all our business with fairness, honesty, and integrity."

"We will offer equal opportunities for all employees, regardless of age, race, or physical ability."

Defining values

Values in business differ from principles in that they are based on the choices made by leaders, external constituents, or the organizational culture. Values are subjective and internal, but develop from our experience of the social environment and the influence of institutions such as schools, universities, religions, and governments. Ethical values relate to areas such as social responsibility, loyalty, and accountability; while business values relate to areas such as competitiveness, innovation, and profitability.

Most larger companies express their values publically in their corporate communications, such as websites and reports: Boeing, for example, espouses business values such as customer satisfaction and quality, but also ethical values such as integrity, diversity, and good corporate citizenship. To make the values more operative, Boeing has a 45-page *Ethical Business Conduct* document to further guide employee behaviour. This document covers most ethical risks for the company.

VALUES
- relate to choice
- used to develop norms
- subjective
- apply to daily decisions
- vary across cultures

"We should keep our promises and maintain our commitments."

"We should contribute to the achievement and well-being of co-workers."

"We should accept personal accountability for our own actions."

Setting out responsibilities

A business doesn't exist in a vacuum. Everything it does has implications for shareholders, workers, the community, and the economy as a whole. The responsibilities businesses owe to society fit into four categories: economic, legal, ethical, and philanthropic, and when businesses fail to address them, conflicts can occur.

TIP

ACT EARLY
Tackle difficult behaviour as soon as it becomes evident – the longer you leave it, the harder it becomes to cope with, and it may affect other members of the team.

Seeing beyond revenue

The notion that a business has a responsibility only to its shareholders was succeeded in the late 20th century by a far broader view of corporate responsibility. Today, maintaining ethical standards and creating a positive rapport with the community is a central part of any firm's long-term success. The wider responsibilities of businesses in today's environment were neatly expressed by management theorist Archie Carroll in the form of a pyramid.

Ascending the pyramid

At the base of the pyramid are an organization's economic responsibilities – its contribution to the economy. From day one, a business needs to be viable, making a profit for shareholders and owners, which in turn drives the wider economy. Businesses that fail to meet their economic responsibilities hinder growth in the economy, and reduce the likelihood that foreign companies will invest.

The second level of the pyramid is made up of legal responsibilities; these are the laws that regulate the way that businesses operate. Businesses are required to obey these laws or face penalties enforced by the government. When a society has expectations that businesses aren't meeting, or when it thinks that a business is acting in an unfair manner, it might take its grievances to court. Legislation may then be passed that regulates the activity in question. Most business laws didn't start off as laws, but as ethical issues that attracted serious and repeated objections.

The third level of the pyramid involves ethical responsibilities. These go well beyond legal responsibilities; they are what the business itself and wider society deems to be right or wrong, or fair or unfair conduct. They are also what shareholders, government officials, customers, and workers perceive as being right or wrong. Unethical conduct may have serious implications that could negatively affect society.

At the tip of the pyramid are philanthropic responsibilities, which are those that improve the community and the well-being of humanity. They are completely voluntary, but increasing numbers of people expect businesses to donate their time and efforts to philanthropic causes; and many businesses are realizing the value of non-profit activities.

The pyramid of corporate social responsibility

PHILANTHROPIC
Giving back
to communities
and society.

ETHICAL
Doing what is right
within your organization,
industry, and external stakeholders.

LEGAL
Abiding by the letter and spirit
of national and international law.

ECONOMIC
Maintaining your organization and taking
care of financial commitments to stakeholders.

Assessing benefits and risks

When you are immersed in deadlines and day-to-day concerns about profitability and employee management, it is easy to ignore ethics. However, implementing ethics and compliance programmes has tangible business benefits, specifically, reducing your exposure to risks, boosting your performance, and enhancing your prospects.

Winning approval

Meeting ethical responsibilities can be just as important for your business as marketing or brand recognition. When you adopt good business ethics you will see four positive results: a greater level of employee commitment, customer satisfaction, shareholder investment, and higher profits.

Employees working in an ethical environment are more likely to feel satisfied. The Ethics Resource Center's National Business Ethics Survey shows that 79 per cent of employees feel that ethics are important and influence their decision to stay with an employer. They tend to care more for product quality

🔍 IN FOCUS... ETHICS, TRUST, AND NATIONAL ECONOMIES

The use of ethical business practices positively affects a nation's economy. Nations with many trust-based organizations tend to have lower levels of corruption and offer citizens a higher quality of life. Trust is essential for the proper functioning of business; when trust is evident customers, employees, and investors experience higher levels of efficiency and productivity. In contrast, when trust is absent, corruption or excessive regulation, or both, may take its place. It has been argued that in economies where trust is high, people can organize and associate with others freely; under these conditions, large corporations can thrive. In low-trust economies, businesses tend to be smaller, family-owned, and run by family members rather than professional managers.

CASE STUDY

The Enron scandal
Established in 1985, the Enron Corporation grew into a huge power, paper, and communications provider, and was hailed by *Fortune* magazine as America's most innovative company. Yet in 2001, Enron was found to be loaded with debt and had no immediate hope of paying off its creditors. This debt was hidden from the public through accounting fraud and other deceptive practices. Thousands of Enron employees had their retirement savings in Enron stock, which plummeted after the scandal was revealed. Ethical misconduct was directly responsible for the sudden downfall of this once powerful organization.

and success when they think the business can be trusted. Employees who are satisfied with their organization's ethics system are much more likely to exceed performance expectations, be more receptive to changes in the marketplace, and be more dedicated to the customers. They focus on creating long-term relationships with customers, which increases customer satisfaction and encourages repeat purchases. An ethical environment fosters mutual trust, leading to better relationships. Team members who trust one another are more likely to make decisions faster and more efficiently.

TIP

EMPHASIZE ETHICS
Boost morale by putting ethics into the workplace; your employees will benefit from the positive feeling that they are contributing to a fair organization.

Attracting loyalty

Studies have consistently proven that a strong ethical culture inspires loyalty from customers if other factors, such as product quality and price, are equal, and so is a real source of competitive advantage. Strong ethics also serve to attract and reassure investors: acts of ethical misconduct, which can cause stocks to plummet and damage corporate reputation, are less likely to occur in an organization that is effective in managing risks; and investors increasingly care about putting their money into companies that demonstrably care about society. The long-term result of meeting your ethical responsibilities is improved financial performance.

Recognizing the risks

While good ethical practice has clear benefits for a business's bottom line, poor standards can result in a downward spiral. As the public's trust for a business declines, consumers begin to look elsewhere for the products they need and in some cases may even start negative campaigns against, and organized boycotts of, the business.

Once a consumer's trust in a business is broken, it may take years to repair, and distrust may spread far beyond the culprit. When one business commits ethical misconduct, others in the industry are suspected simply by association. So remember, ethical misconduct does not just affect you: it creates a domino effect that can involve a whole sector.

Resisting the pressures

Despite potentially serious consequences, many employees still commit ethical violations, and misconduct is not just limited to middle- and lower-level staff. Nearly 30 per cent of employees in one poll said that they had felt pressured in the past by upper-level management to commit an act they knew to be wrong. Even those with good personal ethics are often ill prepared to handle the types of ethical issues businesses tend to face. As a manager, it is up to you to provide a greater focus on business ethics to suppress this negative behaviour. Not only will it prepare employees for ethical issues before they happen, it will help them to resist the pressures to commit misconduct.

Rising to the challenges

Determining the risks for your business and developing systems to manage these risks is not an easy task. In addition to qualities such as honesty and fairness, business ethics include issues such as product quality, safety features, and pricing – all of which vary depending on the organization. Ethical issues may be viewed very differently by different people, so it is important to create codes of ethics to which employees can refer rather than depending upon individual decisions that do not necessarily reflect the company's values.

Employees, especially new recruits, may not be familiar with industry standards, such as product quality or pricing, and their personal morals are unlikely to encompass ethics particular to a certain industry or job. As a result, an ethical employee can violate ethical business standards without intending to. This is why training is essential.

PROMOTING ETHICS

FAST TRACK	OFF TRACK
Establishing solid and specific ethical standards for the business to follow	Establishing vague ethical standards that may be hard to interpret
Creating a comfortable ethical environment for employees	Failing to familiarize employees with standards specific to the industry
Providing training in organizational ethics for all employees	Limiting organizational ethics training to certain employees
Making your ethics systems known to consumers	Assuming that employees will always apply your ethical standards

Looking beyond borders

When you engage in business with organizations outside your home country, you will encounter different systems, which may bring your ethical policies, and your views of what is right or wrong, into conflict with local laws and customs. Conversely, some practices that are illegal in your home country may be legal elsewhere, posing further ethical questions.

TIP

KNOW THE LAW

Take legal advice before offering any type of gift to a business partner: bribery almost always violates the law in the country where it takes place, and penalties can be steep.

Recognizing dilemmas

In a global environment, how applicable are your ethical standards when they are at odds with cultural norms and expectations? For example, in some Middle Eastern countries, it is a common belief that women do not belong in business, and Middle Eastern companies may refuse to do business with female representatives. Should your organization employ only male representatives to negotiate with Middle Eastern businessmen? Does this constitute discrimination against its female workers?

Using sweeteners

In some countries, bribing officials to obtain permissions – for planning or export, for example – is expected and it may be near impossible to do business without bribery. This makes bribery a controversial issue in terms of ethics. The legality of a bribe you pay depends on the country where your company is based; if you are from the US, you may have committed a felony, but if you are from one of several European countries, your bribe may actually be tax deductible. Beware, too, that gifts may be interpreted as bribes in some countries, while in others the exchange of gifts is an accepted and even necessary part of a business relationship.

Price and quality

Ethical uncertainty surrounds the issue of manipulating the prices of goods and services in different countries – price fixing and price discrimination.

Price fixing, which is the deliberate standardization of prices for goods or services, is not allowed in many countries, but multinational companies may operate in territories where the practice is not illegal and where the temptation to elevate and set prices with their competitors is high – especially if everyone else is doing so. Price discrimination occurs when organizations charge certain customers, such as those in other countries, much inflated prices for their products or dump products at low prices to drive competitors out of business.

Global organizations also face ethical dilemmas when it comes to product safety. Some products are illegal in certain countries because they contravene very strict safety standards. Should you sell these "unsafe" products to countries that lack such strict standards? The advantages may well offset the costs. For example, some inexpensive pesticides with harmful properties are banned in developed countries but legal in developing countries.

Attitudes toward gift giving

LATIN AMERICA
Gifts should be given during social encounters, not in the course of business.

CHINA
Gifts should be presented privately, with the exception of collective ceremonial gifts at banquets.

EUROPE
Do not risk the impression of bribery by spending too much on a gift.

ARAB WORLD
Do not give a gift when you first meet someone; it may be interpreted as a bribe.

Chapter 2

Recognizing ethical issues

You can't manage what you don't understand. Knowing the nature of ethical risks, and identifying those that are most likely to affect your organization, is central to any successful ethical management policy.

Developing your radar

The business environment is characterized by change, and one new decision in an organization, or one new development in an industry, can change the ethical landscape. The first step of ethical decision-making is therefore being able to anticipate and identify an ethical issue.

Defining organizational values

Ethical issues can be hard to classify. Values such as fairness and truthfulness are subject to differing interpretations. Therefore, an understanding of what these concepts mean within the context of an organization is important when providing a foundation for ethical decision-making. How these values are expressed in particular areas, such as abusive behaviour, conflicts of interest, bribery, discrimination, sexual harassment, fraud, environmental misconduct, intellectual property rights, and privacy issues, is explored in this chapter.

Overcoming issues

Ethical issues arise when values clash. Conflicts occur on several levels: between organizational values and those of individuals; between organizational values and objectives; or between societal, industry, and regulatory objectives.

Conflict is almost assured if individuals within an organization do not share common concerns about issues and hold common ethical objectives. You cannot expect employees to achieve good organizational ethics simply by relying on their own personal values. What is required is a shared sense of ethical intensity – a term used to describe the importance of an ethical issue in the eyes of individuals, work groups, and/or organizations. Intensity is influenced by the values and needs of the individual making the decision; the characteristics of the situation; and the personal pressures accompanying the decision. The shared perception of ethical intensity requires an understanding of organizational culture, regulatory requirements, and industry standards, and these rules may be complex, requiring guidance and experience. Managers and all employees should be empowered to recognize and respond to the earliest signs of misconduct and a system of reporting must be in place to alert managers to issues that develop.

Spotting the signals of ethical conflict

Everybody does it...

No-one is going to get hurt...

No-one will ever miss it...

Just this once...

Boys will be boys...

Look the other way...

Let's keep this between us...

Don't be such a prude...

They had it coming anyway...

Facing up to your fears

As a manager, it is your responsibility to uncover and assess the activities most likely to be of risk to your business. While many organizations focus attention on the risk from disasters, such as fires, floods, power failures, and data loss, risk associated with ethical misconduct is often ignored.

For many leaders, the fear of discovering misconduct within their organization is paralyzing, and too many simply duck and hide when there is a concern that misconduct has occurred. Some fear that critics, competitors, and stakeholders will use the information to undermine the firm's reputation. They take the stance that if nothing is discovered, then nothing will ever go wrong. This could not be further from the truth.

Discovering ethical issues as early as possible is highly desirable, but no matter how well prepared you are, you are likely to face dilemmas and misconduct at some point, so you also need a plan for response and recovery.

TIP

CATCH ISSUES EARLY

Introduce transparency and openness when dealing with ethical issues. If resolved in their early stages, most ethical dilemmas will not result in a crisis.

IN FOCUS... THE IMPORTANCE OF YOUR REPUTATION

Reputation is more important than ever in today's business environment because of the speed at which news travels and the rate at which an organization's image can be damaged. For this reason, many organizations are choosing to manage actively how they are perceived by the public. This function is known as reputation management. It requires the organization to take into account identity, image, and performance. Identity is how the organization is perceived by its stakeholders. For example, all organizations want to appear trustworthy and valuable. Image is the impression that stakeholders possess of the organization and its actions. Performance involves the organization's and the stakeholders' measurement of reputation objectives. In order to establish a positive reputation, there should be as few gaps as possible between objectives, identity, and image.

Most common types
of ethical misconduct
reported in organizations

- Placing one's own interests over organizational ones
- Discrimination on the basis of race, colour, gender, age, etc.
- Misreporting hours worked
- Misuse of confidential information
- Alteration of financial records
- Internet abuse
- Theft
- Offering inducements
- Abusive or intimidating behaviour toward employees
- Provision of low-quality goods and services
- Using competitors' inside information
- Environmental violations
- Alteration of documents
- Lying to stakeholders
- Safety violations
- Sexual harassment
- Lying to employees

THEFT
BULLYING   BRIBERY
RACISM
DECEIT

Handling conflicts of interest

Within any organization, individuals in a position of trust are sometimes faced with a situation in which their professional objectivity conflicts with personal or other interests. In this event, ethical misconduct is a real danger; a good ethical policy includes measures to avoid or at least minimize the occurrence of conflicts of interest.

TIP

THINK AHEAD
Always award contracts on merit alone and avoid favours to family and friends. If you run a small business, think about how your actions now may be perceived if you choose to expand and seek investors. All your dealings with family members will be closely scrutinized.

Seeing the pitfalls

According to the Ethics Resource Center, conflicts of interest comprise 18 per cent of all cases of observed employee misconduct, reflecting the real difficulty in keeping personal interests detached from professional responsibilities. As a manager, you should always exercise objectivity and avoid favouritism in your judgements. If you feel like your objectivity is compromised, seek the counsel of a third party.

Conflicts of interest among boards of directors can have devastating effects. Directors have privileged information about the stock market that can lead to insider trading; they have control over compensation packages and knowledge of investments and business ventures; and they may serve on the board of more than one company. For some, the temptation to neglect their stakeholder duties in exchange for personal gain is too great.

Following several scandals in the early 21st century, such as the multi-billion dollar accounting fraud at US telecoms giant WorldCom, legislation was passed to address conflicts of interest. The Sarbanes-Oxley Act, enacted in the US in 2002, laid down regulations for all US public companies and accounting firms. Under the Act, directors face increased liability for their decisions: although they cannot be held liable if they exercise due care in their decision-making, they may be held responsible for actions not committed in good faith.

Respecting regulation

The Sarbanes-Oxley Act helps to prevent conflicts of interest, improves investor confidence, and ensures that organizations produce more accurate financial statements. Its provisions include that:

• An Accounting Oversight Board be established and placed in charge of regulations administered by the Securities and Exchange Commission.

• CEOs and CFOs certify that their companies' financial statements are true and without misleading statements.

• Corporations be prohibited from making or offering loans to officers and board members.

• Codes of ethics be put in place for senior financial officers.

• Accounting firms be prohibited from providing both auditing and consulting services to the same client.

• Company attorneys be required to report wrongdoing to top managers and, if necessary, to the board of directors; if managers and directors fail to respond to reports of wrongdoing, the attorney should stop representing the company.

• "Whistle-blower protection" for persons who disclose wrongdoing to authorities must be in place.

• Financial securities analysts be required to certify that their recommendations are based on objective reports.

• Accounting firms rotate individual auditors from one account to another from time to time: two senior auditors cannot work on a corporation's account for more than five years.

• Audit committees should consist of independent members with no material interests in the company.

While the Sarbanes-Oxley Act continues to be a powerful tool in regulating organizational ethics, it has its detractors. Some claim that its very power makes businesses think twice before listing on US stock exchanges rather than less regulated exchanges in Europe.

HOW TO...
AVOID CONFLICTS OF INTEREST

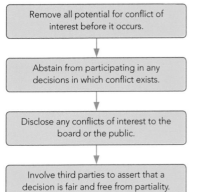

Remove all potential for conflict of interest before it occurs.

⬇

Abstain from participating in any decisions in which conflict exists.

⬇

Disclose any conflicts of interest to the board or the public.

⬇

Involve third parties to assert that a decision is fair and free from partiality.

Abusive behaviour

Abusive or intimidating behaviour is one of the most common ethical problems encountered by employees. Bullying is a kind of abusive behaviour that can cause serious disruptions to an employee's life and to productivity. Many employees feel they have no recourse against the bully because the majority of workplace bullies are in superior positions.

TIP

BE COMMITTED
Keep your nerve and determination when dealing with abusive behaviour. Senior management may shy away from cases because they tend to be long and drawn out, hard to prove, and may damage the reputation of the whole organization.

Recognizing abuse

What is considered abusive varies from person to person. Abusive behaviour can mean anything from physical threats, false accusations, profanity, insults, yelling or harshness, to ignoring someone and unreasonableness. In today's business environment, where working with different cultural groups is the norm, definitions are further complicated by varied meanings of words across ages and cultures. Therefore, a key consideration when analyzing a potential abuse case is intent – was the person concerned striving to harm, or merely clumsy in their communication?

Dealing with abuse

In the past, employees have often been afraid to report abuse because they feared repercussions, such as being fired, but today many organizations are devising safe ways for employees to come forward. Some businesses use suggestion boxes or have telephone hotlines where an employee can anonymously report instances of abuse; others have set up ethics committees, staffed with people trained to deal with situations of employer misconduct. It is important to make employees feel safe so that they will be willing to report workplace misconduct.

Identifying bullies

DIG DEEPER
Investigate thoroughly if you are faced with a case of alleged bullying. Senior employees may be covering up a bully's activities to protect their own reputation.

Bullying is a kind of abusive behaviour where a person or a group is targeted, threatened, harassed, belittled, verbally abused, or heavily criticized. It can use a mix of verbal, non-verbal, and manipulative or threatening expressions that damage workplace productivity. The bully's motive is usually to conceal or divert from his or her own incompetence, and they will often project their inadequacies on to their staff.

Bullying is often a serial behaviour and frequently results in serious psychological damage to the target and poor performance of the team. The presence of a bully is often betrayed by symptoms in a team such as a high turnover of staff, above average absenteeism, high stress levels, and the spread of bullying behaviour to other members as they attempt to meet the bully's requirements. Bullying can occur on an organizational level, where a company forces employees to agree to unreasonable terms or imposes intrusive controls, such as spot checks and monitoring of emails and phone conversations. Companies may also be guilty of bullying by, for example, making unreasonable demands of suppliers in an abusive or threatening manner.

ASK YOURSELF... DO YOU HAVE A WORKPLACE BULLY?

- Does he/she spread rumours to damage the reputation of others?
- Does he/she flaunt status or authority to take advantage of others?
- Does he/she discredit others' ideas and opinions?
- Does he/she fail to communicate or return communications from others?
- Does he/she use insults and shout?
- Does he/she take credit for others' work or ideas?

Avoiding discrimination

Discrimination on the basis of race, religion, gender, sexual orientation, disability, age, or national origin is illegal in many countries, but it remains a contentious problem, especially in the context of the mass migration of people in the 21st century. The best way to deal with discrimination is to be proactive by encouraging knowledge and promoting diversity, rather than relying on legal mechanisms.

Defining discrimination

Giving one person worse treatment than another owing to their colour, ethnicity, sex, age, political allegiance, or other attributes is called direct discrimination. Indirect discrimination involves apparently treating everyone equally, but in a manner that results in unfairness to a specific group of people. An example is failing to provide wheelchair ramps in an office, so excluding people with disabilities from the workplace. In many countries, it is unlawful to discriminate even if that was not your intention; for example, providing conditions that favour male employees over female may be against the law.

BE AWARE OF RELIGIOUS OBSERVANCES
Avoid the danger of religious discrimination by keeping a calendar of the main festivals throughout the year. Don't schedule important meetings or training during festivals.

The role of the law

Most lawsuits brought by employees against their employers relate to some form of discrimination. However, the law has proved not to be a very effective weapon against discrimination. Employees do not often win such cases, partly because they are hard to prove, and may indeed end up worse off, without a job and without good references. Decades of anti-discrimination actions in the courts have had at best a moderate impact on the diversity of executives and senior managers, especially in the private sector.

Managing diversity

Perhaps the best way to combat the ethical risks associated with discrimination is actively to manage diversity. Many companies are implementing affirmative-action hiring programmes. These help corporations recruit employees from a wide variety of backgrounds. The employees have a better understanding of the needs of an increasingly diverse customer and stakeholder base, and many such programmes have a positive effect not only on ethical management, but on company performance and profits.

HOW TO...
REDUCE WORKPLACE DISCRIMINATION

> Write an anti-discrimination policy consistent with local law and distribute this to all employees.

↓

> Provide training on diversity awareness; knowledge will prevent abuses.

↓

> Set up a structure through which instances of discrimination may be reported.

↓

> Take all complaints of discrimination seriously, and give the job of investigating to an impartial, senior staff member.

↓

> Carefully make and keep written records of all investigations.

↓

> Do not discourage employees from seeking help from outside agencies.

Interpersonal relationships

Inappropriate relationships in the workplace can pose ethical hazards. At one extreme, sexual harassment* can result in huge costs in lawsuits and damaged reputations, but there are also risks associated with consensual relationships that may affect professional judgement.

Recognizing harassment

*Sexual harassment *— behaviour characterized by unwanted sexual advances by one individual upon another.*

Sexual harassment can manifest itself as unwanted physical approaches, such as touching, or repeated unwelcome, degrading, or sexist remarks directed towards another person. It may be verbal, written, or graphic, and some non-verbal behaviours, such as gestures or staring, may also be interpreted as harassment. Depending on circumstance, people may view such behaviours as anything from a nuisance to the basis for a lawsuit. Sexual harassment is hard to measure and tough to prove, but there are three conditions that suggest that it has taken place:
• The actions are severe or repetitive; a single incident is unlikely to be viewed as harassment.
• The victim's position at work is impacted by the behaviour. For example, if someone is denied progress, or given a poor review because they have

🔍 IN FOCUS... DUAL RELATIONSHIPS

It is neither desirable nor possible to stop employees from forming and ending relationships with co-workers. However, you should be aware of the ethical risks of such situations. A dual relationship – business and romantic with one individual – is not unethical in itself, but may lead to conflicts of interest and discontent in the rest of the team if favouritism is suspected. Individuals in a relationship with a subordinate should transfer their responsibilities for performance assessments to another manager. Senior staff should notify their employers if they begin relationships with members of the company to head off ethical difficulties.

rejected an advance, that points to sexual harassment. The same goes even if the conduct does not cause economic harm – it is enough that it interferes with your ability to carry out your work or creates an intimidating work environment.

• The conduct is of a sort that any reasonable person would take offence to it.

Taking measures

Many countries have laws that address sexual harassment. As a manager, you should be aware of legislation, recognize harassment early, and take appropriate measures to keep it from happening. At the very least, you should ensure that employees are aware of the definition of harassment and appoint a member of the senior team to act as a point of contact for anyone who has concerns.

TIP

TRAIN FOR COMPLIANCE
Consider setting up a training programme to address the issue of harassment. This could give examples of what constitutes sexual harassment, outline grievance procedures and explain how to use them, and set out the penalties.

RESPONDING TO SEXUAL HARASSMENT

 FAST TRACK

 OFF TRACK

FAST TRACK	OFF TRACK
Telling the harasser exactly what you find to be offensive	Feeling guilty or blaming yourself for the harasser's behaviour
Informing the harasser that his or her behaviour is upsetting you	Ignoring the offensive behaviour
Telling your line manager what you want or do not want to happen	Trying to deal with serious harassment by yourself
Keeping accurate records of serial harassment	Ignoring the organization's grievance procedure

Protecting private data

Organizations are increasingly collecting personal information on their customers to better understand their markets. This data must be carefully managed to protect the privacy of the individual customers and also to safeguard this potentially valuable information for the benefit of the organization that has gathered it.

Managing personal data

*Corporate intelligence — *information gathered by an organization with the aim of monitoring changes and identifying opportunities. This data can include information on customers, as well as on markets, political trends, competition, or new technologies.*

Privacy is a big concern in global business today, and perhaps one of the most difficult to manage. Businesses use technology to collect information about their customers, and maintain huge databases of corporate intelligence* information. Many organizations sell their products over the Internet, requiring their customers to reveal information, such as credit card numbers, social security numbers, and other personal data. Websites can track the types of purchases consumers make, and some companies even have the technology to track the geographical location of consumers.

Understanding the issues

*Identity theft — *using someone else's personal information to assume their identity, for financial gain.*

The ready availability of information raises a number of ethical concerns, and consumers are increasingly worried about the security of their data. Information can be collected on the Internet with or without a person's knowledge. The Internet makes it easy for businesses to share or sell information to other parties. Even worse, the online collection of personal information enables computer hackers to gain access to the consumer's personal details, laying them open to identity theft* – a crime that is resulting in billions of dollars of losses worldwide.

Taking steps

Laws have been created to help protect individuals' privacy with respect to personal data. In Europe, the European Union Directive on Data Protection requires organizations that collect personal information to explain how that information will be used and receive the individual's permission first. The US has no overall law: instead, each business sector tends to have its own data protection legislation. Many major organizations around the world have responded by putting policies in place to address the protection of information. Some reveal their policies in privacy statements that consumers can access.

Setting your policy

Consider how your organization deals with personal data, and if appropriate, take steps to ensure that you are managing your customers' private data responsibly. Some non-profit organizations offer accreditation, which can give customers confidence in your privacy policies. BBOnline, for example, provides a "seal" that businesses can display on their websites to show that they meet certain standards in protecting consumer privacy.

HOW TO... MANAGE PRIVATE INFORMATION

Ensure board/senior management buy-in.

Appoint a project manager.

Determine precisely why you collect, use, and/or distribute personal information.

Review the information you currently have.

Review the methods used by your business to collect personal information.

Keep records of why you have collected the information and the consent to do so.

Appoint a privacy officer.

Develop a firm-wide privacy policy.

Train your staff in data security.

Ensure personal information is secure.

Ensure your third parties and vendors comply with privacy legislation.

Protecting your trade secrets

You should also protect corporate intelligence for the benefit of the business; this is information that could potentially give your organization competitive advantage in its market. With the growth of Internet technology and local networks, trade secrets have come increasingly under threat. Computer hackers break into computer systems to access company trade secrets and use them for their own gain. Hackers also use a technique called social engineering, in which they use tricks to discover people's passwords. Some hackers take a direct approach, watching over people's shoulders as they type in their passwords. Other hackers gain enough personal information about a person to guess his or her password. Some hackers even go so far as to look through a company's waste to find information that reveals trade secrets. Hackers can also break into wireless networks to access information, or can eavesdrop on trade secrets by recording and then decoding a fax machine.

Businesses must therefore take extra precautions to make sure their trade secrets are secure. There are five key steps that you can take to help protect your corporate intelligence and keep your trade secrets secret.

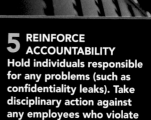

5 REINFORCE ACCOUNTABILITY
Hold individuals responsible for any problems (such as confidentiality leaks). Take disciplinary action against any employees who violate their responsibilities.

4 COMMUNICATE THE CHANGES
Share information with employees and make certain they know exactly who is accountable for what, and what their responsibilities are in protecting valuable company information.

1 CALCULATE THE RISK
Consider whether the information you are collecting and using is crucial for your organization's activity. Would losing the information, even for the briefest period, be harmful to your organization? Is the information restricted or sensitive?

2 DEFINE PROCEDURES
Apply policies that define procedures for system failures or threats to and breaches of security. Create a confidentiality agreement to be signed by all workers that includes information on disclosure practices, data use, and employee responsibility.

Five steps to protecting your corporate intelligence

3 IMPLEMENT ACCESS CONTROLS
Put in place processes that restrict physical or electronic access to sensitive information, such as passwords or firewalls. Use shredders to destroy sensitive documents that you do not need to keep.

Dealing with dishonesty

Lying and dishonesty in all forms – be it giving false information in company financial records, dishonest behaviour or theft by employees, or false or misleading marketing and advertising – can be extremely damaging to an organization. Even if the organization is not prosecuted for its actions, its reputation can be destroyed if it is found to be participating in dishonest practices.

*Fraud — *any untrue statement or form of communication that deceives, manipulates, or conceals facts to create a false impression that can damage others.*

Being alert to fraud

It has been suggested that in times of economic downturns fraudulent behaviour increases. Even in the good times, however, it is important for every manager to understand what constitutes fraudulent and dishonest behaviour, how they can protect themselves from being a victim of it, and how they can avoid participation in any activities that could be considered fraudulent or lead to fraud*.

TIP

STAY ALERT
Always check the accuracy and source of documents, and report any suspicions of improper behaviour to a senior member of staff.

Understanding financial fraud

Fraud in accounting and finance can destroy an organization. It typically involves providing incorrect information in financial reports that contain the key data about a company's financial health – data on which investors and others base their decisions. Providing inaccurate information in financial reports can lead to lawsuits and criminal charges, even if the errors were not intentional. Accounting fraud has frequently been a headline news topic in the 21st century, and as a result many countries have passed legislation to clamp down on the practice. However, there are a number of basic strategies you can use to minimize the risk of your organization participating in financial fraud:

- Elect directors with financial experience in proportion to the size of the company.
- Clamp down on minor dishonesty to create a culture in which fraud is not tolerated.
- Avoid pressures that are likely to encourage fraud, such as unreasonably high sales targets.
- Implement an anti-fraud policy that sets out standards of behaviour, and encourage employees to self-regulate under that policy.
- Provide training for all employees, so that everyone within your organization is clear about what could lead to fraud.
- Conduct regular internal audits.

Detecting employee fraud

Every manager must be vigilant for dishonest and fraudulent behaviour among employees. This can include stealing money or products, taking office supplies, expense account manipulation, and claiming overtime when they haven't worked extra hours.

Theft by employees is an extremel y serious issue, costing businesses billions each year, and in the worst cases, even causing bankruptcy. Studies have shown that 79 per cent of people steal or are tempted to steal from their employers. Stolen items may range from something as small as a paper clip to something as serious as computer software. Sometimes, employees steal copyrighted materials and pass them off as their own.

Employees of all levels are tempted to commit theft; although upper-level managers are not as likely to steal, they have access to more valuable items, and so could potentially cause significantly more damage to the organization. Rarely is theft committed by employees as a result of material need. More often, workplace items are stolen in an attempt to get a thrill or because of greed.

HOW TO... MINIMIZE THE RISK OF THEFT

Do background checks on new employees for problems in previous jobs.

↓

Monitor expense accounts and resources that could be taken.

↓

Encourage employees to report workplace theft they witness.

↓

Consider surveillance cameras for serious problems.

Selling ethically

Marketing is the process of creating, distributing, promoting, and pricing products. Fraud can become a problem when marketing communications, such as advertising, are false or misleading. This is a serious issue because, even if committed accidentally, it can destroy customers' trust in a company – trust that the company may never be able to regain.

Avoiding fraudulent advertising

Deceptive sales practices include providing inaccurate information about your product or misinformation about a competitor's product, so it is very important to be sure of your facts before you devise your marketing strategy. What makes an advertisement fraudulent – or capable of being proved so in court – is not always crystal clear. There is a widespread, difficult-to-define problem called puffery, which involves exaggerations of the truth that no reasonable buyer would find reliable or take seriously. For example, pizza parlours frequently advertise that they have the "world's best pizza". This claim has been made so many times, and can in no way be proven because of its subjectivity, that a reasonable person would not believe it. Puffery also includes the use of words such as "natural" to imply that a food is healthy when its health benefits are, in fact, dubious.

LOSE WEIGHT IN 10 DAYS

THE WORLD'S BEST COFFEE

CONTAINS 100 PER CENT NATURAL INGREDIENTS

Knowing the types

There are two main types of advertising fraud: implied falsity and literally false advertising. Implied falsity is when an advertisement confuses or deceives the consumer. Advertising using implied falsity makes claims that are literally true, but are nevertheless misleading. For example, a company was accused of deceit after advertising that a line of sweaters was made partially from cashmere. The material was in fact made from recycled cashmere instead of virgin cashmere. The company admitted that its label was deceiving because it implied that the cashmere was virgin, but, since it was technically still cashmere, the company maintained that it was guilty only of implied falsity.

An implicitly false claim, while true at face value, needs qualification to prevent it from being misleading to consumers. Literally false advertisements can be divided into two sub-categories:
• Establishment claims: advertisements that falsely cite a study to prove their claims
• Non-establishment claims: advertisements that make claims that cannot be proven.

If one company markets an item as being "better" than another company's, it could be engaging in a non-establishment claim. It would be near impossible to prove one item's superiority over another's because people have different ideas of what constitutes real "superiority."

It is often difficult to distinguish implied falsity from advertising that is literally false.

 IN FOCUS... CONSUMER FRAUD

Organizations need to be aware of, and on the lookout for, consumer fraud, when a consumer tries to deceive a business for personal gain. This dishonest behaviour can be very costly to an organization, and comes in various guises:
• Shoplifting
• Switching price tags for ones from cheaper items
• Lying about age to get an age-related discount
• Collusion – when an employee assists the consumer in committing fraud, such as by giving large discounts to their friends
• Taking back used clothing to get a full discount
• Conspiring with the cashier to get an unwarranted discount.
Dishonest customers typically know the difference between right and wrong, but intentionally use tricks to cheat an organization.

Avoiding greenwashing

"Green" products and "sustainable" business practices are the new buzzwords of the 21st century; but before you make these claims for your own company you must be sure that they are justified. Consumers are becoming increasingly aware of false claims, or "greenwashing*".

*Greenwashing — to purposefully mislead consumers about the environmental benefits of a product or the environmental practices of a company.

Defining the issue

Environmentally friendly products are more popular today than ever before. In the US alone, consumers spend more than $25 billion annually on products sold on their natural or organic credentials. However, as going green has become popular and profitable, more companies have sought to jump on the bandwagon without really changing their environmentally unsound ways. Greenwashing is an unethical, and fundamentally dangerous, practice; consumers have become very savvy about assessing green claims, and will neither forgive nor forget those companies who betray their trust.

ASK YOURSELF...
ARE YOU GREENWASHING?

- Are you selling a product on the basis of its environmental benefits in one area, while ignoring the negative impacts it has in others?
- Can you back up your claim with independent research?
- Do the claims you make really mean anything?
- Are the green claims you make actually true of all products in the category?
- Are you taking credit for a product's specification or performance, which is in any case mandated by law?
- Are you making claims that try to "green" a product in a product category that is not inherently green?

Avoiding risks

When you describe a product or service as "green", "sustainable", or "environmentally friendly", be sure that you can substantiate the claim with specific details and research. Beware of using words in your marketing materials that do not have a clear definition: "eco", "natural", "biodegradable", and "recyclable" are all likely to attract the scrutiny of consumers, and of a number of bodies dedicated to exposing greenwashing.

Today's educated consumers are looking for a real commitment to sustainability, so avoid one-off "green" programmes unless they are truly representative of your company's values. Above all, reach out to your customers and stakeholders. Get their opinions on how you can change your practices to become "greener", and what they consider to be sustainable.

Working to standards

In an attempt to reduce the prevalence of greenwashing and to restore consumer faith in businesses' claims, some organizations have developed certifications to validate and support "green" claims made by companies. One such organization is the Carbon Trust, a UK-based group that works with other organizations to help reduce their carbon emissions. Carbon Trust has developed a green standard that it issues to companies to prove they have reduced their carbon output. The standard does not accept carbon trading as sufficient, as this too has been used as a means of greenwashing. Not only do the companies have to reduce their emissions, they have to continue to reduce them every successive year.

Chapter 3

Implementing an ethics programme

To set up and manage an effective ethics programme you must start with a clear understanding of the factors that influence ethical decisions in your organization, then enshrine agreed principles and values into an enforceable code of conduct.

Setting the context

How are ethical decisions made within your organization? What factors and what people exert an influence on outcomes, and can the process be improved? Answering these questions will help you set a robust framework for ethical decision-making.

Making decisions

All ethical decisions are taken within the context of the needs and expectations of stakeholders; the culture of the organization; and the values and drives of the individuals within it.

Stakeholders – your employees, suppliers, regulators, special-interest groups, communities, and the media – have a wide range of interests, concerns, and potential impacts. These need to be pinpointed, and the intensity, or importance, of each carefully assessed to ensure that your ethical framework accommodates decision-making in all key areas.

Culture and values

Organizational culture consists of the values, norms, and behaviours shared by the organization. It is a collective understanding about what is expected and accepted, and it defines the way decisions are made on a daily basis. In practice, internal culture may be at odds with the values stated in external communications, such as the corporate website; it may allow for, or even tacitly condone, unethical behaviour that boosts profitability.

Most studies suggest that organizational factors are key in the workplace – ethical decisions are most strongly influenced by the internal culture and by co-workers, superiors, and subordinates. Indeed, employees are more likely to be guided by their co-workers'

thoughts than by their personal values; but this does not mean that the role of an individual's personal moral philosophy can be ignored. Everyone has their own perception of right and wrong, shaped by factors such as education, nationality, age, and gender and this will to some extent influence the decisions they make.

The importance of individual factors varies with profession. For example, an environmental engineer working alone on a project has more opportunity to make an independent ethical judgement than a food retailer deciding whether or not to stock a particular brand of coffee; here the judgement is more likely to be made by a board or committee with reference to predefined rules and regulations.

The influences on an ethical decision

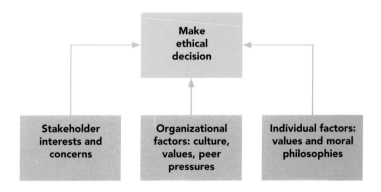

Setting an ethical code

A successful business ethics programme will seek to cultivate shared values within an organization and ensure that staff understand and commit to specific mandated conduct. Excellent leadership, strong communication, and training help achieve these ends.

Identifying principles and values

Before you can communicate your organization's ethical intent or formulate a code of conduct, you need to clarify your principles – those long-standing or "bedrock" beliefs that cannot be compromised – and your values. Starting with principles, develop rules that restrict outcomes and that employees must respect. A good place to start is by reviewing your company's mission statement, objectives, and past performance. Determine what they tell you about your ethical objectives, and identify the key ethical risks to your business.

TIP

BE DIRECT
Remember that the point of an ethical code is not to check a box, but to be helpful to your staff. Use language that is accessible to all and publish the code widely, on paper and electronically.

ASK YOURSELF... ABOUT ETHICAL RISKS

- Are operational procedures in place that help our employees to maintain ethical behaviour?
- Do our employees ever have to break company rules to get work finished?
- Have we ever hidden company practices that would be embarrassing for the public to know about?
- Are any of our products or services described in a manner that could be considered misleading?
- Is there sufficient concern for the community in our company activities?
- Do our concerns about environmental impact address just the issues that we are legally required to consider?

The seven steps of an effective ethics programme

1 Assessing risks and putting in place standards and codes of ethical conduct.

2 Providing high-level managerial oversight to ensure compliance with these standards (for example, the appointment of a dedicated ethics officer).

3 Taking due care not to place individuals with a propensity to engage in misconduct in a position of authority where they can influence others.

4 Using training programmes to communicate the agreed standards to all employees.

5 Establishing systems to monitor conduct and allow employees to report abuses.

6 Enforcing standards, rewards, and punishments consistently across the company.

7 Constantly reviewing the system, and taking steps to revise and improve the way it works.

Supporting ethics

The most effective tool in guiding and developing an ethical organizational culture is your leadership. Managers set the ethical tone for an organization and develop the systems that identify ethical issues. They train and educate employees on how to deal with conflicts, they assign responsibility, and they allow for open communication of concerns and questions.

Ethics in the workplace can also be supported by the consistent use of rewards and reprimands. Quite simply, employees are more likely to engage in conduct that earns them rewards and less likely to engage in behaviour that results in punishments.

Supportive leaders use praise, recognition, and rewards such as bonuses, raises, promotions, and increased responsibility to encourage employees to display ethical behaviour in the organization, and disincentives to discourage ethical breaches.

The past years have seen greater efforts by governments to legislate for good ethics. In the US, this involved corporate governance legislation, which included the Sarbanes-Oxley Act and the revision of the Federal Sentencing Guidelines for Organizations (FSGO). The FSGO guidelines encourage companies to put in place effective ethics programmes and set out steps that should be included in such programmes.

IN FOCUS... WHERE TO LOOK FOR BREACHES IN ETHICAL CODES

Ethical misconduct is more likely to occur with junior and middle managers than with senior staff, because the job security of lower ranking employees usually depends on hitting tight deadlines. There is a temptation to overlook unethical conduct if it means meeting immediate needs. Upper-level managers, in contrast, usually have more job security than middle managers, are more likely to consider long-term goals and so are more likely to abide by the ethical culture.

Assembling the code

With a clear understanding of the ethical risks faced by your organization and how they could be avoided, you can begin to formulate an ethical code according to the following general guidelines:

• Ensure that upper-level management fully supports the code and will provide the necessary leadership to see it implemented: they are the individuals whose behaviour the employees will follow.

• Clearly define the principles and values that lie behind the code.

• Make the code relevant, clear, and credible for employees.

• Make sure that the group that drafts the code is representative of all organizational functions.

• Have a large group of diverse stakeholders review the code, and seek appropriate feedback.

Once agreed, you should communicate the ethical code across the whole organization through effective training, and ensure that it is well supported by strong leadership and other checks and balances.

TIP

BE RELEVANT
Your ethical code should contain "must dos", aspirations, and examples of typical dilemmas that could be faced by staff in your organization.

Leading ethically

Good leaders build, maintain, and revise the systems that support integrity in the workplace, but perhaps more importantly, they lead by example. They need to be knowledgeable and experienced in order to make good decisions that help create an ethical culture based on shared values and behaviours.

Understanding the role of leaders

*Corporate culture — the mix of values, norms, behaviours, and artifacts (tangible signs) that help define an organization's character.

A leader's role is to guide and direct others towards the achievement of a goal. Leaders have the power and authority to motivate others and enforce the organization's rules and policies, as well as their own viewpoints, and so are key in directing an organization's corporate culture* and ethical stance. While most people think of the CEO as the most important leader within a company, the board of directors and mid-level managers play an important part as well.

Leading by example

Being an ethical leader is about far more than drafting, following, and implementing ethical codes. Through his or her actions, a good leader will promote an organizational culture that supports ethical conduct and rewards employees for acting in ways that are consistent with the company's values and ethical standards. This culture will permeate every aspect of the business from its public image and how stakeholders are treated, to the nature of the products sold.

Characterizing ethical leaders

Most strong, ethical leaders have certain characteristics in common. Developing these traits will help you to build an ethical corporate culture, loyal and happy employees, and a successful company.
• Ethical leaders have strong personal character; they possess robust principles that allow them to define a path and lead others along it.
• Ethical leaders have a passion to do right – for their customers and their employees. Of course, they are not infallible, but they do necessarily begin with the right intentions.
• Ethical leaders recognize that good ethics are good for performance and lead to a healthy bottom line.
• Ethical leaders are proactive – they don't just follow policies but make and shape them. This often requires courage – for example, when proposing an unpopular new direction.
• Ethical leaders consider stakeholders' interests. They build trust across the board and profit from the loyalty that this inspires.
• Ethical leaders are positive role models in and out of the workplace. They match their talk about values with visible actions that demonstrate respect.

BE FORGIVING
When you lead an ethics-management programme, it is likely to increase, at first, the number of ethical transgressions that arise. Be understanding when you deal with these issues; staff will look to you for support not censure.

Monitoring the programme

A successful ethics programme must have measurable outcomes; and it needs to be flexible enough to be amended and improved. The function of managing the ethics programme typically falls to senior managers or a dedicated ethics officer within the organization.

Measuring success

You can employ a range of tools to monitor and measure your organization's ethics programme. These include: internal and external audits; surveys; staff questionnaires and anonymous reporting systems, such as online or telephone hotlines; open lines of communication between employees and supervisors; exit interviews with departing employees; and consistent rewards and punishments for ethical and unethical behaviour respectively. Continuous improvement efforts are key to the functioning of the best ethics programmes, and should be a part of your programme, too.

TIP

Appointing an ethics officer

WIN CONTRACTS
Appoint an ethics officer, and you could open up new areas of business. Many governmental bodies will accept bids only from suppliers who have an ethics programme managed by a person of high rank.

If possible, identify a high-ranking manager within your organization to oversee compliance with your own and external standards. He or she should have good working knowledge of the ethical and legal standards expected within your industry. Some large organizations, especially those that are exposed to serious ethical risks (such as drug companies and military contractors) may well employ a dedicated ethics officer to perform this role. In some countries, companies above a certain size are legally required to have an ethics programme and a named individual charged with its management.

The responsibilities

Ethics officers come from a range of backgrounds, such as finance, legal, IT, and human resources, but they are always people who can see value in ethical conduct, both to the business and to the wider community. Their responsibilities vary from one organization to another, but typically include:

• Assessing the risks that ethics programmes must address
• Developing a code of conduct/ethics, and updating it periodically
• Coordinating the ethics programme with other company managers
• Holding training programmes for employees
• Establishing a confidential service for answering employee questions or concerns about ethics
• Ensuring company compliance with government regulation
• Auditing ethical conduct and taking action on possible violations of the code
• Developing, modifying, and communicating ethical codes and training devices
• Monitoring changes in the workplace or industry environment and evaluating how they should impact on the organization's ethical position.

CHECKLIST **YOUR ETHICAL HEALTH**

	YES	NO
• Is there a general understanding of what makes up proper conduct in your organization?	☐	☐
• Do you feel that your organization has a culture that encourages openness between managers and employees?	☐	☐
• Are there rewards for employees who demonstrate appropriate ethical behaviour?	☐	☐
• Do you feel that your employees know how to act ethically during crisis situations?	☐	☐
• Do employees in your organization treat your customers fairly and honestly?	☐	☐
• Do employees treat each other with respect and honesty?	☐	☐
• Are there role models in your organization who demonstrate ethical decision-making for lower-level employees?	☐	☐
• Have you ever given your employees constructive criticism on how to improve their ethical conduct or reprimanded them for unethical conduct?	☐	☐

Training in ethics

Training and communication programmes for employees and stakeholders make organizational ethics transparent. You should view resources for such programmes as an investment, not a cost, because they build trust and long-term relationships.

Setting out the aims

Even the most thorough training programme cannot hope to cover every ethical issue that an employee may encounter. It should, however, equip staff with the confidence to make decisions in line with organizational standards. It should create awareness of key risk areas, inform employees of appropriate contacts for ethical issues, educate them about the rewards for ethical conduct and the consequences of unethical conduct, and set out the benefits to the whole organization of maintaining standards. You can deliver ethical training in a number of ways, each with its own advantages and challenges.

> To help create a culture of openness in dealing with ethical issues.

> To ensure employees and agents understand their ethical responsibility in the context of their job.

PROS AND CONS OF DIFFERENT TRAINING METHODS

DELIVERY	ADVANTAGES	DISADVANTAGES
Lectures and presentations	Reach a large number of people; quick to implement	Trainees are passive and do not experience multiple viewpoints
Case studies and scenarios	Generate discussion and participation	Can have too narrow a focus in the issues addressed
Role playing	Highly interactive and insightful	Some people may be unwilling to participate
Videos	Realism	Too specific and not participative
Computer training	Easy to implement and highly flexible	Limited opportunity for discussion and interaction

Benefits of training for an ethical destination

To communicate the organization's responsibilities and duties, and the need to be accountable and comply with standards.

To communicate organizational standards to employees.

To empower employees to make decisions based on organizational principles and ethical values.

To explain the organizational resources devoted to creating and maintaining ethical conduct.

To communicate an organization's areas of risk.

To encourage individuals to seek advice and information when unsure of the appropriate organizational response in a situation.

To set out the ethical issues that the organization is facing and to explain the business case for an ethics programme.

Caring for your employees

Employee performance and satisfaction are of primary concern to an employer. The ethical treatment of staff, and their knowledge that they are working for an ethical company, have become increasingly important factors in the recruitment and retention of employees.

Understanding responsibilities

The employer–employee relationship has changed radically over the years. Before the 20th century, the employee served the employer and had few rights; but today, in an age of skills-shortages, the employee often behaves more like a consumer than a wage slave, selecting their employer on the basis of many criteria beyond just the salary they offer. Recent research has revealed that as many as one in six people rate an organization's attitude towards corporate social responsibility as the first or second most important factor in choosing an employer. More widely, individuals are increasingly identified with their job, so their choice of employer reflects their own values and lifestyle. To attract and retain employees, companies are having to rethink their offer, building good ethics and corporate citizenship into their brand. Failure to deliver on the declared ethical stance will result in increased labour turnover as employees realize that the initial offer was shallow.

Nurturing your staff

Shifting demographics mean that your organization's ethical reputation is set to become ever more important in the job market. As a good employer, you should take steps to recognize the aspirations and expectations of your team, and ensure they are addressed. Simple measures include recycling more, planting trees to offset carbon output, and publishing your ethical policies. Consider offering volunteer programmes and charitable donations as part of the employment package, alongside benefits such as flexible working and a clear career structure. Actively manage your reputation: most graduates gain their perception of a company's ethical standards through the media and are sceptical about what organizations state in their own published materials.

Another approach is to set up employee stock ownership plans (ESOPs) where staff have a real financial stake in the company. An ESOP provides a clear expression of how much the firm values its employees, and organizations with ESOPs generally have lower turnover rates, higher employee satisfaction, and higher productivity levels. Moreover, companies with a high degree of employee ownership consistently outperform their conventionally owned rivals in pure financial terms.

TIP

KEEP YOUR REPUTATION

Maintain a proactive ethical policy towards your employees: disgruntled ex-staff are likely to go public with complaints about their treatment.

ASK YOURSELF... ARE YOU AN ETHICAL EMPLOYER?

- Are all team members treated with respect?
- Do you use objective measures to determine employees' status and rewards?
- Are you scrupulously honest with your employees about benefits and job security?
- Do you know what motivates your employees?
- Do your staff have a chance to express their opinions?

Managing ethical crises

Instances of ethical misconduct still occur despite the best efforts of managers to implement policies and create an ethical culture. The way that you respond to an ethical crisis will determine the damage your organization sustains and the length of the recovery time.

TIP

HIRE A PROFESSIONAL

When faced with a crisis, consider engaging a professional corporate ethics consultant; he or she will see you as outsiders see you and cut through potentially inaccurate assumptions.

Avoiding crises

By far the best way to handle an ethical crisis is to avoid it in the first place. Companies with well-constructed and effectively communicated ethics policies are better protected against corporate crisis and reputation issues than companies who consider such measures a luxury. It is not enough just to have policies in place – you need to monitor them constantly and update them to match the shifting, and increasingly stringent, expectations of your various stakeholders.

Try to anticipate potential crises, and consider your responses in advance: what would you do, for example, if a hacker gained access to your computer network and stole sensitive customer details? Or if one of your products had to be recalled?

CASE STUDY

Learning from mistakes

In 1995, the campaigning organization Greenpeace protested vocally against the way that oil giant Shell UK chose to dispose of Brent Spar, a storage facility in the North Sea. Shell's failure to present its case to stakeholders eroded the company's well-founded reputation for environmental responsibility. However, Shell learned from the experience, and implemented major stakeholder dialogue programmes, including a website where anyone could question Shell about its environmental standards, and an annual report of its activities in improving social and environmental conditions.

Acting decisively

If a crisis situation does arise, you need to act fast to preserve the organization's reputation. Acknowledge that the crisis exists, assign a team of specialists in all relevant areas to consult on actions, draw up and enact a crisis-management plan, and appoint a spokesperson to liaise with stakeholders and the media. If your organization is demonstrably at fault, accept responsibility and act promptly to compensate any injured parties. It is often in your best interests to exceed the minimum compensation; this shows that your organization cares about stakeholder interests.

Good communication is essential. Establish media contacts, rather than waiting for the media to approach you, and demonstrate that the organization is taking rapid action to resolve the situation. Failure to communicate strongly suggests that your company does not care or is trying to avoid blame.

COPING IN CRISIS

FAST TRACK

OFF TRACK

FAST TRACK	OFF TRACK
Staying calm	Panicking during the crisis
Being honest with the public about the situation	Trying to cover up facts
Accepting responsibility when at fault	Assigning blame to others
Looking at the situation from the stakeholders' perspectives	Focusing on internal politics and preoccupations
Communicating regularly with the public and media	Trying to keep a low profile

Chapter 4

Looking beyond your organization

There are, as yet, no universally agreed standards against which business behaviour can be measured. However, industry bodies, think-tanks, and business theorists have all proposed ways of thinking beyond the bottom line.

Following standards

Just as there are industry standards for the quality and safety of products, so too have industry bodies developed standards for ethical behaviour. These best-practice frameworks provide useful guidelines and give you the opportunity to benchmark your effectiveness against similar firms.

Using the frameworks

The Institute of Social and Ethical Accountability, the Open Compliance Ethics Group (OCEG), and the International Organization for Standardization (ISO) all provide frameworks for ethics accountability. The processes these organizations use tie social and ethical issues into an organization's strategic management and operations. This allows for a more holistic view of corporate responsibility, in which risk, opportunity, and the impact on economy and society are integrated into reporting systems alongside more traditional measures of financial success.

Setting guidelines

Launched in 1996, AccountAbility is a US-based nonprofit institute that brings together businesses, academics, and practitioners with the aim of advancing responsible business practices. The organization has set out, and is continuing to develop, a framework called AA1000, through which companies can improve the quality of their social auditing and set standards for accountability.

Another organization that provides accountability frameworks is the Open Compliance Ethics Group (OCEG). This US-based nonprofit organization has worked with over 100 companies to create a comprehensive best practice model for implementing, managing, and evaluating compliance and ethics programmes. It documents legal requirements, standards, and principles from a variety of sources and provides practices that help an organization address these requirements. Importantly, the OCEG guidelines can be adapted to fit the specific needs and situations of individual companies.

Leading the way

The need for common standards led to the creation of the International Organization for Standardization (ISO), a body of representatives from many national standards organizations, based in Switzerland. Today, ISO is the largest publisher of international standards, many of which have been enshrined in law. The ISO 14,000 series provides environmental standards that help organizations create policies that promote sustainable business practices. Many believe that ISO 14,000 may be a key initiative for worldwide sustainability.

Defining the role of stakeholders

Stakeholders are the individuals or groups to which an organization is responsible. Internal stakeholders (such as employees, managers, and directors) need to understand and participate in ethical corporate culture. External stakeholders (such as communities, customers, suppliers, and shareholders) need to appreciate your organization's ethical principles and take part in upholding standards of conduct.

Characterizing stakeholders

Stakeholders fall into two groups: primary and secondary. Primary stakeholders are those necessary for a business's survival, including suppliers, employees, customers, and shareholders. Secondary stakeholders are those not immediately necessary for a firm's survival, including the media, special-interest groups, and trade associations.

Stakeholders can be classified using three criteria: power, legitimacy, and urgency. Power is a stakeholder's ability to influence the decisions of others. Primary stakeholders usually hold the most

ASK YOURSELF... ARE WE EFFECTIVELY ADDRESSING OUR STAKEHOLDERS' NEEDS?

- Have we identified secondary as well as primary stakeholders?
- Do we take time to listen to all stakeholder concerns?
- Do we have an effective way to gather data on stakeholder expectations?
- Do we take stakeholder complaints and desires seriously?
- Is the message we send to stakeholders consistent with our overall company objectives?
- Do we express our commitment towards meeting stakeholder needs?
- Are we communicating stakeholder needs at all levels of our organization?

power. Legitimacy is an assessment of which stakeholders matter the most. You should base this judgement on criteria that fit within boundaries of what is socially acceptable. If a stakeholder's claim does not seem legitimate, then his or her concerns are not likely to be taken seriously. Urgency refers to the time-sensitivity of stakeholder interactions – some require faster action than others.

Sometimes the concerns of secondary stakeholders become unusually powerful. For example, during a major crisis the media often becomes important to a company, thereby gaining power. What was once a secondary concern to the company has become an immediate one. Therefore, it is important that you anticipate and analyze the needs of both types of stakeholders in your organization.

Communicating effectively

Stakeholders can make or break an organization, so it is vitally important for you to manage them carefully by taking time to understand and address their concerns. Once you are aware of stakeholder agendas, you must work to communicate a clear, consistent message to them.

Communicating with the right stakeholders involves some preparation. You need to determine a stakeholder's concerns and their expectations of your organization, and then tailor your company messages to adequately address these needs. It is important to identify the best means of communication for your message – via your company website, annual report, or advertisements, for example – and make sure the message is consistent.

Effective stakeholder communication in crisis situations is particularly important. Although you will need to act quickly, it is vital that you are aware of the concerns of your stakeholders before you take action.

HOW TO... MANAGE STAKE- HOLDERS

Identify primary and secondary stakeholders.

↓

Use surveys, internet research, or focus groups to determine their interests and needs.

↓

Assess how your organization's activities impact each stakeholder.

↓

Communicate this information throughout your organization.

↓

Take action to address each stakeholder's requirements.

Accounting for your actions

The bottom line in a company's financial statement is the one that shows net income or loss – and was once considered to be the key indicator of an organization's success. But today, the term triple bottom line is increasingly heard in boardrooms of the world's biggest companies.

Defining the triple bottom line

The triple bottom line (TBL) is a measure – both in numbers and in words – of an organization's economic, environmental, and social performance. It gauges how well a company fulfils its responsibilities to all its stakeholders.

There are two good reasons to adopt TBL reporting. First, in today's world, companies are increasingly being brought to task for their wider activities and impacts – for the working conditions of their subcontractors abroad, for the obesity and ill health that their products may cause, and for the environmental hazards posed by their waste, for example. Investors are looking closely at these credentials and demanding evidence of good practice before committing their funds. Second, TBL can help your company reach new, ethically aware markets.

CASE STUDY

Great Lakes Brewing Company
Far-sighted companies have been using the TBL framework to drive policies in all areas of their activity. A good example of this is the Great Lakes Brewing Company of Cleveland, Ohio, which is a craft brewery making all-natural beer. The company prides itself on its commitment to the environment and to the community. It seeks to recycle and reuse the resources used in production and subscribes to the motto "Take, Make, Remake". As the company has worked to reduce environmentally harmful practices, it has been able to save money on operating costs. It also helps the community by donating funds to nonprofit organizations.

Measuring the triple bottom line

ECONOMIC PERFORMANCE
- Sales
- Profits
- Return on investment
- Taxes paid
- Customer satisfaction and retention
- Job creation
- Employee satisfaction and retention

ENVIRONMENTAL PERFORMANCE
- Resource use
- Energy use
- Waste-management practices
- Water and air quality
- Integrity of supply chain
- Compliance with standards

SOCIAL PERFORMANCE
- Labour practices
- Maintenance of human rights
- Impacts on the community
- Taking responsibility for products

Looking beyond profit

The Triple Bottom Line is not an award or a formal certification – it is a process that helps to keep you on track towards running a fairer business. It is still about making a profit, but profit that is in harmony with the principles of benefiting society and the environment.

When you adopt the TBL framework, you broaden the concept of financial performance beyond the traditional measures of profit and loss, to encompass the economic impact that your business has on society as a whole. Consider what economic benefits your business imparts to its host community by asking yourself questions such as:

• Do you pay fair wages and provide flexible working for your staff?
• Have you tried to level out glaring pay disparities in the organization?
• Do you try to source your raw materials locally?
• Have you negotiated fair contracts with your suppliers, and do you work with them to promote your standards?
• Do you support causes and charitable initiatives that resonate with the values of your customers?

✔ CHECKLIST ASSESSING YOUR TRIPLE BOTTOM LINE

	YES	NO
• Do measures of your financial performance assess the economic impact on society?	☐	☐
• Do you have policies that focus on social responsibility and environmental impact?	☐	☐
• Does your organization go above minimum standards of compliance?	☐	☐
• Is there effective communication about the Triple Bottom Line throughout your organization?	☐	☐
• Does your company list the environment and the community among its stakeholders?	☐	☐

Thinking of the environment

To put the TBL model into practice, you should adopt a "cause no harm" approach to the environment. Actively seek to engage in sustainable business practices that will help to preserve the environment, such as reducing energy use and rethinking harmful manufacturing processes. If your business does have environmental impacts, you should accept that the costs of minimizing and mitigating the impacts lie with you, rather than with governments or other agencies. This shifts the burden of responsibility on to your organization, encouraging a more environmentally responsible approach to doing business.

Boosting social performance

The final strand of the TBL model is social performance, a term that refers to the attitudes and actions that your business takes with respect to its workers, consumers, community, and other stakeholders. You need to recognize that the treatment of these groups is entwined with your business performance, and work to the benefit of all these constituents. Review the salaries you pay to ensure they are fair, take every care to maintain a safe work environment, and set realistic working hours.

Beyond your stakeholders, your TBL approach may include social investing initiatives to address healthcare, education, and economic opportunities for the wider community. "Upstreaming" – sharing of a proportion of your profits with the original producers of your raw materials, such as agricultural villages or farmers – is another way of boosting your performance. It can be hard to assess the level of your company's social responsibility: consider working with industry groups, such as the Open Compliance Ethics Group who can help you with ethics audits.

TIP

CARRY OUT LIFE-CYCLE ANALYSIS

If your businesses is manufacturing, conduct a life-cycle assessment of your products. This will determine what the real environmental costs of production are, from gathering the raw materials, through manufacture to distribution to eventual disposal.

Checking your supply chain

Your stakeholders and the media will judge your organization not only by your ethical standards, but also by the behaviour of all the businesses that supply you with goods and services. You should make yourself fully aware of their practices and reputation because you may be held responsible for their actions.

TIP

RIGHTS ISSUE
Before dealing with a new supplier, check if they allow trades unions to operate; a unionized workforce usually indicates respect for rights.

Identifying weakness

No matter how hard you try to steer your organization along an ethical path, you are only as strong as the weakest link in your supply chain; and your exposure to this risk is enhanced if you operate in retail or if you own a brand with a high public profile. A recent example involved toy company Mattel, which outsourced around 50 per cent of its production to manufacturers in China. The discovery of lead paint on some of its product lines led to the recall of almost one million units, and a significant loss of both money and reputation for Mattel, despite the fact that the company required its subcontractors to use paint provided by certified suppliers.

✔ CHECKLIST **ASSURING YOUR SUPPLIERS' ETHICAL CREDENTIALS**

	YES	NO
• Do they provide resources to support the community in which they operate?	☐	☐
• Do they make efforts to attract and retain a workforce that represents the varied background of the community within which they operate?	☐	☐
• Do they promote the protection and preservation of the health of the natural environment?	☐	☐
• Do they actively and demonstrably manage their ethical policies and business conduct?	☐	☐
• Do they have accurate financial reporting and risk-management systems in place?	☐	☐
• Do they work actively to minimize the occurrence of injury, danger, error, accident, harm, and loss?	☐	☐

Ensuring compliance

Developing and maintaining an ethical supply chain is no easy task: the standards you set for your suppliers must have teeth, but also be realistic, and they must work across cultural, language, and legal divides. Many companies have based their standards on independent principles, such as those set out by the International Labour Organisation (ILO), but even having robust standards in place is no guarantee of compliance, simply because suppliers are more likely to conceal their lack of adherence to standards rather than risk losing their contract.

To obtain compliance, you need to work closely with all your suppliers. It is perfectly valid to select your supplier on purely commercial grounds, and then work with them to ensure compliance to your organization's ethical standards. Use training and education to instil in them a real appreciation of the dangers of ethical misdeeds. Make sure that they have the capacity to fulfil your orders while maintaining ethical oversight, and try to involve local regulation agencies who can help the suppliers stick to standards. Examine the purchasing practices in your own organization and identify any conflicts that may exist between ethical and commercial objectives.

Investing ethically

In the 21st century, ever more people are endorsing ethical organizations with their money. In the US alone, it is estimated that three quarters of investors take ethical issues and an organization's conduct into consideration when deciding where to commit their funds.

Getting in tune

*Ethical investing — *an investment strategy that attempts to balance financial return on investment and a positive impact for all stakeholders.*

Ethical investing* is a strategy that is being embraced by individuals, nonprofit organizations, governments, and corporations. As a manager, you have a responsibility both to ensure that your organization is attractive to potential investors, and that your own funds are managed in a way that does not have negative impacts on society.

Ethical investment was thrust on to the world stage in the 1970s and 1980s, when individuals and corporations refused to invest in South African companies because of the human rights abuses of apartheid. Today, many investors refuse to put their money into funds associated with unethical actions, no matter how lucrative the prospects, and conversely, will seek out investment opportunities with clear social benefit.

Seeing new opportunities

The idea of ethical investing varies by country, and depends on the cultural perceptions of companies and their practices. For example, Europeans are far more wary of genetically engineered crops than Americans, so may be less likely to invest in GM technologies. However, some areas, such as renewable energy, are almost universally viewed as an ethical – and in the long term, essential – alternative

CASE STUDY

Creative investment

Ethical investment can be very creative: in the UK, venture capital company Bridges Ventures has provided capital to ventures such as The Gym, a fitness chain based in deprived areas, which offers low charges to its members; and the Hoxton Hotel, a successful operation in a run-down area of East London. It has funded Whelan Refining Limited, a company that recycles waste oil to produce base oil – the base for all industrial and automotive lubricants – and schemes that provide low-cost housing for key workers. Bridges Ventures publishes an ethical charter that encompasses its approach to employees, suppliers and contractors, investors, the community, and the wider environment.

to the consumption of fossil fuels. Recent statistics bear out that ethical investment is more than a sideline to making money: ethical funds have performed well over the years, and the World Trade Organization is set to tighten regulations on companies that exploit people, animals, or the environment, making ethical investment a better bet for reliable investment.

TIP

KEEP IT REAL
Remember that ethical investors are still investors: they are looking for good financial returns and security as well as the promotion of socially responsible strategies.

Choosing your investment

Investments are made on your behalf every day, and you may not be aware of where your money is going. Select financial services providers, such as banks and pension and insurance companies that are transparent about the criteria they use to choose ethical investment. These are likely to be:

• **Negative criteria:** rejecting investment in firms involved in tobacco, the arms trade, and environmental damage, or those recently censured for misconduct.
• **Positive criteria:** seeking out companies that have a measurable positive impact on society or the environment, such as sustainable energy or recycling.
• **Engagement:** using your power as a shareholder to change for the better the ways in which the company engages with people and the environment.

Celebrating best practice

The theory and practice of business ethics is in constant evolution. While it draws upon traditions, laws, and regulations, it is always being shaped by its practitoners – the companies at the sharp edge of business. Some of these organizations have become famous for their good practice, trustworthiness, and integrity and for going well above and beyond their legal duties. Take some time to study their approaches to ethical business and ask if they can be used to benefit your organization.

Championing philanthropy

Some companies have become famous for their philanthropic activities, and their brands are associated strongly with good works. One such company is Google, a hugely influential force in the technology sector. Google believes that businesses have a duty to act responsibly and seeks to decrease the negative impact of business on the environment. As a result, it has created google.org, an organization dedicated to using technology to address worldwide issues, such as climate change and disease.

Google is also working with other nonprofit organizations to create a code of conduct that will help businesses deal with oppressive governments. So far, Google has donated more than $75 million in worldwide grants and investments. As Google chief compliance officer Andy Hinton puts it, "Google is dedicated towards changing the world for the better."

Engaging people

Many companies realize that ethics policies and standards mean little without the commitment of their employees and take measures to ensure buy-in from their staff. Texas Instruments (TI) provides an example. The electronics firm employs more than 30,000 people in over 25 countries and believes that partnership between employees and employer is crucial to an ethical corporate culture.

The company has a special office dedicated to ethics and has established multiple communication channels to inform staff about the latest ethical and legal issues in this fast-changing business. Texas Instruments provides advice on how to assess issues in its quick ethics test, which is distributed to employees. It asks employees to ask the following questions when they are unsure about the ethics of certain situations or behaviours:
• Is the action legal?
• Does it comply with our values?
• If you do it, will you feel bad?
• How will it look in the newspaper?
• If you know it's wrong, don't do it!
• If you're not sure, ask.
• Keep asking until you get an answer.

Going global

Applying ethics consistently in a globalized world is a challenge that has been successfully met by the leading package delivery company UPS, which does business in more than 200 countries. Despite the fact that it operates in so many different territories with their own languages, UPS maintains its high ethical integrity. To make sure that its ethical standards can be understood by different cultures, UPS offers its code of conduct materials in 12 languages.

UPS also participates in many philanthropic endeavours and has won an award from the US Environmental Protection Agency for coming up with innovative ways to reduce its carbon footprint. It has also received plaudits for encouraging diversity and for being one of the best places to launch a career.

Index

Acknowledgements

Author's acknowledgements

We would like to thank Jennifer Jackson for helping to coordinate and develop content for this book. In addition, we would also like to thank Jennifer Sawayda for her work on this manuscript. Their assistance in crafting the final product was invaluable. We also wish to thank John Fraedrich, Debbie Thorne, Bob Chandler, and Lynn Brewer for their insights and depth of knowledge in understanding business ethics. We would like to thank Tim Rhodes for information provided about protecting corporate intelligence on pages 32 to 33. We have been greatly moved by the legacy of Bill Daniels and his inspiration for ethical conduct in business captured by his creation of the Daniels Fund. We would like to thank those at the Daniels Fund who continue to carry the torch and keep his legacy and vision alive, specifically Linda Childears, Barbara Danbom, and Sparky Turner. They continue to "raise the bar" and inspire us to reach out and make an impact in the area of business ethics education. We would especially like to thank Amy Wohlert, Interim Dean of the Anderson School of Management at the University of New Mexico, for her support of this and other business ethics initiatives.

Publisher's acknowledgements

The publisher would like to thank Hilary Bird for indexing, Judy Barratt for proofreading, and Charles Wills for co-ordinating Americanization.

Picture credits

The publisher would like to thank the following for their kind permission to reproduce their photographs:

1 Getty Images: Harald Sund; 4–5 iStockphoto.com: Dean J. Birinyi Photography; 8–9 iStockphoto.com: Jacques Kloppers; 14–15 Corbis: George Diebold/Solus-Veer; 17 Getty Images: Michael M Schwab; 26–27 Alamy: INSADCO Photography; 32–33 Alamy: JCB-Images; 38–39 iStockphoto.com: NickS; 42–43 Alamy: Tom Mackie; 45 istockphoto.com: Paweł Tałajkowski; 46 Alamy: Arco Images GmbH; 50–51 Getty Images: Edwin Remsberg; 52 iStockphoto.com: bubaone; 52 iStockphoto.com: susaro; 57 Alamy: Captured Sight; 61 iStockphoto.com: Simon Smith; 61 Alamy: Petra Wegner; 61 Alamy: Les Polders; 64 iStockphoto.com: Martin McCarthy; 68–69 iStockphoto.com: Kameleon007.

Every effort has been made to trace the copyright holders. The publisher apologizes for any unintentional omission and would be pleased, in such cases, to place an acknowledgement in future editions of this book.

EOIN COLFER

PUFFIN

PUFFIN BOOKS

UK | USA | Canada | Ireland | Australia
India | New Zealand | South Africa

Puffin Books is part of the Penguin Random House group of companies
whose addresses can be found at global.penguinrandomhouse.com.

puffinbooks.com

First published 2015
001

Text copyright © Eoin Colfer, Artemis Fowl Ltd, 2015

The moral right of the author has been asserted

Set in 12/16 pt Bembo Book MT Std
Typeset by Jouve (UK), Milton Keynes
Printed in Great Britain by Clays Ltd, St Ives plc

A CIP catalogue record for this book is available from the British Library

ISBN: 978-0-141-36109-3

www.greenpenguin.co.uk

MIX
Paper from
responsible sources
FSC
www.fsc.org   FSC® C018179

Penguin Random House is committed to a
sustainable future for our business, our readers
and our planet. This book is made from Forest
Stewardship Council® certified paper.

For all the time travellers who followed me into the wormhole

Manchester City Libraries	
C0000020101703	
PETERS	19-Aug-2015
	Â7.99

CONTENTS

NEED TO KNOW

Towards the end of the twentieth century, quantum physicist Professor Charles Smart figured out how to construct tunnels from exotic matter with negative energy density. Simply put, Smart managed to access wormholes into the past at various quantum *soft points*. And, like almost every invention in the history of humankind, this one was quickly exploited by powerful people for their own greedy and violent ends. In this case the FBI established the Witness Anonymous Relocation Programme to stash federal witnesses in the past. This was an idea so monumentally complicated and expensive that it was doomed to catastrophic failure. And fail WARP did when the military tried to take over the programme, and Charles Smart disappeared into the past, taking his secrets with him.

Consequences of the collapse of the WARP initiative included but were not limited to:

- the loss of billions of dollars' worth of equipment at WARP sites through the centuries
- the stranding of several witnesses and their handlers in various historic eras

- the setting-loose of Albert Garrick, a psychotic Victorian assassin, in modern London, where he cut a bloody swathe through the city
- The unleashing of Colonel Clayton Box into nineteenth-century London, where he very nearly succeeded in using his futuristic weapons to overthrow Parliament – and he would have done it too if not for two darned kids, namely:
  - ◊ Chevron Savano, a Shawnee FBI juvenile consultant who travelled to the past to fix the future, which was even more complicated than it sounds, and
  - ◊ Riley, a Victorian orphan who managed to strand his genuinely evil master, the assassin Albert Garrick, in the time tunnel before being instrumental in foiling Colonel Box's plan, which was quite the pair of accomplishments for a fourteen-year-old boy with nothing at his disposal but quick wits and an expertise in stage magic.

No need for newcomers to the story arc to worry about the nitty-gritty. All you need to know is that our two uniquely talented and resourceful teenagers have just discovered that Riley's long-lost half-brother, Tom, has been imprisoned in Newgate Prison and they have rushed over there to liberate him.

I think you can probably guess that things are going to go disastrously awry and much deadly danger will ensue.

Don't fret – there are laughs too, and japes.

But I should not mislead: it's mostly deadly danger.

So, if you are of a sensitive disposition, abandon ye this volume now and find for yourself a book about ponies or the like.

You have been warned.

Also 'ye' is just an old word for 'you', so 'abandon you this volume now' is what I meant to say.

I was going for a mood.

DOWNLOAD SPEED

Professor Charles Smart.

Smart by name, smart by nature?

The man who opened the Einstein–Rosen bridge (that's a wormhole to you and me) and understood as much about it as a chimp does the molecular composition of the banana it has just peeled. Charles Smart poked a *hole* in the banana peel and then tossed people in there, hoping they would come out intact at the other end. In fairness to the professor, most did, but some were changed utterly. There were a few positive changes – such as the time FBI Special Agent Cody 'Cue-Ball' Potter got his hair back, or when stumpy little Jerry Townsend went in five feet one and came out six feet three – but most of the mutations could be judged as negative. Men got spliced with animals: there were dog-men, monkey-men and, on one particularly memorable occasion, a tyrannosaur-guy. Time travellers picked up tumours and lesions and third-degree burns in all sorts of sensitive areas. Doctor Marla DeTroit, who funnily enough was from Detroit, went into the time tunnel a statuesque thirty-something lady and came out a bent-over octogenarian

5

guy. This shook people up even more than the dinosaur incident. And, with every fresh wacky episode, the folk involved realized how little they understood the giant animal they were poking with a sharp stick.

Professor Smart himself said it best: *You want to know how much we know about time travel? Let me put it this way: if we imagine the quantum network to be a giant interlocking system — something like the London Underground, for example — then we are just a swarm of ants who happened to fall through a grate on to one of the tracks.*

Not exactly a vote of confidence. And this is from the big cheese himself. The man who was running the show.

The point being that there were things about the wormholes that Smart could not possibly have known when he hacked into one. There were consequences that the professor could never have foreseen, but as a proud Scotsman he should at least have remembered the lesson taught to him on his pappy's knee: *Nothing is free in this world, Charley boy. Nothing is even cheap. Everything will cost you dearly.*

Pappy Smart was right. Everything must be paid for eventually, and Mother Nature is the cruellest creditor of them all. As a direct result of his meddling, Smart paid with his life. Actually, because of a time paradox, Charles Smart paid with his life *twice*. But Mother Nature was still not satisfied — there were other meddlers in the wormhole from whom blood payment had to be exacted, as Chevron Savano and Riley were about to find out.

Cue creepy foreshadowing music: *Bom-bom-bommmmmm.*

Newgate Prison. The City. London. 1899

Newgate Prison: the most notorious block of lumpen misery ever to put down foundations in old London town. Built on the orders of Harry Plantagenet way, way back at the last gasp of the twelfth century, and refashioned on the say-so of Lord Mayor Dick Whittington himself, which is rarely mentioned in the storybooks.

Constructed in accordance with the principles of the French *Architecture Terrible* school, with deliberate, heavy repulsiveness, the building itself served as a warning, to anyone who looked upon it, of the fate of those who would choose a life of crime. The prison contained not a single elegant line nor a decent patch of natural light.

Outside this forbidding structure, flinching at the sounds of diverse wailings from within, stood the boy magician Riley, not yet fifteen, and his companion, Chevron Savano, warrior-maiden from the future and just over two years his senior, both thinking thoughts along the lines of:

This place is hell on earth.

And:

We must free Tom from here.

'Gold will do the job, Chevie,' Riley said, with a slight tremor in his voice that only a close friend would notice. 'Shillings for killings and pound-letters for debtors. Cash is king in the Gate.'

'Right,' said Chevie in the American fashion, and squeezed his fingers.

For, in this, young Riley was indeed correct.

7

Newgate was every bit as much a financial establishment as Threadneedle's Bank of England. Food, clothing, family quarters. Everything was on offer for cash in the prison, up to the striking of a man's fetters from his ankles or a dram of laudanum to quiet the condemned's nerves on his short walk to the triple gibbet.

And the man to be hanged need not be a murderer. There were hundreds of crimes that would get a man or woman invited to dance the Newgate Jig. One of these crimes was that of defaultery.

London was a city of commerce and, to many of the local business folk, reneging on one's debts was a crime most heinous. A man who would cheat his neighbours deserved no less than a spot of capital punishment while his fellow prisoners cheered and jeered. And, according to all available information, Tom Riley – known commonly as 'Ginger' – was in debt up to the apple of his soon-to-be-stretched neck.

Unless.

Unless the wronged man could be paid off.

In that case it would be all kisses and cuddles and *Off you go, Ginger*, into a bright new tomorrow.

But not so quick, youngster. Not so sprightly.

Negotiating this class of deal was trickier than tying a knot in a jellied eel. One party had the other in sight of the rope that would hang him, and it would take a wheedler of real talent to wring any leverage out of that situation, especially when Tom had defrauded a man of stature – namely, Sir James Maccabee, the finest attorney in London, with more souls on his account than the Great Fire.

Riley could attempt the wheedle himself, but he would be eaten alive by Maccabee, and so he had engaged the services of the famous prison negotiator Tartan Nancy Grimes, who could have outmanoeuvred Bonaparte himself had the wee Frenchman been unlucky enough to have found himself across the barter table.

So Tartan Nancy had come, tested the sovereign advance with a grind of her molars, and then promptly disappeared into the bowels of the prison to see what was what and who was who and, most importantly, how much was enough.

And now Chevie and Riley waited for the wheedler to return. They waited, shuffling and uncomfortable in the teeming shanty town that sprang up in the shadow of Newgate and was dismantled every month or so by the militia, only to grow again like a winter weed between the flagstones. They waited among the destitute families and the visitors and the hawkers and veterans. They averted their eyes from the human tragedy clamouring on all sides, for Riley had troubles of his own and Chevie had not yet convinced herself that any of this was real.

I am in a coma, she told herself repeatedly. *I am in a coma and this is what I get for reading Charles Dickens late at night.*

It was a reasonable theory – much more credible, in fact, than the timeline presented to her by this reality: FBI, time machines, magician assassins, megalomaniacal army colonels and so on.

Coma or not, Chevie had agreed to pull on a dress from the Orient Theatre's costume wardrobe, wearing it over her FBI jumpsuit to spare Riley's blushes. She topped off the

9

outfit with a straw bonnet that hid her dark hair and skin so as not to attract more attention.

I must look like Darth Vader's daughter wearing this monstrosity, she had thought at the time.

Being the only Shawnee Native American in the entirety of England was stare-worthy enough, without being dressed in a fashion shockingly immoral for the period.

Or as Riley had put it: 'We got us plenty of eyes on stalks without you parading yerself like a slattern.'

Chevie was pretty certain that being a slattern was not a good thing and so tied the bonnet tight under her chin, scowling all the time and wondering why it was OK for Riley to wear his magician's cape in the street, even though surely that would also attract attention. But now, as she looked around, Chevie had to concede that there were plenty of becaped guys wandering the area. It was like some kind of old-timey Comic-Con out there.

Some time later the wheedler's stocky frame barged through a side gate and, heedless of the ragamuffins clustered around her voluminous skirts begging for a twist of baccy or a pull of gin, she gestured for Chevie and Riley to join her and they hurried across the street to where Nancy was applying an ember from a nearby brazier to the clay bowl of her pipe. Tough customer that she was, Tartan Nancy held the ember in her bare hand, little finger cocked as though she were pouring cream from a sterling jug.

Tartan Nancy Grimes was not Scottish and neither did she wear the tartan of any clan. While waiting for Nancy to return with tidings, Riley had informed Chevie that the nickname

'Tartan' was a touch of Cockney rhyming slang applied to the wheedler on account of her gassy insides.

Oh, Chevie had said, and then: *Ohhhhh*, when the penny had dropped.

And, though no elaboration had been requested, Riley had proceeded to particularize: *Nancy has been wearing them old skirts so long that they've grown rigid. They act like a bell, they do. Amplifying the sound, as it were, Chevie. Only don't ever mention it as Nance don't like it brought up.*

Being indiscreet like this was not usually a part of Riley's nature, but he was agitated and the words tumbled out. He needn't have worried; Chevie was hardly likely to raise the subject in the middle of a sensitive negotiation, as she had two semesters of hostage negotiation at the FBI compound in Quantico under her belt.

Tartan Nancy Grimes tossed the smouldering ember into the gutter and puffed up a storm cloud on her pipe. She was a stout woman with grizzled ringlets of fading red hair framing her round face as strands of weed might frame a pitted river rock. On her head sat a pristine white bonnet, which seemed out of place with her own self and the rest of the environs, but keeping a fresh bonnet was central to Nancy's credo – if a lady may not have a fresh bonnet, then what in the name of God may she have?

'Have you seen Tom?' asked Riley, and then: 'How did he seem? Hale and hearty?'

Nancy puffed a while longer and said, 'I seen him, young fella. He's a mite battered, but nothing as will put him under, lessen he gets himself infected, which could happen easily enough.'

Tom being still above ground was about the best news they could have hoped for, as it was not uncommon for new fish to croak on the first day – to mix cold-blooded metaphors.

Chevie squeezed Riley's shoulder. 'There, you see? We're gonna be OK. Family reunions by dinner time, right? Or is that teatime?'

Not one of the party smiled, not even the joker.

'And how is Maccabee's mood?' Riley asked the wheedler. 'Has the notion of payment cheered him?'

Nancy knocked out her pipe, then spat in the bowl. 'Ah, now here we arrives at the nub, my young fella, for it ain't Maccabee what has been wronged. It's another gent, a mysterious, shadowy fella what lurks.' Tartan Nancy jammed her thumb into the pipe bowl and worked the spittle. 'And Old Nance hates a lurker. It's the devil of a job to read a lurker. Maccabee is simply his attorney. And for a man to have a man like Maccabee beaking for him inside the Gate itself –' here Nancy whistled between a gap in her side teeth – 'well, that man is a man among men.'

Chevie was confused by this string of men. 'So this guy Maccabee isn't the guy . . . man?'

'Nah,' said Nancy. 'He's a front is all. The gent behind him, the *Lurker*; *he's* your guy and I ain't even seen his face, just boots poking from the shadows. Black riding boots, so black they don't shine where they should. How can a body trust boots like that?'

Tartan Nancy spat into the bowl once more, filling it to

the brim. Chevie must have winced, for Nancy said, 'Pardon my manners, princess, but I don't like to clean me bowl during negotiations.'

Chevie nodded. *Cleaning one's bowl* during negotiations did not seem like a good idea.

Riley had a million questions. 'Does Tom remember me, Nance? Did he say what my name was, perhaps? What in the name of heaven did he do to land himself in these dire straits?'

Nancy pointed the stem of her pipe at him. 'And this is why I am doing the wheedling and not you, youngster. You be tripping over yourself, Riley lad. One at a time, calm and measured, like the world is your teahouse.'

Riley swallowed his impatience. 'Right you are, Nance. The crime, then. What is he accused of?'

'That's a queer one,' said Nancy. 'Defaulting in general is on the bill. But no specifics. And Maccabee ain't talking much. And, as for Lurky Boots, not a word outta his gob. I never worked a job like this. They got your brother in a nice private cell, all ready for bargaining, and then they turns up their noses at gold like it's sewer droppings. A right puzzler, this is.'

Chevie, who had at least theoretical experience in these situations, cut directly to the important question. 'There's always a demand. What is it?'

'The Injun maid has put her finger on it,' said Tartan Nancy. 'They has a demand right enough and a strange one too.'

'Anything,' blurted Riley, already forgetting Nancy's advice that he play his cards close. 'Anything they want.'

'They wants you, young fella,' said Nancy, incredulous at the idea that this stripling could be worth more than shining sovereigns to anybody. 'You seem like a nice chap, Riley, but I offered twenty sovs. I *opened* with twenty.'

Chevie's soldier sense buzzed and something told her there was more going on here than a simple pay-off.

'I don't like it. How does this Lurker guy even know that you exist, Riley?'

Riley was not interested. 'What do they want of me, Nance?'

'Your person. In the cell. They will talk only to you.'

'No,' said Chevie. 'Absolutely not. If Riley goes in there, he isn't coming out.'

'Once again, the Injun is spot on,' said Nancy, looking Chevie up and down. 'You ever think of apprenticing in the wheedle trade, miss? Your exotic appearance could be a real boon, throw the customers off balance. Perhaps you would consider a scatter of facial tattoos?'

'Thanks for the offer, Nancy,' said Chevie. 'However, let's concentrate on today. Purely in terms of bargaining power, it would be disastrous to let Riley into that prison.'

'That is true,' admitted Tartan Nancy. 'But they is not giving a smidge on that front. It's the boy Riley in the box, or go to blazes and the ginger fella swings.'

Riley squared his shoulders and frowned his best determined face. 'I have to do it, Chevron. There ain't no other way.'

Chevie thought that her friend's determined face was pretty effective, and one look at it made it clear that his mind was not for changing.

'OK, pal. But if you're going in there I'm going with you.'

Nancy wagged the pipe stem. 'Just the boy, Maccabee said. And him alone.'

Chevie swatted the objection aside with her palm. 'Yeah, well, Maccabee is going to have to learn to live with disappointment. This is a negotiation, isn't it, Nancy? Give and take? Well, I'm going in there, so you can take that, put it in your pipe and smoke it.'

Nancy snorted appreciatively. 'Strong tone. Good posture, not a sign of a bluff. If you makes it out of the Gate alive, girl, come see me. You're a born wheedler.'

A born wheedler.

Chevie did not know whether to be flattered or insulted. She would, she decided, not worry about it as she was in a coma after all.

A born wheedler?

Which dark corner of her unconscious had that one come from?

Please, doctor, she broadcast as she followed Tartan Nancy towards the prison. *Now would be a good time to resuscitate me.*

Tartan Nancy Grimes led them quickly through the throng to the prison gate. Such was her grease in the Gate that the guards parted before her without so much as a challenge to the identity of her company and with only the most cursory of searches, for it was in everyone's interest, from cook to warden, that Nancy's commerce proceed unhindered.

They passed through a wrought-iron gate and then a reinforced door, both of which clanged ominously behind them, and Chevie could not help but worry that this was a one-way trip for Riley and herself, and the *triple gibbet* she had heard about would be full to capacity by morning.

Calm yourself, she thought. *You have done nothing wrong.*

It was, she realized, becoming difficult to hang on to the coma theory with the black stone of Newgate Prison closing in on all sides.

Riley must have noticed the anxious sheen on her brow as he sidled closer and whispered, 'Fret not, Chev. These locks are cake to me. I got jemmies in me hair.'

Cake locks and jemmies?

Maybe it was a coma, after all.

Onwards they strode, hurrying to keep pace with Tartan Nancy's pneumatic stride. She might have been a steam engine with the pipe as her funnel.

Nancy spoke as she walked, and the wheedler's words drifted over her shoulder encased in puffs of smoke.

'I'll do the talking, boy.'

'Yes,' said Riley obediently. 'Not a peep out of me.'

'And no bawling neither,' added Nancy. 'As far as Lurky Boots is concerned, you don't give much of a fig for this Tom fella. You is only here outta family duty, see?'

'I see,' said Riley. 'Not a fig does I give.'

'That way we keeps the price low.'

In truth, it was for keeping the price low that Riley did not give a fig. He would gladly fork over the last gold sovereign from Albert Garrick's ill-gotten stash to see Tom free, but he knew better than to express this opinion to a wheedler like Tartan Nancy, as the shock could set her bell ringing, so to speak, and nobody wanted that in an enclosed space.

The corridor opened on to the main yard, where prisoners shambled about in fetters if they had not the price to have them struck off. Many of the interned lolled around the gate, scratching at festering blisters, their time served but without the exit fee demanded by the system. Each year many men and women died inside Newgate because they couldn't scrape together the shilling to get out. The sounds and smells were cacophonous, overpowering and uniformly in the negative. Even the famously buoyant Cockney spirit could not stay afloat in such an environment.

I don't belong here, thought Chevie, feeling the horror and historic grimness of the place push her close to panic. *This is not my time.*

In truth, nobody on earth belonged in Newgate, and Newgate did not belong anywhere on earth.

Mercifully, Nancy did not lead them through the yard but turned with marching-band precision into a doorway, marked out from the wall only by a marginally darker shade of gloom, and disappeared into the shadows beyond. Riley picked up his pace and Chevie had little option but to follow, even though her Quantico training buzzed in her skull like a trapped bee at the notion of waltzing into the black unknown, especially since her night vision was one of the qualities she seemed to have lost in the wormhole.

Chevie had noticed over the past few days that this latest jaunt through the time tunnel had affected her in many ways. Nothing big yet – no dinosaur parts – but she was a changed person. Her hearing was not as sharp as it had been and the chevron tattoo on her shoulder had become a straight-edged birthmark. She found running a little awkward and would swear that one leg was half an inch longer than it used to be. And the latest thing on her growing list of mutations was that a couple of times a day, though only for a second or two, she would swear that she had X-ray vision.

Dear Professor Charles Xavier, she thought. *I am writing to you because I think I have what it takes to join the X-Men academy . . .*

Curiouser and curiouser.

And then there were the headaches.

But later for these thoughts.

Now for surviving.

The dark swallowed them and Chevie made herself focus because, whether or not the coma theory was sound, everyone knew that if you died in your dreams you died in your bed too.

Dream deaths are just a wake-up call for people who aren't ever waking up.

Which made zero sense.

Chevie disguised a bitter laugh as a cough. *Sense?* How long had it been since anything made sense?

Chevie realized that she and Riley were holding hands, and not in a young-love kind of way, which would have been weird, but in a white-knuckled, I-want-to-make-sure-my-friend-is-beside-me kind of way.

The poor kid doesn't even know he's dragging me along, she realized. *That's how much he wants to see his half-brother.*

Chevie understood. What would she not do for one more day with her dad? One more shared bottle of orange cream soda?

Two straws, one bottle.

That had been their thing. Then a single spark in a leaky Harley gas tank and it was all over.

One in a million, the highway-patrol cop who'd come to

their little Malibu home had told her. *I ain't never seen nuthin'
like it, miss.*

One in a million, thought Chevie now. *Those kinds of odds
seem to beat me all the time.*

But back to the prison corridor: Tartan Nancy, deadly
danger and so on and so forth.

Nancy stormed ahead with the confident stride of the
powerful or the bluffer, and Chevie wanted to call after her:
Slow down. Don't be so eager.

For they had no way of knowing what awaited them in that
room. Whoever this Lurker guy was, he wanted something
from Riley, something worth turning down cold hard cash for.

Chevie ran through the possibilities while they walked.

An old enemy?

Maybe.

One of Box's men?

No. Too soon to have set this up. Those guys were barely
twenty-four hours out of the picture.

One of Garrick's victims?

No. Garrick's victims were precisely that: victims. They
weren't hunting down anyone, ever. Garrick was the man who
had killed Jack the Ripper, for God's sake. Out of jealousy!

Another witness from the WARP programme, then?

Possible. It seemed unlikely that someone from the future
would care about some kid magician in the past, but 'unlikely'
was a term in which she was fast losing faith.

Chevie found her free hand patting the Timekey that hung
round her neck, underneath her clothes. There hadn't been a
peep out of it for days – it had doubtless been broken by the

various treks across London and a dunking in the city's delightful sewers – but if there was some *future* guy in that cell it could be that this was his endgame: get hold of the key and destroy it.

Funny how nobody from the future wants to go back there. Except me.

But did she really?

I don't even know which future I would be going back to.

Social media and reality shows? Worldwide fascist empire? Or some blend of the two perhaps?

Whatever the future held, Chevie was determined to hold on to the key just in case she needed a way out.

If there's a portal to go in. If there's a pod at the other end.

It would take a dire situation to force her to jump into the wormhole with no sure way out, but she had to admit that dire situations were ten a penny in this century. It seemed to her that here all situations were dire and all smells uniformly terrible. Even the sweet smells were infected by what they tried to mask.

Speaking of terrible smells, they had arrived at yet another door, which was even blacker than the first and seemed to be composed of gathered shadows. The door was guarded by one of the foulest-smelling beings that Chevie had ever been unfortunate enough to sniff. With her eyes closed she would never have guessed he was human by his odour or the snuffling sound of his breathing. The sentry's uniform seemed to have been cannibalized from those of dead soldiers from various campaigns and was topped off with a ridiculous Napoleonic hat, which might have been comical in another setting.

'Broadband,' said Nancy, saluting him with a dip of her pipe.

Chevie was surprised. Had Nancy just referred to this particular guard as 'Broadband'?

Broadband acknowledged the pipe dip. 'Back so soon, Nance. How's the wheedle?'

Nancy whistled through the gap in her teeth. 'Slow connection today, Broadband.'

'Too many users,' said Broadband. 'They is congestin' and stuff.'

Chevie blinked. Were they messing with her brain, or was her brain messing with her?

'Broadband's your name?' she asked, suspicious of a wind-up. 'How come?'

Nancy answered, as if the guard was too slow to remember the reason behind his own nickname.

'On account of this prison vest he used to wear during the frosts. From up north somewhere. Had a broad band instead of the Newgate broad arrow. So, Broadband, ain't it?'

Chevie puffed a sigh of relief. That was a perfectly acceptable explanation. Nobody was going crazy.

'Broadband,' she said with a slightly hysterical laugh. 'What's your download speed?'

The guard considered this seriously. 'I can empty a cart in an hour or so, depending on me boots and gloves and whatnot. A barge takes a day on me lonesome. Less with a chum.' He added to this information a nugget of wisdom. 'I finds that a job is done quicker with more lads doing it.'

Nancy cackled and tapped Broadband's forehead. 'Smart. That's what you is, dearie. Which is for why they puts you guarding the big-knob cells.'

Usually Riley and Chevie would have shared a chortle at this, but not today. In fact, Riley said not a word.

He hasn't spoken, Chevie realized. *Not since the outer corridor.*

She glanced down at her friend. His pale face seemed to glow in the gloom, and the rough and tumble of the past few days had his hair sticking up in a hundred different ways.

Very Manga, thought Chevie. *He's ahead of his time.*

But, in spite of all the life experience crammed into his fourteen years, Riley seemed very much a small boy, squeezing her fingers and staring at the cell door.

What must be going through his head now that he is finally about to be reunited with his only living relative?

In truth, the inside of Riley's head was all a-jumble, with images and emotions falling over one another trying for the upper hand. It was more than his young head could process. At least Chevie knew about the future. At least she had some understanding of the past. Riley had been a wide-eyed ignoramus in the twenty-first century and now felt a stranger in his own time.

Ginger Tom will be my anchor, was the thought that finally broke through the maelstrom in his head. It was a good strong thought and he began to murmur it under his breath.

Tartan Nancy raised her eyebrow at this but made no remark, for she was used to unusual behaviour during the wheedle. One musty sea dog had taken to answering questions in the voice of a small girl, which had been most disconcerting. It was a good ploy, though; the screws couldn't wait to see the back of him.

'Shall we?' she said.

Riley squeezed Chevie's hand again and his fingers felt like a fistful of sardines so slick were they, but she held fast nevertheless – they had been through worse liquids together than honest sweat.

'Let's go,' she said. 'I wanna see what's so special about this Tom guy.'

Broadband pulled out a key on a cord from under his shirt and Chevie was about to do the same with hers and shout *Jinx!* but then wisely decided against it, as in her experience the sudden drawing of cylindrical objects around armed men often led to the *draw-er* getting shot.

Broadband slotted the key into a hole large enough for a mouse to creep through and twisted it two clunks anticlockwise.

'Usual, is it?' he said to Nancy.

Nancy did not speak money out loud, as was her custom with guards, who were technically not supposed to extort over and above what was on the warden's price list. Instead she dipped her pipe twice.

Broadband shook his head. 'Nah. Two ain't enough for this one, Nance. That geezer in the shadows is giving me the willies. You wanna wheedle again today, it'll cost you four sovs.'

With the flat of his hand, the guard barred the entrance to Tom Riley's cell door until, with four dips of her pipe, Tartan Nancy agreed to the price of admission.

THE PRISON TERM

The cell door did not creak like a prison door might in a penny dreadful, for this particular door was well used and the hinges were often greased with animal fat or lamp oil. This door opened into what might be called a *premium* cell, where the fate of special prisoners was decided. Previous occupants of the cell included a senior Romanov and even one of the House of Hanover, who had been led astray after a day at the races with a band of high-spirited Oxford chums and ended up in the hidey-hole.

But now the cell held plain old Ginger Tom Riley, and Nancy Grimes could not help but wonder what was so special about this debtor that a premium cell had been rented for the wheedling.

In the old days, she thought, *a debtor like this common-as-muck cove would have been dumped in the Stone Hall.*

The door yawned open and there was a ghostly candle flicker on the wall that picked out soot-blackened masonry pitted by pocks and cracks. A sour smell oozed into the hallway; it was the odour of despair and persecution.

Either that or damp.

Nancy went through first, as was the protocol, and next walked Chevie, with her fists tightly curled and ready for fight or flight. *Protect Riley* was her prime objective. Generally Riley was more than capable of protecting himself, trained as he had been in the martial arts of master assassin Albert Garrick, but today her friend was distracted and not on tip-top form.

An elephant could sneak up on him right now, Chevie realized, and moved to position herself as a shield between Riley and whatever was in that room.

What *was* in the room was primarily layers of shadows and darkness, which were barely disturbed by the flickering arrowhead of candlelight.

As the newcomers' eyes adjusted (some more slowly than others), they saw that their arrival brought the room's total number of occupants to six, though one of the occupants had to be inferred from the rake of his boots, as not a detail of his actual person breached the wall of shadows beside the cage. Any sense of the hidden figure was gleaned from those boots, and from these came the impression that he was both rangy and spry – the first from the two-foot length of the knee-highs and the second from their splayed stance.

These impressions were stored by Chevie but not Riley, whose attention was utterly focused on the unfortunate prisoner in the cell's cage.

'Tom,' he said. 'Tom, it ain't really you. Could it be you?'

Riley was thinking that it could indeed be Tom. The prisoner certainly sported the copper barnet that Riley remembered, and the face seemed similar to the one he sometimes glimpsed in his dreams, though the features were veiled by grimed blood and distorted by terror.

Riley's own face must have shone with hope, for Nancy pinched the boy's arm, her eyes blazing a warning.

'Hold your nerve, boy,' she whispered. 'Or we lose this battle before a shot is fired.'

Maccabee was the final person in the room.

Sir James Maccabee.

London's most feared attorney. The attorney who had made his name leading the crusade against the scourge of highwaymen almost half a century since. They said that Sir James had *stretched more necks than a turkey farmer*. And, speaking of turkeys, here was the man himself, all buttoned up to his turkey neck and sweating like that selfsame fowl in the yuletide season.

Terrified, Chevie realized. *This Maccabee guy is quaking in his boots.*

This was the exact same observation that had vexed Tartan Nancy, though she phrased it rather differently in her head: *What kind of evil cove is Lurky Boots if he can put the wind up a top gent like Maccabee?*

Riley cared not a jot for the beak or the Lurker. His eyes were on Tom, up and down his body and face, searching for clues. 'Speak to me, Tommy,' he pleaded. 'Give me something to jog me memory. It's been so long and I was so very little.'

Maccabee laced his fingers, resting them on the prow of his belly, and in that stance it was easy to imagine him in chambers sporting the powdered wig.

'No, sir,' he said, his voice deep and rich but nervy like an

26

actor's on opening night. 'He may not speak until our business is concluded. This man is condemned as a debtor, and as such he has no right to life nor any part of it until my client is satisfied. And I must say that bringing this young lady in here is hardly the perfect start to our business.'

Nancy glared at Riley, a warning to hold his tongue, then she stepped forward, took a few puffs to demonstrate her calm and launched into the wheedle.

'Come now, sir. We ain't heathens. We ain't in Scotland or the like. We is civilized Englishmen, God bless the queen and so forth. We is in a negotiation here, ain't we? I brung the boy as you requested, and brought the lady as *he* requested. Now we must confirm whether or not the product is the genuine article, as it were, and not some fakery.'

Maccabee glanced into the shadows before replying to this salvo. The man in shadow did not react visibly to the glance, not with so much as the twitch of a toe, but still Maccabee nodded rapidly as if he had received some orders.

'I am afraid, madam, that this negotiation will not be like the others you have previously, eh, *wheedled*. My master . . . that is to say, my *employer* is not interested in your offer. He has terms, and they are absolute.'

Nancy puffed up a storm, which hung in the eaves like a thundercloud. 'Terms, is it? Terms now? We ain't in the Bailey, Sir James. This here is a wheedle cell, and why for are we gathered here in the sight of God if not to wheedle?'

Maccabee licked his fleshy lips. 'Please, Nancy, please. For all our sakes . . .'

The Lurker stamped the heel of one boot and the darkness

seemed to ripple. The meaning was clear: Maccabee had said too much.

Riley had only one ear on the conversation and the rest of his senses were focused on the man in the cage. Tom had been a boy when they had last met, barely older than he himself was now. Over a decade it had been since they shared a room when Riley was but a tot.

Could this be Tom?

Was it him?

Riley's heartstrings were being tugged right enough. Perhaps his instincts knew what his brain could not fathom.

The Lurker's boot stamp brought him fully back to the wheedle.

'Your Honour,' Riley said to Maccabee. 'Tell your employer to name his terms, for there must be more to it than seeing me stew in this foul place.'

Maccabee sat on a battered stool opposite the Lurker. The stool wobbled and clunked on the uneven floor.

'There are terms,' he said. 'That is to say, a term. One term, which is not open for haggle. You take it or you leave it at your pleasure.'

Nancy spat on the floor. 'Do my ears confound me? One term? No haggling? What class of a wheedle is this? Come you out of the shadows, Lurker, or must I drag you?'

Maccabee was upright so quickly that the stool toppled and the attorney himself staggered forward, off-balance.

'Quiet, woman,' he hissed, righting himself. 'No talk of dragging. Do you want to see us all put under?'

There was a noise from the Lurker's corner then – a dry

rasp, like the sound a rusty blade might produce when dragged along a stone. The disconcerting noise may have been a cough or a chuckle from the throat of a disturbed man. Whatever its origin, the sound did nothing to calm Maccabee's nerves.

'We must finish this business and be away from here,' he shouted. 'We must conclude, I tell you.'

Nancy was vexed and confused. The advantage here should clearly be in her favour, as her opponent was wound tighter than a clock spring, and yet she felt outmanoeuvred. 'Sir James Maccabee? That be you, am I right? The man that cleared the Great North Road?'

Maccabee had apparently suffered enough of Nancy's impudence.

'I said, *Quiet, woman*! Blast you!' he shouted, and for a moment the Old Bailey lion of legend asserted itself. 'The single act that will secure the release of Thomas Riley from Newgate is as follows: one Riley for another. A simple trade.'

Nancy gawped, for this was a condition unlike anything she had heard in her three decades in the wheedle business.

Chevie filled the silence with outrage and blurted her first words since entering the chamber. 'OK. Enough with the garbage. We are so outta here.'

A simple trio of sentences, but their effect was electric. Riley reacted instantly, backing away from Chevie as though she were the enemy.

'No, Chevie,' he said. 'No. This is a decision for me to make. Mine alone.'

Nancy wasn't far behind. 'No one leaves the chamber. Not

29

till a deal is hammered. I ain't having no amateur-like walkouts on Nancy's watch.'

But the most surprising reaction was from the Lurker. Surprising in that he reacted at all. Not that he was flinging himself about or bonking his head on the stonework, but, given that his sole contribution to the negotiations so far had been a tap of his boot and possibly a wry chuckle, it was surprising to see the boots withdraw entirely into the coal-black shadows with harsh scrapes at the sound of Chevie's anachronistic expressions. And even more startling was the sight of the Lurker's dark figure stretching to its full height and a single hand emerging from the corner into the candlelight.

The slow-moving hand hypnotized the room's occupants and they watched it as they might the head of some poisonous snake. The pale hand was cuffed by velvet and fringed with long fingers, which quested through the dark as though seeking to pinch the echoes of Chevie's words. But then they stopped, reconsidered, curled themselves under the shell of fist and withdrew, leaving everyone spooked and none the wiser.

'Well,' said Nancy. 'Well. That was a fine howjadoo, weren't it?'

The man who might be Tom defied the order imposed upon him to remain mute. 'Please,' he said. 'In the name of mercy, please. I didn't do nothing.'

'I'll do it!' blurted Riley. 'I accept. Him for me. A soul for a soul.'

Maccabee bolted across the room, almost stumbling in his haste, and grabbed Riley's hand. 'Agreed,' he said, and spat on the clasped hands to seal the deal, as he had heard once that this was how the lower classes conducted their business.

'A pox on you, Maccabee,' swore Nancy. 'You shift yerself plenty quick when the mood takes you.'

Maccabee sighed mightily, flapping his fleshy lips. 'The deed is done, madam. The shake is shook.'

Normally Chevie prided herself on her quick reactions, but for a person raised in twenty-first-century America's litigious society this deal had been concluded in lightning fashion. There had been no haggling. No mock disbelief. No throwing of hands in the air. Just *bang*, *boom*, done. Shake, spit and that's all. Her friend had condemned himself to death.

'Oh no no no,' she said, as though admonishing a naughty group of children who had agreed to run off to Narnia together. 'This isn't happening on my watch. This deal smells so bad I hardly know where to start.'

Riley was ready for the objections. 'I know what you plan to say, Chevie. It ain't really Tom, perhaps. Or we don't even know what he is accused of.'

'Exactly,' said Chevie. 'And no offence to this so-called *Tom* guy but I don't know him from Lady freaking Gaga. Not to mention the fact that we're all having our chains yanked by some creep in the corner. No, thank you. This stinks. We are vacating the premises. Elvis and his entourage are leaving the building.'

Riley closed his eyes tight, as if he could shut out Chevie entirely. 'I have no choice, my dear friend. None. There ain't no horns and no dilemma. If there is a single chance in a dozen that this is my kin, then I must take the chance. I must.' Riley thought of a devastating argument and opened his eyes to present it. 'Were this your father, Chevron, would you not do anything to save him?'

Chevie stepped back. That was a cruel argument to throw in her face, but Riley was right – she would do whatever it took to save her dad from pinwheeling his flaming Harley on the Pacific Coast Highway, including switching places with him. She would do it in a heartbeat and without guarantee.

Maccabee threw his eyes to heaven and his hands in the air. 'It matters not. None of this. The deal is struck. Our hands shook and that is both legal and final. Consult your wheedler if you doubt it.'

Chevie turned to Nancy, who was fumbling with the makings of a smoke. 'Is he right? Does the handshake do it?'

Nance spat on the floor, and not just a symbolic blobette of spittle: a weighty globule that would have drowned a cockroach.

'Yes, blast the pair of you. Yes, it seals it. And my reputation too. Not one matchstick did I wheedle out of this do. Not a sausage.'

Maccabee seemed to be regaining his poise now that the deal was done. 'You have gained more than you know, madam, believe me. For more was at stake than you could realize.'

Another noise from the shadows. Perhaps a grunt, perhaps a convulsive retch, then the ghostly hand reappeared, index finger ticking like a pendulum. The message was clear. *To business*.

'I agree with the Lurker's finger,' said Nancy. 'I am for finishing this bowl of tripe.' She banged on the door with the side of her fist. 'Broadband, get yer carcass in here and open the box.'

There followed a full minute of clatter and rattle before Broadband stumbled inside, a weighty ring of keys dangling from his hands.

'Apologies for the delay,' he said, shamefaced. 'Only sometimes I forgets which door is locked. Cos there are two doors and I know one is locked, only sometimes I forget which one, so I was endeavourin' to unlock a door what was unlocked already, which is what delayed my arrival.'

The Lurker clapped from the shadows. It seemed he was now in fine form, but he was still not choosing to reveal himself or even speak.

Maccabee's spirits were on the rise too. 'What a capital fellow. Destined for the House of Commons, he is.'

Broadband was smart enough to know he was being mocked but also smart enough not to make a big deal of it, or he might end up on the wrong side of a locked door himself.

'We is finished here, I takes it,' he said.

'Yes,' said Nancy. 'A pox on this day and the memory of it, which I shall carry to my grave.'

Riley pulled Chevie into a corner diagonally opposite to the Lurker.

'I'm going into the box,' he whispered with some urgency. 'Ain't no avoiding that now.'

'You crazy kid,' hissed Chevie. 'What's going on in that thick head?'

'We ain't got time now,' said Riley, his mouth close to her ear. 'Seconds we got, is all. So listen careful. I got the tools for this door and the one outside, but then I'm stumped. Go to Otto Malarkey and ask him to clear a path for me to the wall. After that it's cake, believe me. All I need is the moonlight and a smidge of luck and I will float right out of this hellhole. Coves manage it every day, and none too smart ones neither.'

Chevie nodded. 'OK. I got it, Riley. You mad fool. I'll talk to Otto. I'll drag him here if I have to – but, once you're out, what then? We don't even know what's going on here.'

Riley's eyes flitted towards the darkness of the opposite corner. 'One problem at a time. Dodge the rope, that's my goal for the time being. Once that's taken care of and Tom is safely stashed, then we can investigate this shady character and why my person is so important to him.'

Chevie felt as though events were leaving her behind. She had missed the bus by a fingertip and was now rushing to catch up. Her instincts screamed at her to take control of this room. She was pretty sure she could subdue everyone in here, including the Lurker himself. But what then? Could she break them all out of Newgate? And, once on the outside, where could they go? Unless there was a time portal handy, they were stuck in Victorian London with the entire constabulary on their tails.

The damage was done and she would have to make the best of it.

'Some bodyguard I turned out to be,' she said to Riley.

'I scuppered you myself,' the boy said. 'I put me own head in the noose.'

Broadband had by this time got his keys in order and set

about unlocking the cage, to the visible relief of the ginger prisoner, who was rattling the door, eager to be away.

'Hold yer powder there, convict,' grumbled the guard. 'This lock is sensitive. It don't open unless you approach it just right, and you is throwing me off me diddle.'

In spite of the guard's moaning, the cage door sprang easily enough and swung open on its oiled hinges without creak or whine.

Tom smiled at last and then took to weeping, the sheer relief being too much for him.

Riley took his hand and led him out. 'There now, brother. The ordeal is past. Miss Chevron here has a nice cot waiting for you and a flask of cider to see you off to nod.'

Tom snuffled and said, 'My thanks, mister. Thank you kindly. Bless you, mister.'

Mister? thought Chevie. *A strange thing to call a brother.*

Riley must have thought it too, for he said something, which may have been 'Wait . . .'

But then it seemed as though time somehow expanded to allow for a greater concentration of events than it could usually accommodate. The Lurker was out of his corner with the speed of a flickering shadow and up behind the man called Tom before his image could settle upon the eyes. Then he had Tom by the throat and dragged him to the main door, barricading it with his own body. The shadows seemed to follow him, for he was still not entirely visible – there were just details that seemed not to stand still long enough for classification. Such as the four fingers now clamped round Tom's neck. Thin, white fingers that shone like glow-worms. Fingers

35

that were clearer now than they had been. The long white fingers of a pianist.

Or an assassin.

In that instant Riley knew the truth and all hope left his body with the huff of his breath.

The assassin has returned. Albert Garrick has cheated time and death.

Though he could see but fingers, there was not a doubt in Riley's mind. He knew each nail and knuckle intimately from the many beatings he had endured over the years. How often had Albert Garrick lashed out in a rage? A thousand times over, surely. Most memorably on the occasions when Riley had attempted to flee from his cruel master. Many times those selfsame fingers had been the last things Riley had seen before sinking into the fog of concussion. He had nightmares about those fingers to this very day.

The digits had changed, it was true. They had turned pale and bore some new scar tissue, but Riley felt sure they belonged to the demon Albert Garrick. So certain was he that he blurted it out – 'Garrick! Albert Garrick!' – and in that instant he felt no fear for himself, only a cramping terror that Garrick would kill his brother for the sport of it.

Chevie, who had been moving obliquely to a flanking position, stopped in her tracks, as though petrified by the Medusa of legend.

'No,' she whispered, and then with more force: 'No!' She would not have it. 'Garrick is dead.'

Riley responded with even more force. 'No, that devil is alive!'

And what happened next set Maccabee's heart, already labouring to pump his life's blood through arteries clogged by decades of rich living, into a fatal convulsion. Because Albert Garrick's head appeared, like a macabre balloon, in the space above Ginger Tom's shoulder.

'Garrick is dead!' his head crowed, his face as pale as his hands. Like alabaster it was, except for the deep wrinkles round the eyes that might have been scrawled by slate pencil. Then he added: 'Or perhaps he yet lives.'

It seemed at first glance as though Garrick had been driven stark raving mad, with his face of stone and bloodcurdling shriek, but then Chevie saw that he was not mad but exultant. A man whose dreams have finally come true.

Broadband was a bit confused with all the happenings, and stared at his fingers as though the events could be counted off. Eventually he said, 'Eh?' But this was his final word for some time, as Garrick treated the single confused syllable as a threat and magicked a weighted cosh from some poke or flap and hurled it at the prison guard, felling him where he stood.

For her part, Nancy, who talked for a living and had been in tight spots as a matter of course, straightened her pristine bonnet, cleared her throat and chose her words with considerable caution. 'Now then, Your Honour. Surely you ain't got no need for a wheedler no more . . .'

Garrick did not speak to Tartan Nancy, simply treated her to a devil's glare, which was sufficient to send her stumbling backwards as though pushed.

You stay right here, Nancy girl, she told herself. *Keep yer back to the cell wall and p'raps you shall live to wheedle another day.*

37

But she didn't believe this. She believed that the madman would slaughter them all with no more thought than a child squashing ants.

Maccabee did not trouble the cell with verbals or histrionics, but fell over dead, into the cage as it happened, catching the barred door with a hand so that it swung and clunked behind him. Very neat.

How this could be was not really an issue, as it clearly *was*. This strange Garrick was certainly ghostly, but no ghost. The fist that held Tom aloft was skin and bone, albeit the first the colour of the second.

The hand lifted Tom clear off the ground.

'Family!' Garrick screeched. 'Family? Ain't it?'

Riley could do nothing.

All his nightmares had come true and were standing before him, holding his dream by the neck. He was nine years old again, lying in a West End gutter with Garrick's boot at his throat, waiting for the stamp that would crush his windpipe.

Chevie too was shaken to her core, but she was also trained, and she knew that a sudden attack while Garrick was focused on Riley and his vengeance could be their only chance.

She was wrong.

Chevie bent low and darted towards Garrick's kidney area, hoping to put her knuckles deep in the spongy tissue. Her Quantico instructor, Cord Vallicose, who was to become a woman in this reality (don't ask), had assured her that *there is not a man alive who can shake off a ruptured kidney*.

Perhaps Vallicose had been/would be right, but Chevie was

38

not to confirm her instructor's maxim on this day. Her attack was met with one of Garrick's blacker-than-black boots, which whipped up and stopped her dead in her tracks, leaving her with an indent in her skull that any fool could see was a fatal wound. She fell to the cold floor like a tossed sack of coal and spasmed alarmingly.

'Chevie!' said Riley, and then: 'Tom!'

'*Chevie!*' mimicked Garrick mockingly. '*Tom!*'

Riley wanted more than anything to weep. He wanted to fall to his knees and beg, but he knew from bitter experience that Garrick despised overt displays of weakness or emotion, and so he stood his ground and put together the most complex sentence he could in the circumstances.

'What do you want?'

Garrick laughed, delighted. 'What do I want? No, that ain't it. That ain't the question. The question is, my son: what do *you* want?'

The assassin grinned like a naughty child, relishing his moment of vengeance. 'To know your name, is it?' A curved Arabic blade appeared, curling round Tom's neck like the coil of a snake. 'This fella here. Perhaps he knows your true name. Why don't you ask him?'

Riley did not, for he felt that to play Garrick's game would mean death for Tom.

'ASK HIM!' roared Garrick, hamming it up for the imaginary stalls, and the blade jittered at Tom's neck, drawing a spurt of blood.

'Wh-what is my name?' Riley stammered, the choice taken from him.

39

But all Tom could say was, 'Mercy. Mercy, please. I don't understand. I never even played cards with these gentlemen. I ain't no debtor. Being ginger ain't no crime.'

Garrick was theatrically appalled. 'You don't know my friend's name? Why, it's like you ain't even family. And if you ain't family I don't have a use for you.'

And without further ado he drew the curved Arabic blade crosswise, slicing his captive's throat, then dropped him like a slaughtered animal.

'Tom!' cried Riley, sinking to the floor beside the dying man, whose blood issued from his neck in a broad rippling sheet, drenching Riley's person in a second. Even as Riley tied one of his magician's scarves round Tom's neck he knew that it was futile. There was no help for Tom. The best thing for him with these injuries was a quick death, which would surely be granted.

'Damn you!' Riley swore. 'Damn you to hell, Albert Garrick.'

Garrick's face was serene. 'You tried that, my boy. You sent me to hell and now I have returned.'

Chevie flailed on the floor, blood leaking from one ear. Garrick noticed and affected a sad face. 'Oh, it don't look good for the Injun maiden, does it now? No, not good at all. I would rather have dragged it out a bit, given her part in my – what shall we call it? – inconvenience. But Albert Garrick never did know his own strength, and I had forgotten the little vixen's trademark bursts of speed. As a matter of fact, I had almost forgotten her entirely, believe it or not.'

Chatter and babble was all Riley heard and even that at the

back of his mind. Nothing was making sense to the lad. Tom was dying, perhaps dead already, and Chevie, his dear Chevie, was surely breathing her last.

'Oh,' he said or perhaps sobbed. 'Oh . . . oh.'

Garrick seemed not to care whether Riley paid attention or not, so wrapped up was he in his moment.

'So, my plan in a nutshell,' he continued, 'was to subject your traitorous person to the same pain that poor, betrayed Albert Garrick was subjected to.'

Chatter and babble. Babble and chatter.

Tom spasmed on the cold floor and gave up the ghost entirely. Chevie was moaning with each breath.

'I took you in like a son. But you denied me a family, and so I am denying you a brother. First, however, and this was the genius of it –' Garrick twirled an imaginary moustache – 'I made you beg for his life. I made you value it above your own. This made the killing all the sweeter, for you now realize, Riley, just how much this dead man meant to you.'

Garrick nudged Tom's corpse with his toe. 'And here's the last nail in your coffin, my son. This bag of bones ain't even Tom. You have doomed yourself for a stranger.'

Riley knew the meaning of each individual word but could not fathom their collective gist.

'It ain't even Tom? Not Tom, then?'

Tom or not, there was a dead man on the cold floor and Riley was drenched in his blood and the sour smell of it was in his nose.

And Chevie. Oh, poor Chevie.

Riley had seen an Irish tinker boy kicked by a donkey at

the Islington market several years since. He had never forgotten the sight of the poor Gypsy lad all a-quiver in the mud with his eyes rolled back till they were mostly white and his body racked by convulsions.

She will die horribly, like Tom who ain't Tom. Two dead on my account.

Garrick gloated on. 'How you are feeling at this precise moment, Riley my boy, is unimaginable to most common folk. Lured to a foul pit by a master you had given up for dead. To have the gift of hope granted you, only to be snatched away just as sudden. And then for the awful realization that your dear kin ain't nothing more than a patsy. A ringer, as it were. A common longshoreman stitched up on account of his ginger mop.' Garrick smiled an uncommonly wide smile that was rarely seen but which, when fully extended, bisected his head like a zipper. His ivoried teeth were made all the more yellow by his unnatural pallor.

'Ain't you going to say anything?' said Garrick, his grin gone. 'Just moping, is it? I must say, after all this time, all these centuries, I had dreamed up such an amount of lively conversations we would have. And now all I get for my trouble is a weeping boy. I am quite the disappointed fellow. In truth, I cannot fathom how you outfoxed me on the first go-around. But I was younger then. Now I am the Forever Man.'

This was undeniably a decent villain's monologue, but it was all blah and blabber to Riley. Garrick could have been a huffing gorilla for all the sense the boy could put to his words. And, as for Chevie, she was beyond attaching sense to anything. Her automatic functions would keep her alive for another minute or so, but it was already too late for her brain. Her skull was fractured and leaking fluid like a cracked gin jug.

So fast it had happened. One boot-heel crack in the forehead and she was a goner. After all the diverse scrapes and tumbles she had endured, to be done for almost casually was indeed cruel.

A thought formed in Riley's mind: *Chevie doesn't know what's happening. It's for the best.*

But he would not deal with this notion, would not even glance sideways at it, for that would mean admitting that Chevie was dying.

As will I be presently.

Another thought. This one did not seem so important now. There was only one door in this room and to leave through it meant passing Garrick and that was inconceivable.

Oh, Chevie. Oh, Tom.

But not Tom. Who?

Riley was useless. Paralysed by a flood of emotions, like an insect in a blob of resin. And, more than that, he was sure to be scarred emotionally beyond all hope of recovery if he did by some miracle walk out of this room.

But the universe was not yet done with unforeseen events. Riley would leave this room, but not through the door and not on his two feet.

Garrick stepped into the meagre light and treated the stunned, silent Tartan Nancy to a wink.

'What say you, madam? For sheer melodrama? Top marks, surely. I once trod the boards, you know, all over this fair country. The Great Lombardi they called me.' Garrick held up his palm, which fairly dripped with Tom/Not Tom's blood. 'Or perhaps you will remember my infamous moniker, the Red Glove.'

'Oh, Lord save us,' gibbered Nancy, and executed a strange combination of crossing herself and repetitive curtsying, shaken to her core by the mention of the murderous magician whom most believed to be a mere theatre legend from the penny dreadfuls. But the Red Glove was as real as Jack the Ripper and, in fact, the former had done for the latter.

It was Garrick's habit to bow in a theatrical manner whenever the opportunity presented itself, as it transported him back to his theatre days, which were centuries behind him in one way, and mere years in another. Garrick had always been inordinately proud of his stage bow, and he used to deliver weekly lectures to Riley on the importance of rigidity and sweep.

Fold yerself as clean as the queen's notepaper, Riley my son, he would say.

And thunderheads would brew on Riley's brow and he would think: *I am not your son, devil*.

Garrick bowed now, prompted by Tartan Nancy's botched curtsying.

'At your service, madam,' he said, which both the bow-er and the bowed-at knew was balderdash.

As Garrick silently counted to three, which was his rule for the low point of a bow, his nose passed close to Chevron Savano's chest, within a foot perhaps. And something beeped.

Beeped and then flashed.

Curious, thought Albert Garrick.

It was a strangely electronic beep for the nineteenth century. Unnatural and anachronistic – and yet it was familiar to Albert Garrick and it evoked in him the darkest urges.

His blood-streaked fingers quested towards the flashing light that seemed to emanate from Chevie's heart.

A twist of lanyard glinted on Chevie's collarbone and Garrick hooked a thumb underneath it, pulling out the cord until a flashing teardrop-shaped charm appeared.

'God, no!' he shouted.

For he realized that this was no simple adornment; it was a cursed Timekey. Much like the one that had been used to dispatch him into the time tunnel.

It should not exist!

Garrick calmed himself. *The key is nothing without a pod. Just a lump of plastic.*

And I am protected by silver!

Garrick had discovered quite accidentally that the wormhole could not abide the element of silver. He could feel the time force's pull waning, and sometimes actually recoiling, whenever he wore silver chains or bracelets, which was all the time since he had made the discovery – for the wormhole's pull was like a cloud in his mind that stopped him thinking clearly and set his heart battering a tattoo inside his chest.

But there were quantum facts missing from Garrick's argument. Things even Charles Smart had never known when he'd first entered the wormhole. For instance, once a body had been as thoroughly saturated with quantum foam as Garrick's had, the wormhole did not need a pod to absorb him again. A Timekey would do the job just fine. And, while the wormhole could not take him while he wore silver, the Time-key was more than strong enough to trump the metal's powers of repulsion.

The Timekey grew warm in Garrick's hand, then hotter still, and the assassin was hypnotized by it. The last time he had held a gadget like this one, the wormhole had taken him prisoner for nearly two and a half centuries. Garrick had believed himself in hell, such was his torment. He had barely survived with his wits intact and did not wish ever to repeat the experience.

Flee! he told himself, but it was too late. The device had activated and Garrick's molecular structure was already bonded with the key's; there was no separating them on this plane. He felt that familiar draw, a sickening pull as the time tunnel welcomed him home. And, though it had been some two hundred and fifty years since he had regained his human form, Garrick remembered the sensation well, and the help-lessness that went with it.

Not again! he thought, his ability to form simple thoughts being the only thing left to him. *I cannot survive it again.*

And then: *I never meant to hurt the dove, master.* Which was an unrelated memory from an unresolved childhood issue.

Riley, for his part, did not notice the Timekey's activation; he simply saw the assassin hunched over his fallen friend. The sight brought him round and sent him lurching towards Garrick.

'Leave her be!' he snarled. 'Get away from her, you devil.'

His attack was clumsy and ordinarily Garrick could have

casually swatted the youth away, but now reality was bending and solid matter was phase-shifting to quantum foam.

How? wondered Garrick. *There ain't no pod. There ain't no landing pad.*

The truth was that none of the three would ever know the *how* exactly, no more than the average human can ever truly understand how a bird is able to fly, but that did not change what was happening. A whirlwind rarely stops spinning to explain itself.

Riley's attack was successful in so much as he reached his target, but a failure in that he did not force Garrick away from Chevie. In fact, his lurch bunched them all together, so that when the orange quantum sparks surged from the Timekey's heart all three were engulfed.

Garrick's limbs were already insubstantial. Riley saw his own arms dematerialize and could not believe they were once again being tumbled into the mouth of a time tunnel.

But where will we tumble out? he wondered. *Or, more accurately, when?*

Chevie thought nothing. In her mind, a photographer's flash had exploded and would not fade. In her head, she stared at the sun and began to go slowly mad.

In the last seconds before the three disappeared from the Newgate cell in a swarm of orange sparks, Riley could have sworn he heard Big Ben strike in the distance.

As a matter of fact, the sound came from inside the room.

'Pardon me, I'm sure,' said Nancy, even though there was no one left to hear her.

TIME AFTER TIME

Everywhere. Everywhen

And so Albert Garrick was back in the time tunnel, though to be fair he had never truly been fully out of it, which is a difficult concept to comprehend. To quote Professor Charles Smart: *We don't have a clue about the wormhole. None of us. Anyone who says different is talking out of their backside. And, yes, I'm including Einstein in that. I mean, look at him. The guy doesn't even understand the workings of a hairbrush.*

Simply put, Garrick had been so deep in the tunnel that its particles had permeated his every cell. These elements were more minute than protons, quarks or even black-hole singularities – quantum particles so small that they would be immeasurable for centuries.

Riley and Chevie had absorbed a few million of these particles during their jaunts through the tunnels, but their trips had been over a measured span and through the same corridor, while Garrick had been tossed into the tunnel without an exit visa, as it were. He had floated around in there without purpose or direction, and his being had become saturated with the particles, untold billions of them. They had infiltrated his own molecules, colonizing them until he was as much a part of the quantumverse as he was of the universe. Garrick had truly become a time traveller, remade in his own image but with a connection to the wormhole that could never be broken. Just as the wormhole was forever, so Garrick became forever, and when he fell through the man-made rift (more of which later), he was a changed being. Half mad from his quantum incarceration, for one thing. And when he survived the slings and arrows of good old Father Time, as well as actual slings and arrows and cannon fire, he came to realize that he could not die or be killed.

However, for an immortal to function in a reasonably normal manner, he needs something to aspire to. A goal. So Garrick made it his mission to take revenge on his adopted son, Riley. It was indeed an epic quest, the decision to bide his time for almost two hundred and fifty years to snuff out the life of one boy, but it gave Albert Garrick something to dream about at night and put a smile on his thin lips for near a hundred thousand mornings, which never failed to give the heebie-jeebies to anyone who saw it.

Having never been a slugabed, Garrick did other stuff too. He played quite a substantial role in the East Anglian witch-finding industry (an experience which would shortly prove useful), embarked on a campaign in India, where he found his beloved curved blade in the gut of a disembowelled goat (another story), captained a pirate flotilla out of Tortuga (recycling his Red Glove nickname), and even spent a few decades as a monk in Lancashire trying to change his ways (unsuccessfully, it must be said, as the boredom brought on one of his bloody rages and he murdered half the abbey). There literally is not time to go into the details of all the she-nanigans perpetrated on the human race by Albert Garrick since the wormhole spat him out in 1647. Suffice it to say, for our purposes in this particular narrative, that only the thought of killing Riley in the most inhuman way possible kept his upper lip stiffened on most days. As for Chevie, Albert Garrick had almost forgotten the FBI consultant until she made the mistake of jogging his memory in the prison cell with her distinctive accent. Now, as they entered the time tunnel, Garrick dearly hoped the trip would heal her crushed skull, so that he could kill her again.

Each trip through the wormhole is different, and no two outcomes are the same. On Garrick's last immersion, he had gone deeper than any earth-born being ever had – apart from a prehistoric earthworm who had entered through a rift brought on by a major volcanic eruption, which happened to coincide with extreme levels of solar radiation. That worm went so deep into the wormhole (ha ha) that it emerged sub-stantially enlarged and abides to this day in a Scottish lake.

As regards Garrick, Chevie and Riley, their trip had none of the dream-like, time-bending qualities of previous pro-grammed jaunts. This trip was the time-travelling equivalent of being struck in the eye by a bolt of lightning.

Riley barely had time to see the silhouetted figure of his mother whispering to him: *And you, my son, shall carry the name of your proud Wexford clan.*

All Chevie saw was the cat called Tinder she had owned

with her pop in their Malibu cottage, and the only thought she could form in this regard was: *Miaow.*

The wormhole welcomed Garrick and hugged him close and would have absorbed him utterly this time but for the silver that he had brought with him. Chevie's Timekey had trumped the silver initially, but now it was like acid in the tunnel, even in a dematerialized state, burning great holes in the quantum foam. The tunnel recoiled and Garrick and Co. were left to free-fall to earth, tumbling through the man-made tear in the wormhole through which Garrick had previously fallen. And, where before there had been a cool-down period to ease them back into the swing of things, this time the comfort blanket of quantum foam was ripped off like a blood-crusted bandage.

Simply put, Riley and Chevie fell back into the world screaming. Only Garrick had the presence to recognize the time and place in which they had ended up. A time and place where his authority had once been unquestioned and his power absolute, which had pleased him for a while until he had grown bored. And now he was back.

The Witchfinder had returned.

4

WITCHFINDER

Mandrake. Huntingdonshire. 1647

Mandrake was a small plantation of perhaps four-score brick houses, most with fancy functioning chimneys, apart from a small almshouse and the House of Unfortunates where the infirm, unsound and criminal were expected to hold their noses. Mandrake boasted a broad, hard-packed street running down the centre from its northern gate, bisected by a narrower street that ran from east to west. Earthworks, and more recently a strong stone wall, had been raised between the points of the cross. On the wall's stone buttresses, reasonable artillery had been mounted, which had seen off many a roving band of ne'er-do-wells, pedlars, bandits and plague carriers, with the help of the stout hearts and brawn of the militia.

It was recounted daily in the Huntings Tavern that on one memorable occasion about a year ago the legendary highway-man Colonel Bagshot and his troop of misbegottens had attempted to impose an embargo on the town, only to be repulsed by the visiting Witchfinder, who led the charge when the northern gate was breached. With every passing telling and tankard of ale, the raid grew in stature from skirmish to pitched battle, though the one detail all could agree on was that the Witchfinder had hanged Colonel Bagshot in the town square the following day, ridding the shire of a notorious brigand.

On this spring afternoon, Mandrake's residents were gathered around the stone dais of the same square, engaged in a debate on the town's charter and whether broader permissions were needed to change the town's name, which after all appeared on regional survey maps. Debates of this manner were common in Mandrake and all men were free to voice their opinions, even the African dullard Fairbrother Isles, whose head was currently in the stocks for bullish behaviour. This happened so often that the stocks were generally referred to as the Fairbrothers, as in *Stick that arch-dolt in the Fairbrothers for an afternoon and see if that won't halt his gallop*. It was said that Fairbrother Isles was the only African man on English soil, apart from in London itself, and that he had escaped from a slaving ship.

All other business had been dealt with. It had been agreed that the oil lamps hung outside every house could be lit one half of the hour later in the evenings, now that the sun was keeping its nose up that bit longer, and that the watch could be reduced to a single sentry on each gate after nightfall as there had not been an abomination sighting in several weeks. The menfolk had reluctantly conceded that Bundy Dormouse, the travelling balladeer, should not be admitted to Mandrake, as his ballads grew annually more ribald, and was this not a Puritan community? And now it was time to discuss the town's name and whether or not it was fitting for such a moral town to be named after a plant with magical connotations.

53

The debate would be led, as it generally was, by town constable Godfrey Cryer, who was also the town crier, which could make conversing with the man confusing at times, as he insisted on using the word 'cry' in every odd sentence.

Cryer was not a man to see the humour in this; indeed he was a humourless man, thin of mouth and sharp of bone, with little to differentiate him from a long-handled axe besides the boxy hat he habitually wore as a mark of his various offices.

'As town crier, I decry the name Mandrake,' cried Cryer, to the moans of the assembly. 'I decry it, as the Witchfinder decried it.'

'A crybaby is what you are, Godfrey,' shouted Fairbrother Isles from the stocks.

Cryer, who was as Puritan as they come and considered humour base Satanism, dealt the African a sound kick to the rump. 'Enough of your prattle, dullard. This is a serious issue.'

'This we know,' said the mason and brick worker, Jeronimo Woulfe, who was of good standing as his fingers had a hand in many of Mandrake's walls, so to speak. 'For every week you raise it, when there are other important matters to be discussed.'

'Indeed,' shrieked Cryer. 'Indeed and surely I do raise it, for the Witchfinder himself who cleansed our town not a year since made a point of it on several occasions.'

'He mentioned it once in passing,' said Isles, who'd always had a strange manner of speech and many suspected was a full-dolt as well as an ale-sot. 'No big deal, Cryer. Listen to Jerry and get a life.'

Cryer's hands raked the air. 'Good people of Mandrake, or Mandrake's Groan, to give the town its full and proper name!

It is the sound the root makes when torn from the earth. All who hear it are struck dead and damned to hell. Mandrake is Lucifer's very representative in our soil.'

'Yep,' said Fairbrother Isles. 'And pig bum-blasts are the devil's breath. You're a moron, Cryer. I decry you. Why don't you go and have a good cry?'

General laughter and sniggering ensued. There was no denying that the prisoner had a certain wit about him, though his often confusing use of the King's English was a trial to the brain.

Jeronimo Woulfe, a short, stocky workhorse of a man with outsized hands and flat fingers that seemed too large for the deftness his masonry work required, decided to make peace. 'Come now, Constable. The war has concluded, and did not the Witchfinder move on? Mandrake has known peace this past year. The plague has not crested the hills in many months and our strong bricks are sought after from Huntingdon to London itself. Rejoice, I say. Indeed we all say it.'

Cryer's face swelled and empurpled. 'Rejoice, Master Woulfe? Rejoice, says you. There are creatures in the fens. Abominations born from witches. Have we not seen them with our own eyes? We are truly in the age of darkness, and you would have us rejoice?'

'Not all darkness, surely. Mandrake's red bricks are famous,' countered Woulfe, rubbing his hand over the bristles of his shorn scalp. 'Shall we throw our customers into confusion with a new name for our brand?'

This now was good sense spoken plainly and was greeted with a smattering of applause and even some stamping of feet.

Cryer's shin bone of a face turned brick red. 'Bricks! Bricks, say you? You would place a higher value on bricks than souls? This town has fallen low since the Witchfinder left us. The fens are blighted by weird creatures. Crops rot at the root and our elderly disappear from their very beds. We are being tested. Souls against bricks. Pah!'

This gross exaggeration was the general run of things and would probably go on for some time. Cryer was the last true disciple of the Witchfinder, truth be told. That particular fashion had waned since the Battle of Naseby, to the relief of every good woman in the county. It had got to the point where a mother could not mix a poultice without being accused of witchcraft. Cryer was tolerated for now, but his days were being counted down by the residents of Mandrake and the unspoken plan was to remove him from office by the summer's end before he could attempt to enforce Parliament's declaration that Christmas was henceforth and forever banned. But for now his argument must be at least given a fair hearing and then it would be on to the new name itself.

'Garrwick!' said Cryer, spreading his arms wide, a wedge-of-cheese grin on his pale face, as though the good residents of Mandrake had not heard this proposal a hundred times before.

'Garrwick.' And now he raised a finger as if about to impart a valuable nugget of information. 'Or I am prepared to shake on Garrickston.'

Doubtless a debate would have ensued had not an impish spark ignited itself not half a yard from Cryer's beak of a nose and chased itself into a full-grown fireball.

'Witchcraft!' quoth he, seeming not too perturbed, as he had always enjoyed abetting the Witchfinder.

It was a difficult declaration to argue against, for what else but witchcraft would ignite a spiralling fireball that sucked air from the surroundings and grew exponentially, revealing some forms in its depths? Limbs were perceptible and features, all a-jumble at first like a melting pot of humanity but then separated and vomited forth into the square in three distinct forms that glowed with a dusting of orange sparkles.

Upon which sight Fairbrother Isles quoth, 'Now there's something you don't see every day,' before Cryer struck him from consciousness with his boot heel.

The figures writhed in a jumbled tangle of limbs and trunks until one main form emerged, sloughing off the uncertainty that had made his person hazy, until there was not an adult soul in the crowd who did not recognize him.

'Witchfinder Garrick,' said Cryer, and it seemed like he would weep. 'You have returned to us.'

Albert Garrick shook himself like a hound, his limbs stretching with each undulation to their correct length, then spat a mouthful of blood on the ground. 'That I have, Constable. And just in the nick of time, it would seem.'

At the sight of Albert Garrick, two lasses fainted dead away on the benches where they sat, and three young men also, toppling forward into the mud-like sacks of the bricks Mandrake was so famous for. Only Jeronimo Woulfe had the presence of mind for positive action, stooping to free Fairbrother from the stocks and drag him clear of any potential turmoil.

'I am returned from hell,' quoth Garrick. 'And see what

I have found sneaking into the town – a witch and her familiar!'

There could be no doubt that the materialized female was indeed a witch, for her eyes were those of a cat, not to mention that a bloody wound on her forehead magically healed itself as the people of Mandrake watched. And, as for the boy, if Witchfinder Garrick proclaimed him a familiar, then that was what he must doubtless be.

Garrick pointed at Chevie and Riley with a finger that was accustomed to people looking where it pointed.

'Take them!' he said.

And taken they were with rough hands and no delay.

Riley knew all about the 'Zen Ten' because he had personally experienced those delightful moments when the brain decides a time traveller's phase shift from a quantum-foam state back to bog-standard flesh and blood might be a bit too much for the teeny-weeny human brain to handle, and so provides a gentle pillow of fuzzy happiness to ease the traveller back into the real world. The 'Zen Ten' (a phrase coined by Professor Charles Smart – who else?) was basically the only thing that kept the traveller's brain from short-circuiting on touchdown.

However, when a person has been up and down the wormhole a few times, the brain gets almost blasé about the entire process and decides to divert any emergency power to life support; that is, it puts any available electricity into making certain that the body a person went in with is the one it emerges with, which worked out more or less OK for Riley but not particularly well for Chevron Savano.

As Riley was dragged across Mandrake's main square, he saw the townsfolk descend on Chevie like rats on a sack of offal, their fingers greedy for a limb to tug. Though he was instantly alert and quaked with terror, it was not for himself.

Chevron, Chevie, dear friend, he thought frantically. *What has been done to you?*

For his companion's eyes were indeed those of a cat. Golden and slitted. But there was something more distressing about this new Chevron Savano. She wore not the dreamy smile of the emergent but rather a terrified and vacant expression that displayed not a hint of higher intelligence.

She is more cat than human, Riley realized, and he knew he must help her. It was a compulsion that did not require any thought or concern for his own person, for he had never had a friend like Chevie Savano. And, in that split second of mortal fear for her dear life, Riley felt a spark flicker in his heart and he drooped into action.

For drooping is the proper course of action when beset by multiple assailants; Garrick had schooled him in this.

The curs will be expecting a thrashing resistance, he'd informed Riley during one of their Holborn tutorials. *So we takes our lesson from the drunkards of old London town. Did you ever try to roust a cove in his cups? He is the very devil to catch a grip of, so we must fight our instincts and loosen where we might be fairly expected to tighten. Do you comprehend, my son?*

To which Riley would nod and think: *I am not your son.*

And so Riley employed his ex-master's methods, but added a twist or two of his own. One bewarted fellow he pinched hard in the webbing between forefinger and thumb, which loosened the chap's grip sharpish. And another bowl-cut gent he cracked on the stockinged shin with the heel of his shoe, which Riley was happy to see had made the time trip with him. The others were unprepared for the almost liquid droop of their captive and in a trice Riley was rolling free, towards Chevie, who was hissing at the men encircling her.

She may not even recognize me! he realized, and this thought dismayed him more than he could bear.

'Fight, Chevron!' he called. 'Fight!'

But Chevie would do nothing but paw and hiss and wriggle till her dress was torn from her in rags, leaving her clothed in the FBI jumpsuit. This from the girl who had faced down the Battering Rams gang in their own digs. From the girl who had given Albert Garrick a run for his money.

Riley scrambled towards her until his progress was blocked by two high black boots that seemed to absorb the light. It took no more than the acid foreboding in his innards to inform Riley who was at the other end of those boots.

'I love it,' Albert Garrick said, laughing. 'Fun all the live-long day.'

Before Riley could shift another inch, a boot descended on his crown, crunching his forehead into the ground and rendering him unconsciousness.

Riley woke some time later that same day; the light seemed lower and of a more russet hue as it shafted the arched windows of the stone chapel where he was trussed.

Or possibly it is tomorrow evening, he thought. *For that was quite the bonk on my poor noggin.*

A noggin that still felt thoroughly bonked and swollen.

Then he thought of Chevie and believed he might weep.

What have they done to her?

She was dead, he was certain of it.

Dead, and we never spoke of things. Of feelings. Never nothing but gallivanting and adventures.

Spoke of what precisely? Riley could not say nor even think the word. And so he decided that Chevie would be not dead in his mind until she was dead in his arms.

But for now . . . For now his magician's cape was gone and he knew that he had been thoroughly searched for any picks or tricks hidden on his person. He was restrained in the intractable grip of a most unusual contraption. Some class of double crossbow, with arrows pointed directly at his own neck, and a mess of springs, strings and pins that made the whole apparatus seem a feather away from loosing its deadly bolts. The device extended to milkmaid handles, which held Riley's hands wide in wooden struts that curled upward at each end, and his feet were chained to a half-sunken hoop in the stone altar.

This was Garrick's business, Riley knew, for he recognized elements of the design from his ex-master's stage illusions. *He built it himself or had it done from his drawings.*

Garrick was undeniably alive but changed terribly. He seemed barely human with his alabaster skin and skeletal appearance.

Riley wondered whether or not he was terrified, and was surprised to find that he was almost relieved.

I always knew this day would come and now it has.

But how did Albert Garrick yet live? How?

The *how* nagged at his brain, but not as much as it once had or once would, because he had seen so much in the past year. There were so many *hows* that their intensity faded like echoes. Even *when* did not seem to matter so much.

Chevie.

This was all he had room to care about in his noggin, and all his actions would be driven by that.

To that end, he must attempt to escape this diabolical contraption. Riley sent his senses scurrying outward, across the floor and up the rough walls, trying to glean some information that might help him to break free, though it seemed hopeless with the arrowheads scraping his neck.

A chapel it was, sure enough, but not one of your fancy London cathedrals. It was something altogether more modest, with limed walls and hard benches for squirming on. And there, lounging on the rear bench with those infernal black boots poking from the shadows, which was becoming something of a trademark look, lounged the man himself: Albert Garrick, a cloying odour of tallow and rancid meat drifting from his flesh.

'Welcome to the town of Mandrake, Riley boy. Welcome to the era of witch-hunting. Sixteen forty-something, if memory serves.'

'What are you?' Riley shouted at him. And then again: '*What are you?*'

Garrick cleared his throat. 'I am death, son. Weren't you always proclaiming it to any lawman that would give the time of day to a ragamuffin like yourself? Funny that, because I am the law here, sent from God to weed out witches and their familiars.'

Riley righted himself an inch and heard a cable sing. 'What class of a being are you, is what I mean.'

Garrick, ever the showman, took his sweet time answering, rising silently like a shadow drawn on a string and sashaying into the light. He was a macabre sight to behold: all bones and marble flesh, like a famished statue of his previous self. He turned side-on and performed a casual side shuffle to the altar, then executed a low bow from the waist, his knuckles scraping the floor.

'I told you, my boy,' he said, projecting his voice in his best West End posh. 'I am the Forever Man.'

It was impressive and it was ridiculous and it was pure theatre, and Riley found that the whole performance stirred a pot of feelings in him that he'd just this minute been thinking was empty.

I am terrified.

Garrick saw this and it pleased him, for this entire situation was a new wrinkle in his time. He plonked the length of himself down on the front pew.

'Don't be flinching, son,' he advised. 'For the Cat's Collar is on a hair trigger, so she is. Two hair triggers, to be precise. I suppose it really should be round the neck of your Injun princess; after all, she is the one with cat's eyes.'

Garrick leaned forward and plucked one of the collar's strings so that it twanged, then laughed. 'That, my son, is a G. The fake triggers are tuned as a violin. I would force the captives to play the Alleluia. If they reached the end, then the collar would spring open and God had liberated them. One false note and they would end their own lives and prove themselves Satan's spawn. Now there, Riley, is entertainment at its purest.'

Cat's Collar.

Riley didn't need an explanation that witches' familiars were often cats and believed to be capable of taking human form – and so they would be held in restraints like this one and then forced to fiddle till they died. He also did not need to be told that, in all likelihood, none of the accused had ever survived the device.

The latest in a series of horrors visited by Albert Garrick on humanity.

'It should amuse you to know that I designed the Cat's Collar for you. Not for you in specific, you understand. But with you in mind, for you were the best, most natural escapologist I ever saw, apart from myself. *So*, thinks I to myself, *Albert Garrick, you'd best be coming up with something that even the boy Riley could not wriggle from.* For that would be the height of embarrassment, would it not? To have a familiar slip the noose, as it were.'

This did not amuse Riley one jot. For it made his predicament all the more hopeless.

'I should elucidate,' said Garrick. 'Fill you in on things. For you are no doubt puzzled as to –' the illusionist flapped his hands – 'all of this. Everything that has transpired.'

Riley was happy to let Garrick talk while he studied this Cat's Collar and determined for himself whether it was as escape-proof as Garrick claimed. Maybe he should even charm the devil a little.

'Please, master,' he said, slipping easily into his old supplicant's tone. 'Explain these miracles.'

Garrick laughed again, having himself a fine old time. 'Oho! Master now, is it? And miracles with it. None of your weaselling, my boy. I talk to hear myself talk. For the pleasure of my own voice. So none of your slippery ways, if you please, or I might play for myself a tune on that there collar.'

'Tell me then, devil,' spat Riley. 'Hear your own voice ring out.'

Garrick clapped his hands. 'Excellent. The rat shows his true colours.'

He patted his waistcoat pockets for cigarettes and matches. Finding both, he fiddled with a silver box until a certain cigarette took his fancy above the others and he extracted it. 'These made the trip with me. The wormhole giveth and taketh.'

Garrick struck his match and drew in smoke, exhaled to the ceiling and then told his tale – and all the while Riley plotted his escape, as he generally had whenever his master waxed.

'It was something of a turn-up when you and that American slip of a girl turfed me into the wormhole without so much as a bullseye to light my way and little hope of ever feeling the sun on my face again.' Garrick's lips drooped, a clownish grimace. 'How desolate I was. But then says I to meself: *Buck up, Alby. You ain't dead yet, so there is hope.* And I remembered a quote from an old Chinaman, which ran something like *Keep your friends close, and your enemies closer.* And, having not a friend in the universe, I kept the wormhole close, until it became a part of me, but not so as I would dissolve entirely and become a part of it, if you catch my drift. I held on to my soul, if that's what you want to call it. Bound it up in a skin of hatred.'

He pointed the cigarette at Riley. 'Hatred for you, my boy, if you want to hear the harsh truth of the matter. For it was you, my own squire, who betrayed his benefactor. After an age, or a moment – for there is no actual time in the wormhole – I happened upon a rift that did not close with the same speed as Charles Smart's manufactured portals, and so out I shoots into this godforsaken, blighted land without a decent playhouse for miles. Albert Garrick in the blooming countryside, how's about that? Without so much as a *seel-voo-play* or *howjadoo*. And I arrived just in time to take a pork-sticker in the heart. Right through the ticker. And that was it for Mister Garrick, thinks I. Lying there in the mud, a sword in my chest, dying in dank ignorance.'

Garrick took advantage of this natural dramatic break to stand and squash his cigarette beneath his boot heel. 'But no. It weren't so. Albert Garrick lived.'

You don't say, thought Riley but did not say it, for now he was convinced that it was the devil himself who recounted this tale and his terror had amplified to some never previously experienced level.

'And, what ho, if Albert Garrick did not hop to his feet,

sprightly as a Russian tumbler, and pull that blade out of his own chest and stick it into his attacker's. *Tit for tat*, says I, but he heard me not for he was stone dead.'

Riley had often declared that Garrick could not be killed, but it was hyperbole, for what he really meant was that Albert Garrick with his particular skills would be extremely difficult to kill; now it seemed he had been literally correct.

Garrick is immortal now. Truly. And seems in better humour. Somehow sane.

'I hardly blame the bumpkin for having a go, for had I not appeared from the air in a jumble of sparks? And his companion had informed me, before I rolled him into the marsh to lie with his friend, that they had mistaken me for a witch, as the town was blighted with the creatures and they had been dispatched to fetch the Witchfinder General. *How delightful*, thinks Alby to himself. What a novel way to make use of my talents. And so I lodged here for a spell as Witchfinder.'

He winked at Riley to show his use of the word 'spell' had been intended as a little joke. 'Quite the hit I was, my lad. Standing ovations every night, as it were. Rid the world of a few creatures into the bargain, as more had slipped from the rift than just myself. Horrible things. You wouldn't believe it. And I was happy for a while. However, my boy, the rift's call grew stronger every day and I knew it would have me back, but I would sooner dwell in the rookeries and slums of London town than go back in there where my very being would be forfeit. So, Albert Garrick moved on for himself and travelled the world.'

Garrick paused in his telling. 'On I lived and continued to

live,' he said after a moment. 'Slings and arrows had a go at my person. Not to mention pestilence and plague, but I shrugged 'em all off. And time too. That weren't nothing to me, for I am as the tunnel itself, without end. Oh, the things I've seen and done. The Americas, my boy. I was over there cutting a broad patch through Chevron Savano's ancestors, wishing every one was her. And China too, bringing out opium by the ton. Fortunes I made and lost, and not a fig did I care.'

Garrick stooped to stroke Riley's hair. 'For shall I tell you something, son? It doesn't matter. Nothing matters. Everything is life and death and blood and pestilence. All a fellow can do is take his amusement where he can. And for me, once I realized the tunnel would not let me pass on, I decided to dedicate myself to taking vengeance on you, boy, as a distraction. I will have my little games, you know.'

Riley needed confirmation. 'So, you can never be put six feet under?'

Garrick's expression might have darkened had his complexion allowed it; as it was, his features twisted. 'Six feet under? Six feet? In Sicily I was buried in a crypt for decades by a band of Mafiosi. They took me for some class of ghoul when their musket shot failed to kill me. Grave robbers dug me up not a month ago. Can you imagine my frustration? My rage? I lay there howling at the stone, gnashing my teeth. After all that time and I almost missed my appointment. Not to mention that I missed witnessing my own marvellosity onstage. You might have died in some trivial manner without me there to have a hand in it.

'But I lived just the same in spite of the appearance of my

skin, which is brought about by a reaction between the wormhole's particles and the silver I must constantly wear. And now fate has brought us here where all fear me, and my revenge can be more –' Garrick paused now to choose his words – 'more leisurely. And then I will move on once again, far away from the damned wormhole.'

The entire rigmarole was so twisted and violent that it was somehow worthy of Albert Garrick, and Riley never doubted the story for a moment.

The magician sat again on the low bench, crossing his booted legs at the ankles. 'My first scheme failed to an extent because it grew too elaborate. I was caught up in the mechanics and failed to plan for audience interference, as it were. Little Miss Savano –' Garrick wagged a finger at Riley and leered knowingly – 'I saw it, you know. The gleam in your beadies. Puppy love, ain't it? Forged in the fire of adventure and brought to bloom by the wormhole. You can thank Albert Garrick for that, for who was it if not me who brung you two together?'

For this was the depth and breadth of Garrick's hubris and pomposity – that he congratulated himself for introducing two friends whom he had plotted to murder for centuries.

'But this new infatuation of yours will serve me well, son. For now, instead of forcing you to witness your so-called brother perish at my hands, I will force you to watch your Injun princess burn as a witch, before we see whether or not you can pluck your way out of the Cat's Collar.'

Garrick stretched creakily to his full height, slapping his knees on the way up. 'Simple, ain't it? Simple as jam.'

Riley had enough steel in him for one little barb. 'Simple as jam, less you touch Chevie. You touch her and yer gone into the wormhole, ain't that so, *master*?'

As soon as he said it, Riley realized that he should have kept his trap latched.

'Right you are,' said Garrick, instinctively rubbing a thick silver cuff bracelet on his wrist, where it was almost invisible against his skin. 'By times the wormhole calls to me, loves me and hates me all at once, but the silver kept her at bay till now. But that accursed Timekey could have me swimming in foam, right enough.'

He tapped Riley's head. 'My thanks to you for the reminder. It seems my very proximity is enough to light up that accursed device. So I will not lay a hand on your beloved. I will have my acolytes lash her to the pyre and the accursed Timekey can melt and run like tallow down the stake along with the meat on her bones.'

With that, Garrick spun on his heel and left whistling a merry tune, which it took Riley a few bars to recognize as a music-hall favourite: 'The Mad Butcher'.

5

FAIRBROTHER ISLES. GEDDIT?

Constable Godfrey Cryer was watching over the prisoner in the town jail, which was reserved for troublesome reprobates who could not be trusted in the House of Unfortunates; it was little more than a woodshed with a stout door and a single-barred window overlooking the square's gibbet and stocks. The jail was situated within stumbling distance of the Huntings Tavern, which historically supplied most of its occupants, who, though Puritan, were not against a tankard or two of a hot afternoon – or a cold one for that matter. Indeed it was said among Mandrake's locals that the jail's wooden bench had absorbed enough beer dribblings over the years that any prisoners who went in sober came out drunk from the vapours.

Since Cryer's guard duty had commenced not one hour ago, three times already the constable had nipped round the back of the jail hut, where none could see him but the birds perched atop the town wall, for what could be described as either a gibbering weep or perhaps a gnashing series of sobs. Godfrey Cryer was enveloped in a whip-storm of emotions. Witchfinder Garrick had returned after a year-long absence, and this was what Cryer had wished for, had prayed for nightly, but now he felt that he was not worthy to serve Albert Garrick. Indeed, was not his lace collar being laundered this day? The very day that Master Garrick returns, his constable is found without a trimmed collar and with only his stout hat to proclaim him constable. What must Master Garrick think?

I am crying, thought Cryer. *Cryer the crier is crying. It is enough to make a man weep. Oh, they would laugh now; how they would guffaw. Jeronimo Woulfe and all the rest who secretly scoffed at the very existence of witchcraft.*

But now . . .

But now there was a witch barricaded in the jail and none could deny it, for she had the eyes of a cat, and all had witnessed them flash gold.

A demon dragged hissing from hell she was, without a doubt. Cryer's chest swelled with a fierce pride in his master's unprecedented accomplishment, but in that moment he felt the witch reach out to him, trying to exploit his sin, and Cryer's very skin crawled.

'Witch,' he shouted, pounding on the wall behind him. 'Begone. Leave my mind!' Though, of course, the only thing stirring in Cryer's mind was his own imagination.

'I think you already left your mind, Crybaby,' said a voice behind him. Godfrey Cryer whirled round with such speed that his hat spun a quarter revolution further than his person.

'Nice look, Crybaby,' said Fairbrother Isles, for it was he

72

who had spoken then and now. 'Hat all askew and such. Very constable-like.'

Cryer straightened himself, his tunic and his hat. Then he scowled that he should be so compromised by such a fool as the African man, Isles, with his weirdness of speech and softness of head.

It was true that Fairbrother Isles's shaggy appearance did nothing to dispel the general opinion that he was indeed an arch-dolt and slave to the grog. For as long as Cryer could remember, the man had made his home in a shack in the fens. Though Cryer had never cared about the man enough to brave the abomination-infested bogs, he had no doubt that the shack reeked even more than Isles, which was a considerable amount.

The duffer in question stood, or rather leaned insolently on the jail wall, with his customary smug grin skulking behind a spade of beard, which remained as dark as his own skin in spite of the rampant grey in the unkempt hair that was brushed back from his forehead. His boozy habits had set his frame running slightly to fat but he was a broad man nonetheless and Godfrey Cryer had often given secret thanks that Isles put up no resistance when thrown in the jail or stocks. He was a maudlin drunkard, given to rambling and fantastical weepy stories about ships that could fly or paintings that moved, or how much he missed creatures that he named *hot dogs*.

'Isles,' snapped Godfrey Cryer, 'begone from here. Important matters are unfolding. Witchfinder Garrick has called an assembly and you'd best be attending.'

Isles made no move to leave. 'Witchfinder, whatever. I have a bone to pick with you, Cryer.'

Godfrey Cryer cared for the man's brazen tone not one bit nor his bone comment for that matter – Cryer was well aware that his skin's tone and sheen lent him a bone-like quality.

'Bone, is it? You have a bone to pick with me? That is not the way of things, Isles. A sot-pot does not *pick bones* with the town constable.'

Cryer attempted to loom over Isles, but the man seemed of greater heft somehow on this day and even greater uncontriteness than was normal.

'Yeah, well, this sot-pot is supposed to be spending the night in that jail, right? That was the deal. I was disorderly, so I spend a day in the stocks and a night in jail. You pronounced that, Cryer. You cried it loud and clear.'

Another mocking of his name in a day overflowing with mockery was too much for the constable and he lashed out with the back of his hand, the very boniness of which he was sure would raise a pleasing welt on Isles's cheek. But the blow did not strike flesh, only the wooden wall of the jail as Isles's head moved sharply out of reach.

Cryer cried out, which drew a chuckle from Isles even as he chopped the constable's neck with the side of his hand in a move that would be known as the *brachial stun* by US marines in several hundred years. Cryer dropped like a falling log.

Fairbrother Isles chuckled again and thought how long he had been waiting to knock Godfrey Cryer on his backside and how it had been well worth the wait.

'Crybaby,' he said, and stepped over the fallen constable to the jail door.

Isles checked for any eyes that might be pointed his way, but the street was deserted.

'All packed into the House of Unfortunates,' he muttered to himself. 'Attending the great weirdo Albert Garrick's magic meeting.' Isles did a little spooky face here that would have earned him a lashing had Cryer been conscious to witness it, but Cryer would not awaken for several minutes and it would be several more minutes before he had gathered the courage to admit to Witchfinder Garrick that he had failed in his duty. While it was true that the Witchfinder had no official authority in Mandrake, being a mere freelancer, Godfrey Cryer had witnessed Master Garrick perform such feats that he revered the self-proclaimed Witchfinder as he would Saint Peter himself.

Constable Cryer's unconscious state afforded Isles all the time he needed to congratulate himself on his one-blow knockout by whispering 'You never lost it, baby' to himself and to slide back the bolt of the jail door and slip quietly into the cell, which he did without delay.

Inside was something he had almost given up on ever seeing again. Three gold letters on a blue uniform. Not the kind of jumpsuit he remembered, but close enough.

Say them aloud, he thought to himself. *Make it real*.

So he did. 'F . . . B . . . I.'

If Isles expected a reaction of some sort from the person, *creature*, wearing the federal uniform, he was disappointed. The cat-girl was alive, but she huddled in the corner and did

75

nothing more than stare into space and shiver slightly. So Isles leaned closer. 'FBI,' he repeated, then tapped his own chest. 'Fair-brother Isles. Geddit? I'm Club Fed.'

The poor cat-girl apparently did not *geddit*, and so, sighing, Isles lifted her bodily.

'Goddamn wormhole mutations,' he said to himself, he supposed, as it was obvious the unfortunate time traveller over his shoulder did not understand a word coming out of his mouth. 'Better get you back to the field office.'

Isles left the cell with his cargo slung fireman-lift-style over one shoulder. He thought about kicking Cryer in the rump on the way past, but decided against it, not out of the goodness of his heart but because a sharp pain in the rear end might actually wake up the snoring town crier. So instead he stepped over the constable, slipped through the unguarded western gate and disappeared into a copse that ran through the fens, displaying a level of sneakiness that could only have been learned in Quantico.

6

ON WITH THE SHOW

Albert Garrick had indeed summoned the townsfolk to a meeting, though he had no authority from Parliament, the king, Levellers or any of the other factions currently claiming dominion over England. Indeed, not since the tribal age had the country seen such turmoil, which suited Garrick to perfection. King Charles was being jostled from one prison to another like some prize bull, and local lad Oliver Cromwell was struggling to hold a divided Parliament together. Outlaws and brigands raided the county, plague was forever rising in black waves that could consume a town in days, and the dispossessed roamed the country roads like staggering corpses, their hollow eyes pleading for food, their stick-thin arms outstretched for alms.

Mandrake survived because it was too small and remote to be of any strategic use, surrounded as it was by fens, bogs and thick wedges of forest, and too large to be overrun by bandits. The watch was vigilant, and the militia was trained and armed with cannons and four-foot matchlocks that sat in notches along the walls. In peacetime Mandrake was situated in the worst possible place for a town, being far from main roads or river transport, but in dark times there wasn't a safer band of goodly souls than the residents of Mandrake's Groan, tucked inside the town walls with their faith and deep wells to sustain them.

But then came the abomination and the whispers of witch-craft. Of course people were not fools; whenever days were dire the first cry to arise was that of *Witchcraft*, usually from the hysterics and zanies. And most days these cries were treated with the contempt and scoffing they deserved.

However, two years ago a creature had come stumbling into the town from the fens with steam rising from its hide. A creature that was undeniably the work of some dark power. The head was human and so was part of a shoulder, but the rest . . .

The rest was a great lizard with hooked talons and a broad, powerful tail that swung like the reaper's scythe, slicing flesh and breaking bones. It blundered through the market gate and sliced two horses to bloody shreds before it was herded back the way it had come by militiamen, and it shambled into the marsh fog, howling a scream of the damned.

The entire town had seen it. The escaped slave, Fairbrother Isles, had watched from the stocks and nearly tore the restraints from their hinges in an attempt to remove himself from harm's way.

It was recorded in the parish diary that:

A great beast, with aspects of man and lizard, emerged from the white mist and did make a great rampage through the fair, doing an amount of damage to beast and produce. Though stout-hearted men set upon it with musket and stave, no mark could be made on the beast's hide and it fled to the marsh and can still be heard screaming by night.

This account was signed by a dozen witnesses and marked with an X by twice as many again who could not write.

There were monsters in the world and none could deny it. Word was sent to Huntingdon and help sought, but the government officials had matters of more import on their platters than wild tales of devil spawn, and not a single soldier was sent to aid the besieged townsfolk. Next a petition was sent to Matthew Hopkins, the notorious Witchfinder General, but it seemed as though Master Hopkins was wading through a good body of witches himself and so sent a man in his stead. A man in whom he placed the utmost trust: Witchfinder Albert Garrick. A man on the rise, so they said in the witch business. A man who could sniff out Satan, wherever he lurked and sniggered.

It was said that Oliver Cromwell, whose own aunt was purported to have been killed by a coven of witches, once consulted Albert Garrick, though publicly he denied any specific opinion on the witch-hunts.

Garrick came and paused for barely an hour to tear at a loaf of bread and down a jug of bitter wine before off he went into the fens at moonrise, with the light glinting on the twin swords in his fists. The townsfolk lined the walls, following Garrick's path across the moors, then into the whiplash rushes and then into the deep snarls of the fens, where his rangy figure merged with the dark shapes. For three days the Witchfinder was gone, but return he did, dragging the beast's corpse behind him; the creature's eyes were like burning coals, shining through a crust of lizard blood.

Garrick had stood outside the northern gate to the town

and declared that he would not enter unless his terms were agreed to.

There be witches here! he had stated. *This creature is witch-born. And I must have payment to deal with the devil's crones.*

The townsfolk agreed without quibble and so Garrick's reign of purification began.

Seven women Garrick sniffed out and forced confessions from. They confessed to witchcraft and collusion with spirits and casting curses upon their neighbours and calling forth monsters from the earth. The common folk of Mandrake were horrified that these evildoers had lived for so long in their midst. The midwife Millicent Lewis, so trusted for her gentle nature and healing elixirs, now admitted to secretly baptizing babies for Lucifer once they were in her arms. Christabella Clopton, always believed to be nothing more harmful than an old bedlam, now professed that she danced with spirits at full moon. And the dreadful list went on.

More abominations emerged from the fens. A giant ape with the arms of a man, for instance, and, worst of all, a flying snake that could not breathe fire, as the story was now told in the Huntings, but which did have foul and sulphurous breath. Garrick dispatched them all, with a degree of enthusiasm for the combat that drew queasy glances from the townsfolk. Often it seemed that the Witchfinder was so grievously wounded that he could not possibly survive but, following a night's vigil, Albert Garrick would emerge from his spartan room, without so much as a scratch where there had been a wound or gash the previous night, and take his trademark deep bow to the assembled citizens.

For a full year Garrick held this post, amassing quite the purse of gold for his labours.

His *Herculean labours*, as his lackey Godfrey Cryer often described them, skirting blasphemy by citing false gods.

Then, one morning, off he went into the fens for his customary morning patrol, with his high leather boots to protect his breeches from the snap of reeds, and a leather satchel of meat and bread, and he returned not.

Days passed. Then weeks. A trepidatious search party poked through the marshes, hallooing the Witchfinder's name but without success.

Most presumed him dead, for he took no gold with him, but Cryer always believed his spiritual master would return.

There is evil yet abroad in the fens, he said when he wasn't wasting good working hours trying to change the town's name to Garrickston or some such variation on his hero's name.

And now the constable was proven right, for Garrick had indeed returned, with a witch in one fist and her familiar in the other. And when Albert Garrick, the scourge of evil, called a meeting in the House of Unfortunates, then brave was the individual who took it upon himself not to attend.

The House of Unfortunates was the place where the infirm, unsound and lawless were interned on the upper floor with only the most casual guard, for most were happy to be there. The alternative was desolation outside the town walls with nothing but skin-and-bone rabbits and sour berries to sustain them. The ground floor, or long hall, was used for the serious business of visiting masters, magistrates or coroners and such. Above the yawning hearth there was inscribed in the stone: FOR JUDGEMENT IS WITHOUT MERCY TO ONE WHO HAS SHOWN NO MERCY.

As for Garrick, he was more interested in the *judgement* section of that Biblical quote than in the *mercy* part.

For judgement I do so enjoy but mercy not so much.

This is not to say that Albert Garrick had never shown mercy in his year as Witchfinder. In fact, he had twice granted women their freedom, but only because he suspected that they might actually be witches and would in some way cheat death, as he himself had, and return to do him grievous harm.

Only kill the innocent, became his motto. It was not always practical, he knew, and so he tagged on the addendum *where possible*. For sometimes even the guilty cannot tell themselves apart from the innocent.

But not I, thought Garrick, as he gazed upon the congregation, their eyes rapt, marvelling at his dramatic return. *I am the bad man. I am the worst man. And now that I understand what is occurring here, I intend to take full advantage of it.*

For Albert Garrick now had greater plans than simply taking revenge on a boy. Yes, he had dreamed about this day for centuries but only as a whimsy, a distraction from the pressures of eternity, from the constant siren song of the wormhole, which promised him such power if only he would return to its soft embrace.

But power ain't what Albert Garrick is after, thought the Witchfinder/illusionist/assassin. *Magic is what I crave.*

Jeronimo Woulfe was the mason whose hands had fashioned the gargoyles that adorned both the hall roof and the mantel of the fireplace that warmed Garrick's back — for he had been so cold since the Sicilian grave robbers exhumed his corpse-like frame. Now, this man, Woulfe, cleared his throat and stepped from the crowd.

'Master Witchfinder,' he began, then paused, from nervousness perhaps or uncertainty about how to proceed. He parsed the phrases in his mind before continuing. 'Your return is most welcome. *Most* welcome. But the manner of your return. Your materialization from the very ether —'

Garrick cut him off. 'Master Mason. Jeronimo, ain't it? See how I have not forgotten your name, even after all this time.'

Woulfe nodded agreeably, though the Witchfinder had been away barely a year, which was not such a very long time for a grown man to remember another fellow's name, 'less he be a blunderbuss altogether.

'I see, course I do, how my arrival could cause consternation, as it were,' continued the self-appointed Witchfinder. 'Flash, bang and here's Albert Garrick right back where he started from.'

The assembly nodded along with the rhythm of Garrick's words, though more than a few were confused by his accent, which was obviously London in origin but different in some inflections from that of the petty chapmen who often passed through from the capital.

'So what's to set Albert Garrick apart from the other demons? Who's to say that Master Garrick ain't himself a class of witch or warlock, if you will, come to sow confusion and breed hatred?' Garrick raised a rigid finger to emphasize his final point. 'For he looks different, don't he now? His appearance is much changed. All ghostly and pale is the Witchfinder.' Garrick appeared agitated by a sudden thought. 'And what if it ain't Garrick at all,' he said with pantomime horror, 'but some shape-shifter come to tempt the good people of Mandrake's Groan?'

Woulfe spoke again, seemingly the only resident with the gumption to do so. 'We all witnessed it, Master Garrick. A thing of wonder it was, how you appeared from the mysterious fluxes, dragging those infernal beings behind. But your own argument, though sarcastic it was, I suspect, is well made. Anyone with working glaziers can see, plain as warts, that you are no longer the man you were. And it has been so peaceful here, this past year. Some diverse howlings from the fens, yes, but peace in the town. The war is over now apart from some straggling skirmishes. Even Matthew Hopkins labours no further. So in this time of rest and prosperity and, may I say, godliness, it seems a touch strange that the Almighty would send us a Witchfinder. So perhaps all is not as it appears.'

Garrick noticed that the townsfolk's heads nodded with a greater rapidity now, especially those of the young women who had no wish to be accused of witchcraft and don the Cat's Collar. Now Garrick was on the knife's edge and it thrilled him. There was no danger of death, but he could be discredited and driven from here, which would be inconvenient. Now was the time to set on stage the Great Lombardi, who had thrilled the West End, setting hearts a-thumping with his fantastical presentation and feats.

'Yes, good sir mason,' he cried, leaping atop the long hall's stone table so all could appreciate the nuances of his performance. 'All is not as it appears, for this is not a time of true peace, for were it truly so, would I have been sent here? Mandrake is in the eye of the storm. There are thunderclouds behind us and more gather on the horizon. For I have seen the future and it is turbulent.' Garrick paused and the moment was still and silent as a crypt. 'War!' he shouted to the rafters. 'The king shall be free, and once more the rivers will run red with English blood. And, while Cromwell fights the king, Satan's forces will mass unopposed.'

Woulfe had enough gumption for one more objection. 'But all this is talk, surely. Words and blather. Surely you travel with some form of confirmation that you have been sent? An envoy could ride to Parliament perhaps.'

Garrick was surprised. 'To Oliver Cromwell himself?'

'He is a good and reasonable man, I have heard.'

Garrick laughed a little to himself. 'Yes, this revisionist notion has been gaining popularity of late, but you may find Master Cromwell not as cheery a cove as advertised, and he might not appreciate the mistreatment of his ambassador.'

'Nevertheless.'

Nevertheless, thought Garrick. *This mason is a plucky one. Fearing for his daughter, no doubt. Time to silence my critics.*

Garrick grasped his head as though in sudden excruciating pain, letting out a blood-curdling scream that saw the assembly shrink away from him.

'Evil!' he cried. 'Evil is surrounding Mandrake!'

Evil! The cry echoed through the long hall, penetrating even to the upper storey. Women already fraught with fear broke down weeping and sobbing.

Garrick pointed a crooked finger at one of Woulfe's leering gargoyles. 'I see you, demon!' he called, and at that very instant a tongue of flame issued forth from the creature's stone mouth.

A collective *Oooh* rose like a mist from the hall.

This is prime stuff, thought Garrick. *The punters would gladly pay five shillings for this*.

'And you, devil!' This to the second gargoyle. 'You cannot hide from me.'

At this, another gout of flame came from the stone creature's mouth, aimed directly at the Witchfinder's head, though he skipped aside to avoid its lick.

Garrick stretched to his full height. 'This town is under my protection. The protection of Albert Garrick, Witchfinder and exorcist.'

A low moan swirled around the feet of the Puritans. It rose to become a howling screech that seemed to envelop the Witchfinder, challenging his power.

'Begone!' shouted Garrick stoutly. 'Begone, creatures. You shall not harm these people.'

Flares of white light shot from Garrick's hands as he battled the invisible spirits that surrounded him, and from the flares great puffs of powdery smoke rose in a broad column above the table. In seconds the smoke settled to reveal that the

Witchfinder had been taken. Swallowed entirely by the powers of darkness.

But then came Garrick's disembodied voice booming the length of the hall.

'No! You shall not have them, witch! You shall not have me!'

And there came a mighty flash in the hearth and from the belly of it rolled Albert Garrick himself, doused in sweat and heaving of chest.

'Stronger,' he panted. 'Stronger it grows.'

Even Woulfe was now convinced. 'Tell us, Master Garrick,' he said, helping the Witchfinder to his feet. 'What must we do?'

Garrick disguised his grin as a grimace. 'Thank you, good sir mason. Thank you for your trust.' He shook off the man's arm and turned to the stunned congregation.

First the stick and then the sugar, as his old dad had often said about training fighting dogs.

Time for the sugar.

'Good people of Mandrake. Know that there are no witches among ye. All here are pure of heart and soul. But we must burn the cat-witch with all haste before she spreads her evil to your daughters.'

'Burn?' said Woulfe. 'But hanging has always been our method. It is more humane.'

'Burn!' thundered Garrick. 'She must be destroyed entirely. I have returned from the gates of hell to save this town and I will not be thwarted now by a witch fragment. One fingernail is enough to infect another. Would you have witchery spread to your own daughter, sir?'

Woulfe's girl grabbed her father's elbow. 'Papa,' she pleaded. 'I would not be a witch. I would not.'

There was no argument left to Woulfe. Outplayed and outflanked, he was.

'Very well,' he said with a tinge of resignation in his voice. 'We burn the witch.'

Garrick's smile was gentle and paternal, but inside he gleefully gloated and congratulated himself for taking the time, all those years ago, to manufacture for himself the bag of tricks to which he had treated these bumpkins on this day. Fortunate too that he had left them behind in Mandrake, for if not they would have been long spent before now.

You get what you pay for materials-wise, Alby, he told himself. Another personal maxim.

His moment of triumph was rudely truncated by the sudden intrusion of Godfrey Cryer, who barged into the chamber, panting as though pursued by the hounds of hell.

'The witch!' he called to Garrick, his voice hollow with fear, for the news he was about to deliver would likely enrage his master. 'She has been taken. Isles took her. Bewitched he was. Africans are susceptible to magic, I have heard.'

Garrick was momentarily peeved at this news, but then he conceded to himself that it was a most satisfyingly dramatic turn, which could have leaped from the pages of a penny dreadful.

The show must at all costs go on, Alby.

'The familiar!' he cried with the authority granted him by

his disappearing act. 'She will attempt to free her familiar. To the chapel!'

And, from the table, down he went in a single lurching leap that covered half the distance to the door. With a barge of his elbow, he knocked Cryer aside, making a note in his mind to deal with the fool later, and out into the night he ran, his black boots and pale skin making him seem like a legless ghost floating down the main street of Mandrake's Groan.

THE FIELD OFFICE

Meanwhile, in the fens. Huntingdonshire. 1647
Fairbrother Isles's actual name was Fender Rhodes Isles, thanks to his mother's adoration of legendary funkster Stevie Wonder, who favoured Fender Rhodes electric keyboards. His mother had actually wanted to name her baby boy Wonder but Fairbrother's father, to his credit, baulked at the notion that his son should be forever taunted as 'Wonder Isles'.

'Sounds like something outta *Star Trek*' were his actual words, and so they settled on Fender Rhodes, which wasn't great as names go, but it was better than the alternative.

Fender had jettisoned his own first names on his arrival in the seventeenth century and replaced them with Fairbrother, hoping that any other undercover time travellers might put two and two together and get FBI – but no one had, leading Isles to believe either that his code was too subtle or that he was stranded back here in the age of Roundheads and witches.

Isles had been at this end of the time tunnel for so long that sometimes he wondered if he might have dreamed up the whole future thing.

Computers, cellphones, space travel, Power Rangers.

It was beginning to sound nuts, even to him.

Gradually, as the first years trudged by, he forgot all about his real name and began to think of himself as Fairbrother and even to buy into his cover as the town's drunkard-cum-halfwit. He bought into it a little too much and spent more nights in the jail than he did in the field office, a fact that annoyed the professor quite a bit. But what was the prof gonna do? Fire him? The prof was a civilian anyway, so technically he wasn't Isles's boss.

But, even as he told himself this, Isles knew that this particular civilian was not just a normal guy. This civilian was extra special, or as they might say in the good old twentieth century: *a high-value asset.*

So all alone he had been, without brother or sister agents, unless you counted Pointer, who hardly qualified as human company any more. All alone until today, when this kid materialized with a magician and the Witchfinder, as far as he could see, but the kid wore the blue and gold. OK, her eyes were weird, but he'd seen a lot weirder in the past twenty years. In fact, the good people of Mandrake probably considered him far weirder than the cat-girl. Yes, he'd been forced to blow his cover to spring her, but what was he going to do? Leave the girl for Garrick to lynch in the square? *Hardly.* Once a Fed, always a Fed. Though this kid looked a little young to be an agent. Maybe that meant he was getting old.

'Old and outta shape,' Fairbrother said aloud, patting his blossoming stomach. He would cut back on the ale, he decided. And the pies. Maybe do a little cardio.

Hey, he realized, *I feel . . . What is this feeling? I feel switched on. Plugged in. I've got purpose.*

It had been a long time.

Isles negotiated a path through the forest clumps that dotted Mandrake's perimeter, though to be honest the term 'path' barely applied. 'Trail' would perhaps be a more accurate word, for he varied his route, as his drill instructor in Quantico had impressed upon him and his classmates by following them back to their secret off-base beer stash one night and trussing them all up with plasti-cuffs.

Never take the same route twice in a row, kids. Twice in a row is a pattern and a pattern leads to your beer being confiscated at the very least.

Isles had learned the lesson well and now had over a dozen routes back to the field office, which were rigged with trip-wires and bear pits in case anyone was on his tail. Low-tech stuff but very effective.

Isles switched the mewling figure he was carrying across to his other shoulder as he left the forest proper and moved into the marsh. The waist-high reeds drummed his thighs as he waded through, spraying him with a fine mist that he generally appreciated as his head was often fuzzy, but today he felt sharp and connected, as though something important might happen.

The falling night and thick fog that habitually hung over the fens soon enveloped him, and Isles felt confident enough in this natural cover to take the most direct route back to the office. As he walked, he softly whistled the five notes made famous by the twentieth-century movie *Close Encounters of the*

Third Kind and within seconds a sleek brown hunting dog appeared at his side, keeping pace easily but sneezing whenever a reed flicked against his nose.

'I hate these rushes,' said the dog. 'Right at face level for me, you know?'

'Yeah,' said Isles, patting the dog's head with his free hand.

The hound twisted away from the touch. 'Quit it, Fender. I swear, you do that again I will bite your hand off.'

Isles laughed. 'Come on, Pointer. You love it, boy.'

'And don't call me "boy". I ain't no dog, man,' said Pointer. 'I'm a mutation. Have a heart.'

Isles relented; after all, Donald Pointer had once been his partner and was the only person/dog who still called him Fender.

'OK. Sorry, partner. How's the old man?'

'He's the old man, you know,' said Pointer. 'Still trying to set things right.' The dog sniffed Chevie's leg. 'What you got there? Lunch?'

'Yeah, you're not a dog, right?' said Isles.

Pointer barked once. 'Darn. These animal instincts, you know. It's been twenty years, partner. I'm forgetting what it feels like to be a federal agent.'

'Well, what I have on my shoulder here might just be able to remind us what that feels like.'

'Yeah?' said the dog doubtfully. 'She looks a little young. The FBI are doing daycare now?' Pointer loped alongside quietly for a minute, then said, 'And I'm getting a vibe, man. For some reason I don't like this female.'

Isles laughed. 'Hah. Maybe that's because she has cat's eyes.'

93

The dog stopped in his tracks, growled, then shook himself and fell in beside his partner.

'You are not a dog,' he told himself. 'You are not a dog.'

Not yet, thought Isles. *But more and more every day. Pretty soon there'll be nothing left of my partner but the colour of his hair.*

Isles and Pointer had once upon a time been two of the FBI's go-to guys in the field of witness security. During their spectacular tenure at Wit Sec they managed to shepherd twenty-five crucial witnesses into the witness box without losing a single body. Isles was the strategy guy and Pointer was the muscle, which was not to say they couldn't trade roles when the situation called for it. Their most famous case in Bureau circles was when they avoided a bunch of mercenaries surrounding a Florida courthouse by sneaking the witness through the sewer system. Afterwards the witness, a low-level driver by the name of Stickshift Rossini, had said, *Hey, guys, that was one close encounter*, which led to Isles and Pointer adopting the five famous notes as their theme tune.

When they make the movie, Donald Pointer used to say, *Denzel plays you. Stallone is the only man alive who can do me justice, and they gotta recycle the* Close Encounters *music.*

The movie never happened.

What happened was they got assigned to a very special professor guy in London, of all places, and took a time jaunt back to the seventeenth century that didn't quite go as planned.

Isles's shoulders were starting to ache with Chevie's weight, no matter how many times he switched her over.

'Hey, Don, buddy. You don't think . . .'

The dog trotted a few steps ahead. 'Don't even ask, man. You shouldn't even let that question form in your mind.'

'Hey, you didn't even let me speak, partner.'

Pointer turned on him. 'Oh, it's *partner* now you want the cat-girl to ride on my back. I ain't a donkey neither, got it?'

Isles was always amazed that his partner had taught himself to talk with a dog's vocal apparatus. It shouldn't have been possible, but maybe there was a human larynx in there. However, even though Pointer could talk, days could go by when he spent his time engaged in more dog-like activities, like chewing on stuff and chasing rats. And he could deny it all he wanted, but sometimes in the evening Pointer loved nothing more than a good tummy scratch.

'OK,' said Isles. 'Loud and clear. You ain't a dog and you ain't a donkey neither.'

'Yeah,' said Pointer miserably, his long face making the expression more effective. 'But what am I?'

Isles shrugged with one shoulder only. 'Hey. I'm a special agent but not that special. I can't answer that question, but maybe the old man can wake this kid up and get us a few answers.'

Pointer sniffed the air. 'Well, our luck is in. The old man is out of bed. What do you say we go and see if he can put some of his sparkles to work?'

'I say that's a plan, Dog. I mean, Don.'

Pointer jogged off in disgust. 'That ain't funny, Fender. That and the patting on the head. Neither of those things are funny.'

Isles's eyes were serious as he said, 'No. Course not. Sorry, pard. No more pooch jokes.' But, behind the beard, his lips were drawn back in a grin.

The FBI Mandrake field office was actually a swamp treehouse that Isles had constructed in the branches of an unusually tight cluster of English oaks that seemed as though they might even pre-date the marsh itself. Isles's history as the son of a master carpenter and a graduate of Fort Benning Sniper School made him literally the best-qualified person in the world to construct and camouflage the makeshift federal HQ. Pointer didn't like the ladder much, but he got used to it after a while and now trotted up it like a goat up the side of a cliff. The door was not at the top of the ladder, where a person might reasonably expect it to be, but rather three precarious steps along a winding branch and forty degrees round the girth of a massive trunk. The door itself was virtually invisible after all these years and yet Isles's hands could have found the recessed latch in the dark with his senses clouded by ale, which they often were.

But no more ale. I've been reactivated.

He shouldered in the door, which was not designed to swing easily, and Pointer trotted into the office before him, resisting the urge to mark his territory, both because it was a base animal instinct and because the scent could be used to track him. Inside was what could be described as an exceptional example of a log cabin; building them had been Isles's father's bread-and-butter business, though he could also knock up a nice deck or patio. There was a large central room, complete with fireplace and stone chimney, and passages leading to a bedroom, workshop and armoury. The interior was lit with electric lights that were run off a small generator hooked up to solar panels way up in the copse canopy. Huddled over a table, gazing at the screen of a clunky laptop computer, was what seemed like the ghost of an old man in a laboratory jacket, shimmering and semi-transparent, his sparse strands of white hair crackling around his head like lightning bolts.

'Hey, Prof,' said Pointer. 'What's up?'

'What's up?' said the old man without raising his head. 'What's up is that the rift is opening more frequently and we can expect a cataclysmic increase in the number of incoming mutations any day now. That, my friend, is what's up.'

Isles lowered Chevie on to a wooden sofa padded with blankets and straw. 'I think the wait is over. Three warm bodies came through today. I got one right here.'

Now the elderly spook did raise his head. 'What? Three bodies you say?'

'Yeah. Popped out right in the town square. First time that's happened. I had to break cover to get this girl out.'

The old man's accent was Scottish and his expression was concerned. It was a look that seemed etched on his face, as though he'd died with it and had come back from beyond the grave with it locked.

He hurried over to the sofa and hovered over Chevie.

'This girl. I know this girl. Somehow. I've met her. Perhaps the other me.'

Pointer coughed. 'Yeah, the other you. Right, Professor.'

The professor tried to test Chevie's temperature but his spectral hand passed straight through her.

'This is so infuriating. I hate this foam state.' He glanced sharply at Isles. 'Any mutations, Special Agent?'

Isles knelt beside Chevie and gently pulled back one eyelid with his thumb. 'Just the eyes, as far as I can see.'

The professor nodded. 'I see, I see.' He put an ear close to Chevie's chest, then actually lowered it *into* her chest to better hear her heart.

'Come on, Prof, man. That is utterly disgusting,' said Pointer.

This from a guy who licks his own butt, thought Isles but did not say it. He had given his partner enough grief for one day.

The ghostly professor withdrew his head. 'How long has she been catatonic?'

Isles closed one eye, calculating. 'Well, she came through a few hours ago. There was never that much going on, you know, but at least there was some verbalization and movement. But now, these last thirty minutes, not a peep. Just shallow breathing.'

The professor hovered six inches off the floor. 'Something traumatic happened to her, besides the wormhole. She's still mutating. In flux. Get me the medi-kit.'

Isles pulled a Kevlar pack from under the sofa and unzipped it to reveal a comprehensive medical pack that was about two-thirds empty.

The professor tapped his own chin and there were orange sparks at the contact. 'I need the defibrillator and the local anaesthetic.'

Pointer raised one of his paws. 'It's all down to you, partner. These paws aren't going to be much use.'

Isles pulled the portable defibrillator battery from the pack and flicked the switch to CHARGE.

'OK, that will take a minute to warm up. Where do you want the anaesthetic injected?'

'We discovered accidentally that the anaesthetic seemed to be quite effective at halting or even reversing mutations,' said the ghost-professor. 'I don't know how it works. I don't know how anything works. The more I find out, the less I know.'

'Hey!' said Isles sharply, pulling the plastic cover from a loaded hypodermic. 'You're babbling, Prof. Where should I stick this?'

The ghost blinked nervously and if he could have sweated he would. 'At the mutation point. In the eye.'

Isles began to sweat profusely himself. 'You want me to stick this big old needle into this little girl's eye?'

'Yes. In the middle. And then hit her with the defibrillator, which will hopefully wake up her brain.'

'Hopefully?' said Isles.

'I don't know,' said the ghost. 'Sometimes it works.'

'I gotta say, Professor. Your expression isn't really selling this needle-and-shock idea.'

'That is unfair!' said the ghost. 'I'm stuck with this face and you know it.'

'Go on, you sissy,' said Pointer. 'Just do it. She's only a cat anyway.'

'And you're *not* a dog, right?'

99

The professor levitated three feet from the floor and glowed fiercely. 'Please, Special Agents! Time is of the essence here.'

The defibrillator beeped. It was ready.

'OK,' said Isles, and used one massive hand to both hold Chevie's head still and gently open her left eye. The other hand held the needle, which he moved into position slowly until it hovered above the eyeball. 'In the middle, right?'

The professor swooped closer. 'Yes. But not deep. A quarter of an inch, no more.'

Isles rolled his own eyes. 'One quarter inch, right.'

'Give her every drop. Then hit her with the paddles.'

'Inject then paddles – got it.'

Isles hesitated a final moment, then thought, *What the hell*, and pushed the needle into Chevie's eye. He felt the slight resistance of the cornea before the needle slid into the pupil.

'Far enough,' said the professor, who had tilted and swivelled so that his head was inside Chevie's.

That's not distracting at all, thought Isles.

'Now hit the plunger.'

Isles did so, being careful to hold the body of the syringe steady so that the needle intruded no deeper than it needed to. He pressed the plunger firmly and steadily until the hypodermic was empty and pulled it out.

He turned to find Pointer with one of the defibrillator's paddles in his mouth.

'Good dog,' said Isles automatically, and just as automatically followed with an apology. 'Sorry, partner.'

Isles took the paddle, then reached for the second. 'Clear!' he shouted, because that's what you're supposed to shout, right?

'On the temples!' yelled the professor, his voice crackling like an overloaded speaker. 'Not the chest.'

Temples, thought Isles. *This kid is gonna love me.*

He placed a paddle on each side of Chevie's head and gave her the full thousand volts in a two-second blast.

The effect was immediate. Chevie's back arched from the initial shock.

'That's very cat-like,' Pointer pointed out.

And then she began to spasm, clawing the air and swallowing furiously.

'She's going to swallow her tongue!' said the professor. 'Put something in her mouth. A stick. A spoon. Anything.'

'I can't believe I'm doing this for a cat,' said Pointer, and jammed his forepaw into Chevie's mouth only to be bitten for his trouble.

'Nothing wrong with her jaw,' he said through gritted teeth, and then could not suppress a howl.

Chevie thrashed for a full minute, and would have broken her own bones had Isles not weighed her down with his forearms, but slowly her convulsions subsided and her breathing settled into a steady resting rate and Pointer could remove his chomped paw.

The professor stuck his head into her chest once more. 'The heart is normal. She's a strong one.'

'She's a Fed, Prof,' said Isles. 'We breed 'em strong.'

They stepped away from the sofa and watched and waited

in silence. Even the hunting hound gave his voice a rest so he could lick his paw.

Nothing happened for a long moment, but then Chevie stretched as though coming out of a long sleep and opened her eyes, which were still the sunrise gold of a cat's with arrowheads of dark pupil. But there was something behind them, something that could be intelligence.

The professor hovered close enough to whisper.

'My dear, can you understand me?'

Chevie sat up slowly. 'Professor Smart. But you died. I saw you dead. Twice.'

The spirit of Professor Charles Smart, the man who had opened this entire can of wormholes, sighed and sank half into the floor.

'Dead,' he said. 'Then I am truly a ghost.'

Chevie stood with great difficulty. 'Riley. We need to save Riley.'

But all her strength was gone after a single step and she tumbled into Isles's waiting arms. He laid her gently on the sofa and Pointer gripped a blanket between his teeth and tugged it over her length.

'She's going to be out for a while,' said Charles Smart. 'And no doubt she will have a million questions when she wakes up. You should both rest. I have a feeling you're going to need your strength.'

Pointer studied his injured paw. 'Hey, partner. Maybe you could bandage this for me, since you're playing doctor.'

Isles smiled. 'Sure thing. That was some quick thinking.'

The dog wagged his tail, which was his version of a happy

face. 'Thanks, Fender. How about a beer to celebrate reviving the cat? There's a jug in the refrigerator.'

Isles shook his head. 'No. We're on the job now, Donnie. Clear heads all the way.'

He turned to Professor Smart, who was still moping down in the floorboards. 'Hey, Prof. Sorry to hear about you being dead and all.'

Smart studied his own hands, watching the spectral bones within. 'Twice no less.' He raised his eyes to meet Isles's. 'And it's only going to get worse.'

Mandrake. Huntingdonshire. 1647

Riley sat cross-legged in the Cat's Collar contemplating escape. He had been sorely tempted to simply give in and sink into depression. It would be so easy to accept his fate. It was inevitable that Garrick would do him in and he'd always known it. Chevie had been so certain that Garrick was gone for good.

But I always knew that Garrick could not be killed, for he is death.

He gingerly tapped the wooden neck of the Cat's Collar restraint.

The Alleluia, he thought bitterly. *Ain't it an irony that the devil should pick a song of praise to get his dirty work done?*

Riley had some rudimentary knowledge of the violin and had even been known to saw the folk fiddle for Garrick's amusement – but the Alleluia?

'Not a bloomin' prayer,' he said to the rafters. 'Never in a million years.'

But the notion of dear Chevie enduring some terrible torture made him almost willing to give it a bash, so he racked his brain for the tune and wondered if he could pick out the notes without even testing the strings.

Impossible. Even for a magician.

He sat there, chained to the altar, humming quietly, when the chapel doors burst open and Albert Garrick himself charged through and hurried, nay, *ran* down the aisle. His screwed-up features relaxed when he saw Riley still trussed and helpless.

'Ah,' he said. 'In time, then.'

Then Riley knew by the hurried entrance and the obvious relief on Garrick's face what had happened. In general at least, if not specifically.

'Chevie escaped!' he said. Now it was his turn to feel relief, and it felt as though a shackle round his heart had been unbuckled. 'Hah! Albert Garrick, Witchfinder. Your witch has escaped.'

'He confesses!' declared Garrick to the crowd that had followed in a babbling jumble behind him. 'And in this holy house.'

'To me those words seemed spoken in mockery more than confession,' said one man, standing forward.

Garrick turned on him. 'You would judge a confession, Jeronimo Woulfe?' he thundered in his best menacing stage voice. 'You would presume to divine the workings of a familiar's mind?'

The man stepped back into the throng, reaching to find

the arm of a pretty young woman. 'No, Witchfinder. No, forgive me.'

'Chevie is in the wind, ain't she, Albert Garrick?' said Riley, and a glowing pride in his friend was all there was room for in his heart. 'She's given you the slip. And *you* the great escapologist. The mighty Albert Garrick.'

Garrick knelt before his one-time apprentice, but did not seem unduly upset by either the turn of events or the level of cheek. In fact, his worried frown was quickly replaced by an ebullience that seemed out of place on his blanched features.

'Ain't this fun, lad?' he said, rapping the Cat's Collar. 'All these shenanigans. It don't make a whit of difference to me, so it don't. It's a distraction, as it were, from the sameness. From the eternal. It ain't like I can make a fatal mistake, now, is it?'

Riley knew there was no point in trying to talk sense to Albert Garrick and so addressed the congregation.

'Would you put your faith in this creature?' he shouted. 'Do you believe him sent by God?'

Garrick laughed. 'Oh, the sauce of him! You are a scamp, my son. And no mistake. I am sent by Oliver Cromwell himself to deliver these godly folk from the abomination that is your mistress. And you, her familiar, would try to turn them against me.' Garrick sat back on the front pew. 'Go ahead, my lad. The stage is yours. Do your worst.'

Riley stood gingerly, careful not to jar the Cat's Collar. 'People, please. I have confessed to nothing. Things are not as they seem in this place; surely you must feel the wrongness. Albert Garrick ain't no Witchfinder. He's a stage magician, no more. A common conjurer. And Chevie, my friend, well, she ain't no witch. She's a mutation from the future is all . . .'

Riley's speech petered out as he saw that his words were not having the impression he desired. In retrospect perhaps he shouldn't have used the words 'mutation' and 'future'.

Nicely played, dullard, he told himself. *You just lost your audience.*

Garrick applauded. 'Hark at him, good folk of Mandrake's Groan. His mistress ain't no witch; she's a *mutation* from the *future. Oh! what a tangled web we weave/When first we practise to deceive!*'

That *was* nicely played, Riley admitted to himself. To eloquently quote a poem not yet written.

He stared glumly at the *audience* and it occurred to him that generally people dressed as these were, in jerkins and doublets, would be on stage in a Shakespeare play or the like and *he* would be the audience. And so Riley, pushed beyond the point of reasonable endurance, said quite belligerently: 'Actually, good folk of Mandrake, if this be the ghoul in which you choose to trust, then you deserve everything that comes your way, for I trusted this man once upon a time and all he brought me was doom and gloom.'

Garrick applauded. 'And still the boy has a spark in him.' He stood and faced the townsfolk, who were clustered at the rear of the small chapel like sheep before the butcher. 'And, yea, I sayeth to you: the servant of the witch shall deny his sins to the end, for that is his curse. And only death itself may redeem him.'

And, yea, I sayeth? thought Riley. *Albert Garrick truly relishes his role in this place.*

'So it's damned if I do and it's damned if I don't,' he said to Garrick's back.

Garrick spun on his heel, almost dancing with delight. 'No, boy. Not damned at all, do you see? Redeemed you shall be. Saved, as it were. A confession is all that's needed. Three little words.' Garrick bent low so his face was level with Riley's; the dead stink of his crypt breath was full in the boy's face, and the coffin white of his skin seemed to glow with a sickening light. '*I am guilty*. Admit it, boy. For you are certainly guilty of some such or other.'

Riley was so scared in that moment that his stomach felt as though it might split and he could barely stop the confession tumbling from his lips, but he forced his fear down for Chevie, and instead spat a denial.

'I ain't no familiar, nor any class of demon. You are the devil here, Albert Garrick. Hell hangs upon you like a shroud. One look upon you is all that's needed in the way of proof. One look, or one sniff of your brimstone stench.'

Garrick sent a long finger twitching forward like a white worm and plucked one of the Cat's Collar's violin strings, and the note sang in the chapel's nave. 'Ah, the loyal familiar. Damned by denial. It seems more persuasion is needed. Perhaps when I have your dear Miss Savano lashed to a stake you will say anything, *anything*, to save her skin.'

Then suddenly Albert Garrick was stretching to his full height and was all business.

'Fairbrother Isles took the witch, ain't that so?' he said to Cryer.

'Aye, master,' said the constable, who stood shamefaced now by the door. 'Into the fens, no doubt. For that is where he dwells without fear of beast nor monster.'

'And how did the witch greet her rescuer?'

'I don't imagine she greeted him at all, master. Out of her senses, she was, when I last looked in.'

'Good, then perhaps she's harmless for the moment,' said Garrick. 'So merrily into the fens go we at first light. I will take twelve men of the militia with whatever ordnance we can muster. Except you, Constable.' Garrick pointed one of his stripped-twig fingers at Godfrey Cryer. 'You have brought disgrace to your office. Overpowered by a bumpkin indeed. You shall remain here and guard the familiar with however many men remain. Your watch begins forthwith and you shall neither sup nor swallow till the witch is recovered.'

'But, Master Witchfinder . . .' began Cryer, but his words trailed off as he could not muster a reasonable objection. He had been bested by a drunkard. 'Yes, Witchfinder Garrick. As you command.'

Garrick bent low for a wink and whisper to his one-time apprentice. 'Riley boy. Hark at this. I have always wanted to speak the following lines.'

He stood ramrod straight, threw back the folds of his black greatcoat and thundered: 'Citizens! Prepare yourselves for the hunt. At first light we go!'

With that, he took dramatic flight down the aisle, drawing

a wedge of townsfolk in his wake as though he were some class of Pied Piper.

In moments the small chapel was empty but for Riley and a handful of guards, and two notions occurred to the tethered boy in quick succession.

The first was grudging: *That indeed was a stirring performance. Albert Garrick has this audience in the palm of his hand.*

Then: *If Garrick left bludgers to watch over me, he must believe that escape from this contraption is possible.*

The glinting of the arrowheads aimed at the tender flesh of his own neck gave Riley pause. He would not begin plucking strings just yet. In any event there was a disgruntled constable and his cohorts to be overcome even if he could dislodge the device.

And then a third notion:

Fairbrother Isles.

Fair Brother Isles.

FBI?

Could he be a member of Chevie's Pinkerton-style organization?

How had Chevie referred to her brotherhood of lawmen?

The Federal Bureau of Investigation or, with a witticism that Riley had never understood, Club Fed.

Perhaps they were not alone.

Perhaps there was hope.

Once again the arrowheads flashed in his vision.

A sliver of hope. A whisper.

But they had survived on less.

THE BIG PICTURE

The field office. The fens. Huntingdonshire. 1647

Chevie opened her eyes.

Eyes that now had eight times more photoreceptor cells than they once had, so, even though the light in the cabin would barely register in the pupils of the average human, to Chevie everything in her field of vision was as clear as high noon. This was because Chevron Savano was no longer the average human. She was a mutation. Not that she realized this at the time. All Chevie knew was that it was daytime as far as she was concerned.

It felt good to be *concerned* about anything. Her memories of the past day, if that was even the correct way to describe the time span, were a jumble of pain, sorrow and animal terror. It felt as though the wormhole had stretched her consciousness behind her on an elastic band and it had only just snapped back into her head.

The tangle of thoughts began unravelling into a linear order and Chevie brought herself up to speed.

Garrick kicked me.

I was dying.

Then the wormhole took us and I thought of Tinder.

Then I was alive somehow and further in the past.

They locked me up and took Riley.

Oh, Riley. My Riley.

Chevie knew the tunnel had done something to them both. Made them see what could be. It had never even occurred to Chevie before – after all, Riley was more than two years younger than she. And, as far as teenagers are concerned, two years might as well be two centuries.

We could be . . . we could be . . . happy.

It was something Chevie had never even considered for herself: actual happiness, beyond not being in fear for her life. Beyond taking a swim in clear Californian water.

And he felt it too. I felt him feeling it.

But later for all of that. There was more urgent information to be processed.

Someone had rescued her from that wooden cell.

An agent? Could it be?

And then . . . this must have been a hallucination.

A talking dog and the ghost of Professor Smart.

Wormhole dreams, surely.

That was the only explanation and Chevie would have banished these last faux memories to the dream section of her mind had not a large brown hunting hound's head loomed in the corner of her eye.

'Hey,' said the dog. 'Look who's awake.'

A fizzling man-shaped spectre rose through the floorboards, illuminating the entire space. 'I imagine you have some questions, my dear,' said the ghost of Charles Smart.

'Emmmm,' said Chevie. 'Ehhhhhhh.'

The dog sniffed Chevie's leg. 'I dunno, Prof. She still smells stupid to me. Sounds stupid too. Like a cat.'

'It's a dog!' said Chevie, sitting bolt upright. 'A dog with human talkings.'

'That ain't great sentence structure,' said the dog. 'Plus you hurt my feelings with the *dog* crack, and also you might wanna take a look at yourself in the mirror.'

'Ehhhhh,' said Chevie again, and augmented it with: 'Oooooooh.'

Professor Smart raised his transparent hands. 'Now, now, my dear. I can explain.'

'Sure,' said the hound, then snuffled. 'He can *explain*. He's been *explaining* for years.'

Chevie jabbed a finger at Pointer. 'Dog!' she said.

'Cat!' responded Pointer. 'And how come a floaty ghosty is no problem but a conversational canine you can't abide? You better watch your mouth, kid.'

The confrontational tone kick-started Chevie's natural moxie.

'I never punched a dog before, pooch,' she said. 'But, if there ever was a day for new experiences, this is the day.'

Smart clapped his hands and they sparked at the contact. 'Wonderful. Signs of intelligence.'

'I don't know about that,' muttered Pointer.

Smart did his utmost to soften his perennially harsh features. 'I know this must all seem very strange, young lady.'

'You think?'

The professor persisted. 'As you seemed to know, my name is Charles Smart –'

'I know. Professor Smart,' said Chevie, interrupting. 'Don't you remember me? Agent Chevron Savano? Or Chevie maybe?'

'We met, I take it? We were friends perhaps?'

'Not exactly,' said Chevie. 'Once I saw you dead, stabbed, and once I was sent to kill you.'

These confessions were met with a growl from Pointer and a lowering in Smart's wattage so Chevie hurriedly added, 'Which I didn't, by the way. Someone else murdered you. Both times.'

The dog slapped a paw on the floor. 'Hey, don't sugar-coat it, whatever you do. Heartless. Ain't that just like a cat?'

Chevie wrinkled her nose. 'Why's he talking about cats?'

'I always hoped I might get home to my family,' said Smart forlornly, ignoring the question, perhaps not even hearing it. 'Be reunited with myself, you might say, but I never really believed it.' He held up his glowing arms. 'I suppose this is all that's left of me now.'

'Where's the other guy?' asked Chevie. 'The one who rescued me?'

'Agent Isles is checking the perimeter,' said Professor Smart. 'To use federal lingo.'

Chevie closed her eyes, took several deep breaths, tried to think about flowing water and gentle breezes, then opened her eyes again. The dog and the ghost were still there. That was OK because, if they were still there, they were probably real and she wasn't losing whatever mind she had left. Maybe.

After all, she had seen some weird stuff since her FBI special-consultant days in Los Angeles.

But nothing this weird.

'OK, there's a reasonable explanation for all of this,' she said with a depth of calm to her voice that only Tibetans and Californians can achieve. 'It's all wormhole-connected, I'm pretty sure about that.'

'You got that right, kitty,' said Pointer.

Chevie kept her focus on Charles Smart. 'My strategy is to ignore the dog because he really bugs me for some reason, so what I would like is for you to tell me where I am, why I'm here and what the hell is going on. In your own time, so long as it's right now.'

Smart settled into a lotus position, hovering before Chevie. 'You are here because there is a tear in the wormhole. A rift, if you will –'

Chevie interrupted after only two sentences, which was doing well for her. 'Yeah? Let me guess. You tore it.'

Smart's miserable expression deepened. 'Yes. Yes, I did, heaven forgive me. I thought it was science, you know. I thought that if I followed Einstein's quantum theory then I could stabilize a transversable wormhole through space–time.'

'Maybe you should dumb that down for the dog,' suggested Chevie.

Pointer growled. 'Maybe I should dumb *you* down, kitty.'

'That doesn't even make any sense,' snapped Chevie.

'And so I built a time pod that opened a negative energy hole,' continued Smart, moving his hands rapidly so they created a ball of energy that hung in the air. 'And I thought that when we pulled the plug the energy would dissipate or be absorbed by the wormhole.' The glowing orb dissolved slowly, strands floating upward like a cobweb in a chimney. 'But . . .'

'But the energy wasn't absorbed?' Chevie guessed.

'No, it wasn't,' said Smart miserably. 'It was anomalous and so couldn't mix with the wormhole's dark matter.'

'Oh,' said Chevie. 'I hate it when that happens.'

Pointer raised a bandaged paw. 'Let me take over, Professor. I'll make it simple for the kitty cat.' He turned his long face to Chevie. 'Imagine the wormhole is like a big toilet and all the plumbing that goes with it.'

Chevie nodded. She was prepared to swallow a few insults for the sake of clarity.

'OK, puppy dog. A big toilet, got it.'

'Right. So if you flush a jug of heavy acid down the bowl, where's it gonna collect?'

As it happened, Chevie had once flushed her phone down the toilet and so knew the correct answer to this question. 'In the U-bend. That's where all the blockages end up.'

'Ten points for the kitty cat,' said Pointer. 'In the U-bend is right. So all this exotic matter the professor was using to open doors in the wormhole ended up in the U-bend and bored right through to the world underneath.'

'Which is here,' said Chevie.

'Right again. So now all these quantum mutations, which have been floating around for who knows how long, are being pooped out in seventeenth-century England.'

'I was so wrong about everything,' Smart wailed. 'So wrong. I thought the tunnel was a tunnel. It's not a tunnel; it's an inter-dimension. I thought it could be calibrated and controlled but it can't. It has a consciousness, for heaven's sake. Now I'm not saying it's sentient – it would be premature to say that – but it can interact with time travellers. It seduces them.'

'Seduces them?' said Chevie. 'Like with dinner and a movie?'

Pointer chuckled. 'That's funny, for a cat.'

'No, missy,' said Smart. 'Not with dinner and a movie. With dreams of immortality. With promises of understanding beyond the dreams of man.'

Pointer actually winked at Chevie. 'Which is catnip for a scientist.'

'I was in the wormhole more often than anyone, even Albert Garrick,' Smart continued.

Chevie forgot all about the cat–dog repartee. 'You know Garrick?'

'I was aware of him,' replied Smart. 'I felt his evil spirit. He has more dark matter in him than I have. There is no telling what he might do.'

Professor Smart was silent for a moment but for the cracklings of small sparks in his innards, then he continued his story.

'So, yes, I know Albert Garrick. And I hate to say it but he is a stronger man than me. Garrick's core was so solid, so bright, that he was a beacon to all souls adrift in the quantum foam. He took what it had to offer but would not give of himself.' Smart drooped mournfully so that half his torso disappeared through the floorboards. 'Which is more than I can say for myself.'

Chevie reached out gingerly and stroked the professor's arm, and felt pins and needles at the contact.

'What happened to you, Professor?'

'I was weak,' muttered Smart. 'On the surface I held fast to my mission, but underneath my subconscious couldn't resist. I had to know, to be made aware. And so on my last trip back from Victorian London my unconscious mind peeled away, like a pale shadow, and the wormhole showed me everything.'

Chevie was fascinated. 'What did it show you?'

Smart sank even lower. 'It showed me what I had done. How my tamperings had ruptured the inter-dimension, creating a dumping ground here in this time. All these splicings that come through are my fault, or the fault of a version of me from some other reality. My body continued on into twentieth-century London but my subconscious was sucked down through the rift and it brought my FBI escorts, Special Agent Pointer and Special Agent Isles, and our field kit along with me.'

The dog saluted. 'Special Agent Donald Pointer, ma'am. Fidelity, bravery and –'

'Integrity,' completed Chevie.

'I imagine the rest of me wrote the agents off as casualties,' said Smart, and his expression perfectly suited his voice.

'No,' said Chevie. 'You shut down the programme shortly after. Then you disappeared into the tunnel and took all your secrets with you.'

Smart levitated above the floorboards and brightened considerably. 'That's right. Of course I did. Well done, me. Sometimes it's difficult to distinguish other people's memories from their dreams.'

Now that Chevie was as up to speed as she was likely to get, given her limited understanding of quantum science, she felt it was time to summarize so they could press on with the business of rescuing Riley.

'OK, so the time tunnel isn't a tunnel and there's a hole –'

'Rift,' said Smart.

'Rift. Got it. There's a rift in it so that anything floating around in the tunnel –'

'Inter-dimension,' corrected the professor.

'Anything floating in the *inter-dimension* gets dumped –'

'Pooped.' This from Pointer.

Chevie expected Smart to correct the correction but he simply shrugged. 'Pooped is pretty accurate.'

'So anyone or anything or any mutation floating around in the inter-dimension gets pooped out here in –'

'The infamous decade of witch-born monstrosities.'

Chevie knew she should probably know about this from social-studies class but after all the trips through the inter-dimension she wasn't even sure which history was the real one.

'Except they aren't witch-born monstrosities,' she said. 'They're mutations from the wormhole.'

Smart opened his ghostly mouth to correct her but Chevie cut him off.

'I'm used to saying "wormhole", OK? Or "time tunnel".

118

Those are catchy phrases. So let's just take it that I mean "inter-dimension" and not correct me every single time.'

'Yeah,' said Pointer. 'Kitty has a point. You do that a lot, Prof. That whole *correcting* bit. It's getting old, man.'

Smart smiled sheepishly. 'Sorry. I'm an educator. It's in my nature.'

'And this has been going on for how long?' Chevie asked.

'Years,' said Pointer. 'Decades, actually. Which proves I am still part Donald Pointer. If I was really one hundred per cent dog, I wouldn't be alive any more. I'm just a dog-shaped guy.'

The professor drew another spark-shape in the air, which reminded Chevie of the zip on her old book bag that had split in the middle. 'But recently it's got much worse. The rift is open almost continuously now and is expanding as more and more energy collects; soon it will be visible to the human eye. If it opens permanently and I can't figure out how to close it, then . . .' The zip split wider and wider until a tumult of sparks spilled out and exploded in the air.

'I get the zip and the sparks, but what does the explosion mean?' asked Chevie, afraid that she already knew.

'Oh, that's the earth,' said Pointer conversationally. 'End-of-the-world kind of thing. We all get absorbed by the inter-dimension.'

'Not necessarily,' said Smart.

'Yeah, I remember. Either the earth is absorbed completely *or* it's ravaged by mutations before being sterilized forever by dark matter.'

'Correct,' said Smart. 'Nothing could survive, except me, of course. If you can call this surviving.'

'And Garrick,' said Chevie.

Smart nodded. 'Oh yes. Garrick. He would be king of the mutations. His atoms are saturated with quantum foam.'

'Inter-dimensional foam, I think you mean,' said Pointer, wagging his tail.

Chevie rubbed what she still thought were her own eyes. 'I feel like I'm in one of those shampoo advertisements.'

Pointer pranced, suddenly excited. 'Yeah, kitty. I know exactly what you mean. Here we are, all cool and attractive, waving our hair around and whatnot, then in comes Professor Sparkles with the science bit. Boring.'

'You don't seem too worried about the world being sterilized and all that other bad stuff,' said Chevie.

'That's the dog genes,' explained Pointer. 'I can't get too concerned about the long term. Not much of a concentration span, to be honest. It's all about the next meal with me, kitty.'

Chevie snapped. 'What's all this kitty stuff?' She jerked a thumb at Pointer and spoke to Smart. 'Is this a thing with him because of his condition, or am I special for some reason?'

Smart and Pointer exchanged a loaded glance and Chevie got the feeling she would not like what it was loaded with. Following the glance, Pointer gave a nod, which Chevie interpreted as: *You tell her.*

So she said, 'Tell me.'

Smart did not speak. Instead he held up one palm in front of Chevie's face and concentrated so that the density of the sparks increased and the palm became a reflective surface.

Chevie took a second to be amazed at this clever parlour

trick, but it took less than half a second more for her to notice that her eyes were not what could be called *human*.

'Oh,' she said, stunned. 'Kitty. Fair enough, I guess.'

Chevie was morosely silent for a long moment and Smart filled the vacuum with science.

'The inter-dimension deconstructs the physical body and reassembles it according to the host's subconscious wishes, so if the host happens to be thinking about something –'

'Not the time,' said Chevie. 'Unless you can fix it, I don't want to know right now.'

Smart apologized. 'Sorry, I can't fix it. We tried.'

Chevie was almost afraid to ask. 'How did you try?'

Smart winced. 'I'll tell you later when you're feeling stronger, but the truth is there's only one way to fix your mutation and that's to go back into the *wormhole*, as you insist on calling it. And even then it might not work. If it's any consolation, when the rift ruptures entirely, if you concentrate really hard you will be yourself again for a few seconds before the dark matter obliterates you.'

'Because you're worth it,' quipped Pointer, flicking his ears.

'That is no consolation, Professor,' said Chevie. 'Zero.'

Smart lowered his hand. 'No. I suppose not.'

Chevie patted Pointer's head. 'So, I'm a cat and you're a dog. What a life!'

Pointer twisted away. 'I'll give you one head pat, because you didn't know. But never do that again unless you want me to start leaving out saucers of milk for you. I ain't a mutt, got it?'

'Yeah. I got it. You ain't a mutt. And I ain't a kitty.'

Pointer held out a paw. 'Fair enough, Chevron.'

'OK, Special Agent Pointer,' said Chevie, and shook the paw.

A shadow fell across the group as Fairbrother Isles ducked through the doorway. 'Well, ain't that cute. A truce in the animal kingdom.'

'Meet my partner and your saviour,' said Pointer. 'Code name Fairbrother Isles, if you can believe that. His wormhole mutation is that he's a tactless moron.'

Isles grinned behind his dense hedge of black beard. 'That's bull, Pointer. I was a tactless moron long before the wormhole got hold of me.' He waved away Smart's objection before he could make it. 'Yeah, I know. It's an inter-dimension. I'm just a field agent, so give me a break.'

Chevie would have smiled at the effortless camaraderie between the federal agents, but she could not allow herself to be happy when Riley was in danger. God only knew what horrors Garrick was subjecting him to now that she'd escaped his clutches. Plus she had cat's eyes.

'Good to meet you, Agent Isles. Agent Chevron Savano. I know that a thorough debriefing is the standard protocol. I'm sure you have questions.'

'Yeah,' said Isles. 'Like how a teenager gets to be an FBI agent, for one.'

'I'm not an agent exactly,' admitted Chevie. 'I'm more of a consultant. A lot of stuff happened in the years after you guys skipped out of the twentieth century, but I can bring everyone up to speed later on the internet and *Terminator* developments, etc. For now, we need to come up with a plan to save *my* partner. Albert Garrick has him captive back in the town and you can bet your last dime that a slow, painful death is part of his plan.'

Smart was immediately panicked, his luminosity increasing until Chevie was forced to shield her eyes.

'No, no. I will not have another death on my hands. That boy must be saved. I will go. I will play at being a ghost and scare them silly.'

'No,' said Pointer. 'You are our mission, Professor. I cannot allow you to put yourself in harm's way.'

'But, if the professor can help, couldn't he at least try?' said Chevie. 'Riley tried to save him once upon a time.'

Isles made certain the door was tightly sealed and then turned the solar-powered lamps out altogether, which didn't make much difference since the professor was lit up like a firework.

'He can't help,' said Agent Isles. 'The rift moves around a little but it's more or less right over the town, as you found out.' He nodded at Smart. 'This little ball of energy goes anywhere close and he'll be back in the wormhole quicker than you can say: *It's not a wormhole; it's an inter-dimension*. In fact, the only reason that he isn't sucked up from here is that I managed to rig up a magnetic field around the field office when the rift grew too powerful. Am I right, Professor?'

Smart took ghostly spectacles from a transparent waistcoat pocket and settled them over his glowing eyes. 'Aye, it's true. The tunnel wants me back. I'm like a runaway sheep, shedding quantum wool all over the material world. I live in the office and sleep in a silver-lined, battery-powered box. Soon my power will run out and the rift will have me. But not before I figure out how to close it. All I need to do is generate a small field of dark matter and I could sew up that rift for good. If only there were two of me, then I'd have the power.'

Sheep. Wool. Sew, thought Chevie. *An extended metaphor. Not baaad.*

Then she giggled. *I've got cat's eyes.*

A thought struck her. 'What's with the silver? Doesn't the inter-dimension like silver?'

'It certainly does not,' said Smart. 'I would go so far as to say that the inter-dimension is allergic to that particular transition metal. Silver is its Achilles heel. And perhaps if I knew why then it would help me to understand quantum material. But so far my tests have failed to yield any positive results.'

'So, you're stuck in a box, Riley is stuck down a hole probably and I've got cat's eyes.'

Fairbrother Isles's features softened. 'Hey, kid. I know this is hard. We've all had to make adjustments.'

'Tell me about it,' muttered Pointer.

Isles glared at him. 'Not now with the self-pity, OK, Donnie? I'm trying to give a motivational speech here.' He focused on Chevie. 'As I was saying, we've all had to make adjustments but we have each other. And we will get your guy out of there, but just not right now.'

This hit Chevie like a slap in the face. 'Why not now? He could already be dead.'

Isles moved around the treehouse, checking the shutters were sealed. 'Because Garrick is leading a witch-hunt through the swamps, heading right this way. And guess who the witch is?'

Chevie fluttered her eyelids in what could have been the first sarcastic eyelid fluttering in history. 'Oh, I dunno. Who could that be, I wonder?'

'So we sit tight until they pass by.'

Pointer raised his nose and sniffed. 'They got dogs, Fender.'

'I saw,' said Isles. 'A couple of pointers.'

Pointer sniffed again. 'That's Rosco and Duke. Clowns, both of 'em. Smaller versions of me. Let me go pee on a couple of tree trunks, maybe show them my butt. That drives them nuts.'

'Yeah,' said Isles. 'Go pee, partner.' He stepped on a knot in the floor and see-sawed one of the floorboards to allow the sleek brown hunting dog to slip out.

Isles chuckled. 'Pointer loves secret hatches and all that spy stuff. Makes him feel like an agent.' He winked at Chevie. 'Maybe I should make a hatch for you too?'

Chevie glared at him. 'I appreciate what you're doing, Special Agent. Including me in the back and forth. But my best friend is in danger. So pardon me if I don't join in.'

Isles nodded seriously. 'Understood. Let's do some banter later on, though. I got a feeling you have a talent for it.'

Chevie smiled in spite of herself and remembered an old saying of her father's, which went: *Even the toughest shell has a sweet nut inside* – his variation on *Every cloud has a silver lining*. Chevie's dad generally trotted out this saying when they were down to their last nickel and the refrigerator had nothing in it but mould.

Isles turned his attention to Professor Charles Smart. 'And,

Professor, if you wouldn't mind dimming the lights as much as possible, in case I missed a crack in the walls.'

'Of course, Special Agent,' said Smart, and turned down his glow until he was no more than an outline of himself.

'Anything in the vicinity I should be aware of?' asked Isles.

Smart floated round the desk to his computer, checking his scanner read-outs. 'Nothing on the surface. But Rosa is due back in town.'

'Rosa!' said Isles. 'You know, for once I hope she does show up. I would love to see Mister Almighty Witchfinder deal with that witch-born abomination.' He chuckled, then settled on to a bench that seemed familiar to Chevie. It took her a moment to realize that there had been one just like it in the WARP pod that had taken her to Victorian London.

'Might as well relax,' said Isles, closing his eyes. 'Best way to keep quiet.'

Chevie could hardly believe it. 'How can you relax at a time like this?'

Isles opened one eye. 'Because I've been in a time like this for quite a while now.'

Fair enough, thought Chevie, and sat beside her fellow agent, but, even though she tried for several minutes to clear her mind, Riley kept popping up.

Is he hurt?

Is he dead already?

Where would Garrick keep him?

And one non-Riley-related thought:

Who's Rosa?

9

ALLELUIA

Mandrake. Huntingdonshire. 1647

Riley slept as best he could, delicately tilting the Cat's Collar so its left arm touched the stone floor, and in that diagonal slump he snatched short fits of slumber, swapping one nightmare for another. When he awoke, seized by a dreadful cramp in his calf, it was only his training as an escapologist and magician's assistant that enabled him to completely relax his body in spite of the stabbing pain.

The cramp had passed, though Riley could still feel the knot like a clenched fist in his calf, and he sat there on the cold stone, hunger like an empty cauldron in his belly.

'Food,' he said to the hard-faced men watching over him, for they had bread and ale laid out on the pews. 'Water, at least.'

Constable Cryer forbade it. 'You shall have nothing, familiar. If I shall neither sup nor swallow on the Witchfinder's orders, then neither shall you.'

Riley grunted and rattled his chain. 'Fool,' he said. 'You would follow Garrick to the gates of hell, and he would toss you into the flames without a thought.'

They made for strange adversaries.

Riley and Cryer did not have many things in common, apart from gender and current location, but they were both endeavouring to make the best of a bad situation and each would have proclaimed that their own circumstance was the worse of the two.

Riley, most would accept, was probably right on that front – after all, he was chained to the floor, with steel bolts on delicate triggers pointed at his neck, and surrounded by hostile men wielding sharp tools. But Godfrey Cryer saw his wounded pride as a far greater injury than anything that could ever be visited upon a mere witch's familiar, even unto death itself. For had he not been shamed in the eyes of his master and hero? And for this humiliation he blamed the familiar himself. The boy in the Cat's Collar. The boy now chained before him. And he wondered if there was some way in which he could provoke the lad into tampering with the device and unleashing the bolts into his own throat, for Constable Cryer felt sure that this would improve his own mood. So every once in a while he would take a run at Riley and then pull himself up short, hoping to startle the boy into triggering the Cat's Collar. Riley, being a smart lad, did not fall for such bully-boy tricks and held himself stock-still while he considered his predicament.

Think, Riley, old son. Use the noggin.

For Riley had a working theory and it unfurled as follows: *Garrick has never trusted a soul on this earth besides his own self, and even as he constructed this contraption I know full well he would have imagined his neck by some reversal of fortune placed in it.*

128

For it is the nature of man that he will turn on his saviour, and Albert Garrick had surely styled himself the saviour of these gullible country folk. Even though they could not kill Garrick, they could certainly cause him considerable pain, no matter how many strings of coloured kerchiefs he pulled from his sleeves.

And could Riley credit that Garrick would lumber himself with plucking out the entire Alleluia as an escape plan?

No, it beggared belief that a master illusionist would not leave himself a way clear of this death trap.

But if Garrick had constructed this collar with Riley in mind, then it would be a way that Riley would not be privy to.

What could that be?

Cryer made a sudden run towards Riley, brandishing a cudgel and howling like a loon, but Riley was as a statue and treated the constable to nothing more than a stony stare.

'Bah,' huffed Godfrey Cryer. He dared not nudge the boy or even verbally encourage him to fidget, for Albert Garrick had ordered him guarded, but still he coveted the boy's death as though it were the throne of England.

'You best be circumspect, Godfrey,' advised Thomas Cutler, one of the guards, whose very life was built around circumspection. A boy who, it was said, would not risk so much as a single bun for a kiss from Lizzie Woulfe, surely the prettiest maid in Mandrake. 'The Witchfinder wishes him alive for trial. To kill the lad without absolution would be to set him free.'

To set me free? thought Riley. *How were my own countrymen ever so gulpy?*

But Garrick had a most persuasive way about him. Had he not convinced Riley that he was the devil himself? How difficult would it be for a performer of his calibre to persuade a town under siege from Royalists, bandits and beasties that he was an agent of heaven come to save them?

But to the nub of the problem: *How would Albert Garrick free himself?*

It would be an escapologist's trick, of that Riley was certain. But which one? The hidden button? A secret key? Or perhaps a simple manipulation of one's own digits.

Riley explored as far as his reach allowed, which was further than the average person's, for as Garrick had often joked during his lessons: *Manual dexterity is a trump card in the escapologist's hand, if you will pardon my little joke, Riley my boy.*

Garrick had always loved his little jokes. Riley could not remember having laughed a single time.

When they had lived in the Orient Theatre, Garrick's instruction methods were all his own, for he believed himself something of an innovator. For manual dexterity he had fashioned a miniature iron maiden lined with dull tacks, which could be screwed into any of a dozen constellations that Riley learned by heart from a chart. Riley would insert his hand into the iron maiden and in the second before Garrick slammed the lid down he would name the tacks' configuration and if Riley could not manipulate his fingers accordingly then his flesh would be pierced and pinched. And, even when he did manage to position his fingers in time, he would be forced to endure the awkward position for long periods, often while Garrick went off on a job.

Well done, my boy, Garrick would say when he eventually unclamped Riley's hand. *Soon your hands will be as nimble as mine, and then no man will ever hold you captive.* He would then wink merrily. *Excepting, of course, my good self. You can never escape from me.*

Well, it appears that Albert Garrick was right on that score, thought Riley now with a certain glumness. *Even time itself cannot set me free.*

He shook off the glumness with a mental shake and not an actual one and set his fingers a-roaming round the lip of the Cat's Collar. It was slow labour with the constable and his comrades scrutinizing him, but even so Riley was able to give the implement a good poke and squint and there was nothing.

Then the key is in the mechanism, he thought. *Something in the strings themselves.*

This was no common-or-garden musical instrument, for the strings had a double purpose: to make music and to launch the cross bolts.

Riley could see a complicated tumbler mechanism set into the wooden body, but there was no way to influence the rotations with his reach.

Riley racked his brain for some form of clue.

What has Garrick's weakness always been? Historically, as it were.

This was an easy question to answer.

His vanity.

Garrick had always believed himself the finest illusionist who ever lived and when he'd had a jug of red wine the self-pity would come tumbling out of him. He would forget his theatre vowels and speak in the accent of the rookeries where he'd grown up, in spite of cholera and near starvation.

People ain't got a notion, boy. People don't know that among them, in their very midst, is living a man — nay, more than a man — who could wipe the stage with any of the so-called greats. Pinetti? Robert-Houdin? Amateurs, flashy hucksters. Albert Garrick could have the world in the palm of his hand. Kings, emperors, the lot.

Garrick's promising career had been literally cut short when he had sliced his beautiful assistant in half during a perform-ance, on account of a perceived slight, and he dared not return to the stage for fear of being recognized.

But give it another few years, he often said. *And perhaps a nicely waxed set of whiskers, then I shall re-emerge from the shadows and you shall be my assistant, boy. And, oh, the wonders we shall see. No more skulking around this hellhole. And I shall have a black carriage drawn by plumed Arabian horses, with my initials in gold on each door.* He would hold his hands high, imagining the scene. *No fancy monikers for me. The world shall know my true name. Albert Garrick.* He would close his eyes, then, seeing the gold initials: *A . . . G.*

And then Riley had it.

Of course.

But he could be wrong.

Even if he was right, though, that only gave him half a chance, for there were two sets of strings. And, even if Lady Luck smiled on him, there was still Cryer to be dispatched.

Which is a task, Riley thought, *that I shall relish.*

Did he have the gumption in him, he wondered, to take

on such odds? To possibly unleash the bolts into himself and end his own life?

Perhaps I am immortal now, like Garrick?

But he knew that he was not, for he felt no different in himself than before.

Except about Chevie. Except in that respect.

As it turned out, Cryer made up Riley's mind for him. First the dolt made another one of his dashes towards Riley, hoping to startle the boy with his stamping feet and zany hallooing, but when that did not produce the desired results he resorted to insults and threats.

'You are hell spawn, boy. There is no creature on this earth lower than the familiar of a witch. Lower than a snake, you are. For at least the snake knows not its sins.'

Riley was still pondering the risk and whether he would take it when Cryer squatted before him and said, 'I promise you this, familiar. Your witch will scream when they burn her. And I shall see the flames are kept to a low flicker so that her hellish screams will echo long into this night. Then we shall see if you are ready to confess.'

All doubt disappeared from Riley's mind. Chevie would not be harmed by this fool's hand, not while he drew breath.

So he flexed his fingers and, upon hearing the knuckles crack, Cryer was surprised. 'You would attempt the Alleluia?'

'No, Constable,' said Riley. 'I believe I know a shorter tune.'

Then without hesitation he plucked the right A string and left G string simultaneously.

A. G. Albert Garrick.

The world shall know my true name.

'Hah!' crowed Godfrey Cryer, as though his dreams had come to pass, but his celebration was short-lived as the Cat's Collar tumblers tumbled and clicked.

'Faith!' he gasped, but for an officer of the law his reactions were slow and he merely watched slack-jawed as the hinges of the collar swung open, releasing Riley's neck and hands. Hands that would, in the case of a normal prisoner, drop like heavy anchors from their positions of confinement – but these hands rested steady as those of a statue, fingers resting on the violin strings.

Which control the cross bolts, thought Cryer. *Which are no longer pointed at the familiar.*

'I think I'll try the Alleluia now,' said Riley, and twanged a random string.

One bolt flew from its cradle like a streak of light and took Cryer high in the shoulder, driving him backwards into the front bench, which set off a domino effect of crashing pews.

Riley lifted the second bolt from its groove and jammed the head into the padlock securing his shackles, into which it fitted perfectly, as he had suspected it would. One quick turn and his feet were free, after which he replaced the second bolt in the crossbow and sent it whistling past the earhole of Thomas Cutler, giving the man such a fright that he turned and left the building, almost outpacing the arrow such was his haste.

The other guards were made of sterner stuff and hefted their cudgels, doubtless reasoning that although the familiar had perhaps some tricks up his sleeve he was still a boy and could be laid low with a knock to the bonce.

While it was true that Riley was indeed a boy, he was no ordinary boy, having endured several years of rigorous training in stage magic, escapology and martial arts – and so was more than a match for two part-time members of a rural watch with no more qualification than a willingness to take a shilling and stand on a wall. It took Riley barely a half minute to relieve the first man of his cudgel and strike them both senseless with it. He felt a touch guilty for laying low two of his own countrymen in a chapel, of all places, but they would wake up in a short while with nothing to show for their assault but the flushes of bruises and shame. And there were lives in the balance.

Chevie's in particular.

From the tumbled pews Cryer moaned, then called, 'Demon! Devil! There is nowhere you can run that the master will not find you.'

Riley ran down the aisle, grabbed his cape from where it was draped over a pew, and dashed out into the morning mist, thinking: *For once Garrick ain't trying to find me; I am trying to find him.*

10

ROSA

The fens. Huntingdonshire. 1647

Albert Garrick was not too far away as it happened, for progress through the diverse thicketry, woodlands and now boggy fens was proving slow. The would-be witch-hunters were hampered not only by the East Anglian landscape but also by the dense fog, which refused to disperse with the morning sun and seemed tinged with a sickly hue that had the men mumbling it was *witch-summoned*. A muttering that amused Albert Garrick no end.

These fools, he thought, not without fondness, for after all they feared and adored the same Albert Garrick. *These fools and dullards. Witch-summoned fog indeed.*

It seemed the hounds were just as dull as their masters, for they dithered from one tree trunk to the next, sniffing and slobbering, and if Chevron Savano had followed this hound-suggested path then she was indeed witless, as was her rescuer.

No, he thought. *We are being bamboozled here. Led astray by some means or other.*

Garrick was mildly surprised to find that the red mist of

rage did not rise behind his eyeballs; in fact, the more twists and turns this tale took, the more it delighted him.

You are amused, Alby, don't you see? he told himself. For it had been so very long since this world had distracted him. Time had seemed to dissolve into a succession of blood-soaked trudges, with the faces of the dead blending into one.

Riley's face.

And yet, when he had Riley in his very grip, he had realized that this was no monstrous betrayer. He was a mere boy who'd had a lucky escape. And also Garrick caught a glimpse of what lay beyond Riley's demise.

Centuries of sameness.

Nothing.

He would kill Riley. Yes, he would. No doubt of that. It had crossed his mind to rehabilitate the boy, reinstate him as his assistant. But that would be folly. He'd taken many assistants over the decades. Assistants, sidekicks, wives, servants, pages, slaves. Albert Garrick had indulged them all and always with the same result: they died. Either by his own hand or from natural causes.

So, yes, he would kill Riley and the girl Savano. They had wronged him and that could not be allowed to pass without vengeance, but he could not deny an unexpected twinge of regret that the great adventure was almost over.

What then for Albert Garrick? What great magical destiny?

Garrick almost smiled at the memory of his younger self. The naive assassin who had stumbled into the quantum elements with lofty ideas of magic and greatness. He'd even gone back on the stage for a few years but it all seemed so pointless now. Longevity was all there was. The rest was inside the wormhole, if he might call it that, and he would not allow himself to be dragged back inside.

I could not resist her again, he thought. *I would be consumed entirely.*

And, even though Garrick had tired of life, he did not yet crave death.

Moreover it would not be true death, for the tunnel would spread me along its velvet length until Albert Garrick was nothing more than a paste of electrons.

Garrick was pleased to have remembered the word 'electrons'. Once upon a future time he knew much of the twenty-first century's science, but, in truth, science bored him, beyond the trickery applied to his stage machinery, and much of his knowledge had faded. But he still held on to snatches and looked forward to aeroplanes and espresso machines.

For I have tasted future coffee and it is wonderful.

He had abandoned his notions of a great destiny, though, for what could he ever rule but men who would wither and die before him?

But this now: these shenanigans with Riley and Chevron Savano. This is entertainment on a strange and broad stage. And there is tunnel magic involved, for have I not been deposited here twice now? I sense a weakness.

Which was why Garrick had confiscated every silver bangle and pin in the town to protect himself from her pull.

Though precious metal would not be enough if I were to touch the Timekey.

No one shall touch it, he vowed. *Savano shall burn at the stake with the key round her neck.*

But until then he would enjoy this distraction.

Up ahead the tracker hounds snuffled and abandoned their previous course, taking a sharp right turn towards a wide expanse of green-skimmed bog, which glistened with reflections that promised hidden sinkholes and unsure footings.

Enough, thought Garrick. *I will not be made a complete dunderhead.*

He cast his eye ahead of the dogs and saw their target. A third hound, sleek and brown, his forequarters poking from the reeds.

'Aha!' he called to the handler, a portly, bow-legged fellow whose feet were jammed into some form of wooden clogs, which were proving most unsuitable for a hunt in the fens. 'Look, man. Look! A decoy.'

The handler was confused. 'It's a dog, master. A decoy dog is you saying? Another familiar?'

Garrick looked closer at the brown dog and realized with a jolt of excitement that there was an extra element in his *seeing* of the dog. He was feeling its presence like a tug at his innards.

There is kinship between us.

The dog was from the wormhole. A mutation.

Here now was a new gift from the wormhole, which was just awakening in him. There was so much of its cursed *foam* in his make-up that he was able to detect other mutations, for he supposed that he was a mutation himself, just as Chevie now was and, without doubt, this dog. Garrick looked harder with his extra senses and thought he could see the ghost of a man shifting inside the hound.

I can see that which the wormhole has changed. The previous being, as it were.

Garrick knew what had happened. This man was of weak stock and had allowed the wormhole to reassemble him according to the desires of his subconscious.

Pathetic fool.

What other gifts do I possess? he wondered. *What more could I be?* This was indeed a time of surprises. The previous dawn he had believed his elaborate quest for vengeance at an end, and yet here he was feeling curiosity for the first time in an age.

Garrick gave no sign that he saw anything in the animal other than what it appeared to be; he simply whistled and clicked his fingers as any good fellow might do upon spotting a handsome animal without tether or rope upon him out in the wild.

'Good chap,' he called, kindly-like, as though there were a treat in his pocket. 'Come over here now, and don't be leading our boys astray.'

Garrick wondered whether he should skewer the beast with one of his throwing blades, for he had several about his person, but thought, *No, there is more to be gleaned here, Alby.*

Questions first. Painful death later on.

He whistled five notes that he felt hanging in the air around the dog, and its flat head came up and their eyes met. They each felt the other's knowing, and the dog tensed for flight.

Garrick cursed his impulse to whistle the tune that his brain had simply plucked out of the air.

Even the air has information for Albert Garrick, he thought. *I am a superman*.

And yet the dog might run and there would be chasing. And, whereas earlier he had not minded a pursuit, now he had questions – serious ones at that – which might change his entire future and that of the world, come to think of it.

As it was, the dog *would* have run had not the shallow lake directly between it and Garrick's troop exploded in a geyser of slime, sludge and tentacles.

'Hah!' shouted Garrick, enjoying the spray that engulfed him, while the others cowered or were tossed backwards. A phrase came to his mind that he had heard Chevie Savano use once upon a time: 'Now we have ourselves a party!'

Donnie Pointer had been having himself a ball for the past hour, leading Garrick and his dumb mutts all over the marshlands. Messing with people was one of the only perks of being stuck in dog form. As a matter of fact, Pointer had had himself a little too much fun and got cocky. When he ran out of pee, he thought he might show himself to the hounds, just to drive them insane altogether. In the name of accuracy it should be said that he actually intended waggling his butt at the canines, as that was just about the most insulting gesture in a dog's arsenal.

While Pointer was scoping out his target for the rear-end wiggle, Garrick caught a look at him peeking out of the rushes, and the Witchfinder's gaze sent a shiver running from the tip of Pointer's nose to the point of his tail. There was something about that look. An intensity. Like he knew what was really going on here. Plus the man was as creepy as hell with that pasty face.

You know what? Pointer thought to himself. *Enough fooling around for one day. Time to get old Donnie to a safe distance.*

A prudent notion, but one that occurred to Pointer a single second too late, for even as he shifted his weight to his rear legs something surged from the scum-skimmed lake before him.

It seemed as if the entire bog erupted, and Pointer found himself borne aloft on a thick shaft of water, marsh mud and sludge while his body was spun and juggled by rubbery tentacles.

Oh nuts, he thought. *Rosa*.

Rosa Fuentes had been just about the brightest star in the Puerto Rico FBI field office and had made such an impression on the higher-ups that, instead of promoting her internally where her local knowledge was invaluable, they shipped her to London to get a little European anti-terrorist experience before a ticker-tape parade back home, where she was expected to take over before she hit forty. The only thing the brass didn't like about Rosa Fuentes was the large intricate tattoo of a giant squid that adorned her back and shoulders. Of course they had no way of bringing this up in interviews and, strictly speaking, they shouldn't even have known about it, but Rosa was proud of her tattoo and claimed it had been a symbol of good luck in her family for generations. There was a legend that one of her forefathers, way, way back, had actually been rescued from the Caribbean by a giant squid, who had looked deep into his eyes and seen the goodness there and deposited Alejandro Fuentes on the timber wreckage of his own boat. Rosa's tattoo was based on the charcoal drawing sketched by Alejandro on a loose plank from the gunwale as he waited to be rescued.

So the tattoo was disapproved of but tolerated, and meanwhile Rosa was setting the bar high in the London office – until she was lent out to the sci-fi-sounding WARP division in Bedford Square and her climb up the career ladder stopped abruptly.

Rosa was sent to Victorian London along with Agent William Riley to look after a Mob banker. Bill Riley made it through intact, but Rosa had been lost in the tunnel.

Such was the strength of Rosa's will that it took on a form of its own in the wormhole: that of her forefather's saviour. Rosa's human form was abandoned and her mind was embodied as a gigantic squid, which was routinely dumped in the marsh or lakes dotting the fens and just as routinely sucked up into the rift again. Unfortunately for Pointer, Rosa chose this moment, which was already pretty stressful, to reintroduce herself to her one-time colleague, though they both looked a lot different from how they had been back in London.

Pointer found himself wrapped in thirty-foot tentacles, with the life being squeezed out of him by razor-edged suckers. He was face-to-face with the dinner-plate eyes of a monstrous squid that reared impossibly from the lake, water gushing in rivulets between its rows of suckers, and a howl that belonged to neither human nor sea creature emanating from its beak.

'Hey, Rosa,' said Pointer through gritted teeth. 'What's up?'

What was up was apparently Pointer himself, as the squid tossed him high in the air, bashed him with the knobbly clubs on its longer tentacles, then wrapped him tighter than a mummy in its eight arms.

Pointer could not help it. He howled like a dog, but quickly got a grip on himself.

'Come on, Fuentes,' he said. 'I know you're in there. It's me, Donnie Pointer.'

Every Fed in the London office had heard about the giant squid tattoo and, after what Pointer himself had gone through, it took him about two seconds to make the connection to Rosa Fuentes. Also the squid had an eyebrow ring over its right eye, even though it didn't have an eyebrow. But the ring had been another of Rosa's trademarks.

'Rosa,' said Pointer, making sure not to bark the name. 'Rosa. It's me. A brother Fed. We have a mission, Special Agent Fuentes.'

The squid did not release Pointer, but it did not squeeze any tighter either. Instead it held him there, suspended in the marsh mist, and watched him closely, waiting for any sign of treachery.

'You can trust me, Fuentes. We used to shoot pool, remember? In the rec room. I beat you every time, right?'

This was the wrong animal to tease. Pointer howled as his bones creaked.

'OK, OK. You won a few racks too. In fact, it was pretty even.'

The pressure eased a little and Pointer thought he saw something in the squid's eyes. Recognition maybe, or probably just a slight dulling of the crazed hatred.

'And remember that music you liked? The swing jazz stuff. Mulatu Astatke. That guy was cool, Rosa. We danced at the office party, remember? I stood on your toes.'

The squid huffed and a ripple ran along its tentacles. It might have been a laugh.

'We're on the job, Fuentes,' said Pointer. 'We took an oath, remember? We got a motto. Fidelity, bravery and . . .'

'Integrity,' said the squid. Well, it didn't say the word exactly, just snapped its beak four times. Once for each syllable. But there was definitely intelligence there.

Pointer kicked his paws in the air and pressed ahead. 'Our principal is in danger, Special Agent. We have a hostile in the vicinity.'

The squid rose a full thirty feet higher, tentacles shivering with rage.

'Oooooh?' it said, spraying Pointer full in the snout. 'Ooooh?'

Pointer stuck his nose earthward in Garrick's direction. 'You see that pasty-looking streak of misery who thinks he's some kind of tough-guy pirate?'

The squid swivelled its eyes till they fixed on Albert Garrick.

'Sssssss,' it said, nodding repeatedly. 'Sssssss.'

'That's our guy,' said Pointer. 'You got the green light, Fuentes. Take him out. Extreme prejudice.'

The squid spared one tentacle to tumble Pointer into a bed

of moss and lichen while the rest of it descended on Garrick like a mottled megaton bomb.

Pointer thought he must be stunned or mistaken, because it seemed from his vantage point that, just before impact, Garrick threw back his head and laughed.

The squid came down on Garrick and drove him into the soft earth, throwing up a great shower of mud and sod that engulfed the hunting party, and it seemed clear that even the Witchfinder, who had battled witchcraft in all its sly and obvious forms, could not emerge unscathed from this tussle. Backwards along the border of the lake they drove, the squid's great legs powering them onward with an undulating corkscrew motion. It was a fierce struggle that saw the battling pair plough through soft ground and sharp shale.

Garrick's skull cracked more than once as the squid forced him down on to blunt rocks and even dashed his brains against a tree trunk, but, although the Witchfinder's frankly ghoulish laughter had trailed off, still his face held a rictus and his hands strove for the squid's cauldron head. Inch by inch he hauled himself closer, repeating over and over in his loud voice, 'I smell magic. I smell magic.' Words that boomed like cannonshot across the fens in spite of the chaos.

Garrick was pinioned inside a whirlwind of destruction, but no sooner was he wounded than the quantum particles in his very marrow clamoured to heal him. With the activation of the healing foam, he felt the colour return to his cheeks.

Oh, happy day, he thought. *A ghoul no more.*

But later for vanity, Alby, Garrick scolded himself. *Now for action. The audience has a certain expectation of their Master Witchfinder.*

For any other human this would surely have been a fatal entanglement. Most humans would simply have died of fright at the sight of the giant squid, a monster from their nightmares come to thrashing, sinewy life. But Albert Garrick was not most humans. In fact, he was not mostly human. He was a mutation and, unlike the mutation he was fighting, Garrick had been augmented. He was better, in ways he was discovering as he went.

I sees different, he thought, thinking in Cockney. *I sees magic.*

The monster with which he grappled had an aura about it. *Nah. Not 'it'. Her.*

Rosa Fuentes. The information was coming through her fingertips.

More FBI. Will they never learn?

Apparently they would not, so now Garrick applied himself to his task with glee and fervour, hauling himself along the squid's grapplers, ignoring its hissings and thumpings as best he could. Time after time he was knocked back or ploughed under, but, strong as the creature was, Albert Garrick was tireless and steely.

The world seemed a maelstrom around him, yet somehow here in the belly of the struggle it felt strangely calm. Garrick sank his fingers into the very matter of which the squid was composed and saw that the quantum foam was his to control; he took it into himself and felt stronger with every gulp of matter that he stole from the squid. So, as his strength grew, the squid lost its power.

I am growing the hair of Samson, thought Garrick. *This matter is mine to control.*

The squid sensed the loss of its mightiness and tried to discard Garrick, but it was futile. He was now like a tick in her flesh. What had once been Rosa Fuentes panicked and increased her thrashing, a keening squeal erupting from her beak, and still Garrick dragged himself forward, ignoring the piercing sound and batterings.

Round and round they went, inscribing great circles in the soft ground, throwing up great wings of atomized lake water. And somehow Garrick was in the ascendant, beating down the giant squid until their revolutions slowed and they slid to a blubbery halt against a slab of moss-covered rock.

'I wants it,' he hissed at her, forgetting his toff's theatre voice, all barrow boy now. 'I wants it, d'you hear me, creature?'

He crawled along the squid's shrinking form, reeling her in like a fisherman's rope until he was at last at the bulbous head. The eyes darted this way and that but could not escape Garrick. He sank his fingers into the dissolving flesh of the creature's head and took the quantum foam from it, absorbing it into himself, his chest heaving from the effort, feeling sparks of information and energy rattle through his veins.

Knowledge is power. Energy is understanding.

Garrick felt the particles speak to him, and understood now the wormhole in its entirety and knew suddenly what his destiny was.

Of course, he thought. *Of course*.

He continued to siphon foam from the creature. The squid shuddered and shrank, becoming amorphous and vague, its limbs flopping ineffectively and its giant head deflating – yet still Garrick bore down, greedy for every drop. A shroud of mist collected around them and glowed orange, strange shadows flickered alarmingly, and the hunting party shrank back from the otherworldly show.

Inside the cocoon, the giant squid disappeared, reduced to a two-dimensional representation on the back of a young Latin lady, lying in the mud on the brink of death and wearing the neoprene jumpsuit of the WARP unit.

Garrick's hand clasped her skull as though he might crush it, as indeed he intended to do, but not before delivering a gloating message.

'My thanks to you, Rosa Fuentes,' he said, all showman once more. 'You have given me the key to this world. And I shall use it to destroy everything you love.'

Rosa Fuentes blinked, then coughed, and the blood that ran from between her teeth was tinged with orange sparks. 'Hostile,' she said. 'Hostile.'

Garrick chuckled. 'Oh, I see. Yes, I am a hostile. I could be fairly called that.'

'Hostile,' said Rosa again, and from her side she pulled a large handgun that seemed like a cannon in her small fist and Garrick was so surprised that he could do no more than make a small 'O' shape with his mouth before Rosa raised the gun and pointed the barrel at his face.

'Green light,' said Fuentes, then shot Garrick between the eyes, sending him flying through the air and into the slimy depths of the still-churning lake, where he floated rapidly towards the middle like a punt poled from the bank. As the lake calmed, it was a strangely peaceful scene, with the sun finally poking through and the chirp of birdsong and the plume of smoke drifting from the hole in Garrick's head.

'Hostile down,' said Rosa, and her arm flopped into the mud and the remaining seconds of life in her began to tick down.

Pointer was the first to move, possibly because of his training; he disentangled himself from the greenery where he had been deposited and ran straight to Rosa Fuentes, frantically nudging her.

'Come on, Rosa,' he said, though he was so upset that his voice had more dog in it than man. 'Come on, Special Agent.'

Rosa dropped the gun in the mud. 'Hey, hey, Pointer. Is that really you, compadre?'

Pointer licked her face; he couldn't help himself. 'Yeah, Rosa. Yeah, it's me.'

Rosa smiled and her eyes flickered. She was barely there any more. 'I was a squid for so long. It was torture.'

Pointer was miserable, his big doggy eyes matching how he felt. 'I'm sorry, Rosa. I didn't know. I would never have sent you in.'

Fuentes coughed again, then she was peaceful and opened her eyes. 'No. No, thank you, Donnie. I'm free now. Free. And we got him, didn't we?'

Pointer cast a quick glance over his haunch at the lake, where the men of Mandrake were wading towards Garrick. He noticed that the Witchfinder's arms were already thrashing in the water.

Not dead, then.

'Yeah,' he said. 'We got him. The hostile is down. Area secure.'

Rosa laughed, though it cost her. 'Area secure? You sound like one of those Secret Service dummies.'

Pointer nuzzled her cheek. 'Yeah, they wish. Those guys should get a real job. Sunglasses models is all they are.'

'You know it,' said Rosa, and she patted Pointer's head; for once he didn't mind.

Three pats she managed, each heavier than the last, and with the third her hand rested on Pointer's head and her chest heaved no more.

Pointer whined a little and nuzzled Rosa's cheek, but his nuzzling was not to last long as what was left of Rosa Fuentes dissolved into a series of orange sparks that spiralled upward into the mist. Pointer followed their flight for a moment and then was almost overcome by the desire to attack Albert Garrick, but there were bigger factors to consider than his desire for revenge. And he wasn't an animal. Not yet.

Pointer threw a growl at the band of men wading into the lake to rescue Garrick, then he clamped Rosa's pistol in his jaws and disappeared into the mist like a ghost hound, leaving only clouds of breath hanging in the air where he had been.

He made it maybe a hundred feet before his body reminded him that, even though the giant squid had been a friend of his, she had almost squeezed the life out of him. Suddenly the tree trunks were all a-wobble and a buzzing filled his brain.

I'm going under, he thought, and staggered into the nearest clump of shrubs for cover.

What a professional, he thought, before collapsing on to the cool moss.

11

HUNTER AND HUNTED

Mandrake. Huntingdonshire. 1647

Riley would have preferred to make good his escape from Mandrake during night-time, for the dark is the magician's element and he had spent countless hours blending with the shadows of the Orient Theatre. One of Garrick's many unorthodox training methods was to lock the doors, bar the shutters, and give his apprentice five minutes' head start.

You may hide in any nook or cranny inside the theatre, Riley my boy, but take care that I do not find you . . .

For, if he was found, Riley would suffer six licks of the strap and a twelve-hour fast. This was a game that Garrick named 'Hunter and Hunted' and in all the times it had been contested Riley had never succeeded in avoiding the strap. It seemed as though Albert Garrick could see a spider in a hole, so adept was he at pinching the boy's collar, no matter how gloomy a corner or precarious a ledge Riley chose. In the interest of fairness, according to himself, Garrick would often play the role of hunted and give Riley one hour of the clock to find him, but the lad never laid eyes on Albert Garrick. There was no punishment for failing to find his master, for Garrick found his own smugness reward enough itself.

Slipping out of Mandrake in daylight would prove a small enough challenge for a lad schooled by such methods; there were shadows aplenty cast by the brick houses along the narrow streets. Though there were small clusters of militiamen on duty, Riley flitted past some and sauntered round others and was even brazen enough to snatch a small loaf from the baker's cart. It pained him to thieve from an honest labourer but he had not had a morsel since 1899, which logically meant that he would not be hungry for some two and a half centuries. Nevertheless, his belly was up in arms, so to speak, and the bread was nicked to quiet the gurgling, if nothing else, for that was how Garrick had found him more than once in their game of Hunter and Hunted.

Riley would have liked to have taken some time to survey the town while he chewed, and to get a lie of the land. It would be easily done to pull his cape tight to conceal his Victorian get-up and *walk the grid*, as Chevie might say, but there were two factors that precluded this activity. First, the constable and his men were surely already raising the alarm, and so any strange youth strolling the town backstreets would be detained for interrogation. Second, and infinitely more important, was the fact that Garrick was on Chevie's trail.

And, if he finds her, he will drag her back here for burning, no matter who tries to prevent it.

Riley knew that he could not allow that to happen to his dearest and truest friend, especially when she was addled, to say the least. On a normal day Chevie would have a fighting chance against any villain who might cross her path, but in her current state of mind she would be easy prey for the self-appointed Witchfinder.

But how to prevent it? How to stop a man who could not be stopped? A demon who, according to himself, could not be killed?

Well, thought Riley, *that's all blather and theory, ain't it?*

Perhaps those who had attempted to do Garrick in hadn't tried the right methods.

With a shock Riley realized that he was giving consideration to how he would murder Albert Garrick.

Then with a second jolt he saw that if he succeeded in his mission, then he would use all the trickery Garrick had instilled in him to become what Albert Garrick had always intended him to be.

An assassin.

And his teacher would be his first victim.

Now if that don't have a touch of the ironies about it, nothing does.

Riley arrived at the town wall and sidled along till he came to a hefty gent chopping up a pallet of firewood, enough to see him through the following winter.

Quite an expert the fellow was by the looks of his axe selection. A long-handled swinger for the big logs and a short-heft chopper for the kindling.

Riley waited till the man switched to the smaller axe and busied himself hacking quarters, then with a magician's sleight of hand he spirited the longer axe under his cloak and was away over the wall in less time than it takes for a hangman to pull the lever.

So Albert Garrick cannot die, he thought as he dropped to the ground and ran towards the trees. *That may or may not be true, but I'll wager he will have a hard time living with his head burned to a cinder and buried in a hole far away from his body.*

With this thought Riley took the first step towards becoming that which he had for many years despised.

If Albert Garrick had been travelling on the sly, leaving the scene of a grisly murder of his own doing, as he often had, no man on earth could have tracked him. Perhaps a particularly keen-eyed hawk might have kept pace in daylight, but other than that the trail would quickly run cold.

Fortunately for Riley, Albert Garrick was not his usual skulking self. He was a righteous champion of justice leading a group of zealots on a crusade and, while there was some due paid to stealth, there was no time sacrificed to covering their tracks.

Soon Riley found the path left by the group of clodhopping men. He quickly determined that there were in-and-around ten men, with two more ranging ahead after a couple of dogs. Generally when hounds had a scent in their nostrils the path ran as the crow flies – that is to say, straight-wise – but this pursuit ran from pillar to post and from zig to zag. Riley concluded with a grin that someone was playing games with Garrick's *posse comitatus*. The notion that Garrick would be infuriated by this made him grin all the wider.

Riley caught himself in the act and was instantly chilled to his marrow, for he knew his cold expression was that of a killer, even though it was born out of love. But had not Albert Garrick's first kill been a crime of passion? The difference being that Riley planned to kill to save the one he now loved, whereas Garrick had killed the one he loved for not returning his passion.

Good luck explaining the difference to Saint Peter at the Pearly Gates, he thought.

Then he said aloud: 'To hell with that and to hell with me too, if it means that Chevie will live.'

And that was it. Riley's mind was made up and he knew he was willing to pay whatever price necessary to save Chevie, up to and beyond his own life.

Riley had always been a city boy and he found the fens and the accompanying hoots and whistles from the wildlife downright spooky, as his only experience of moors and such came from the images conjured by candlelit readings of penny dreadfuls featuring daring highwaymen and ghoulish undead creatures that roamed the countryside. The fens seemed totally alien to Riley and he could not help but think that the rules of nature would not apply in this particular marshland. The fog too was different from the heavy soot-laden pea-soupers that regularly enveloped London, which could render the city itself almost invisible from Primrose Hill. This fog had a taste of the country in it and Riley found it actually quite bracing, though it did throw up strange shadows and flickerings as the sun endeavoured to break through from above.

Still, like any London dweller of his day, from common muck-snipe to the royal widow herself, Riley was accustomed to navigating through fog. At least this one didn't have soot flakes in the mix, which could half blind a fellow if one caught him square in the eye.

At any rate, his tracking skills were not required for very much longer, for from up ahead there came fearsome, terrible sounds. Riley had never before heard noises like this but he felt sure they were produced by an enormous, enraged creature.

Run away! said Riley's sensible voice. *Flee!*

But that voice had grown very faint of late, and Riley hurried towards the inhuman sound, for he knew that was where Albert Garrick would be.

Riley's enormous-enraged-creature theory soon proved to be spot on when he emerged into a soggy field. And at the far side of a green-scummed lake loomed an enormous creature, which first put Riley in mind of the tentacled Martians described by H. G. Wells in his terrifying serial *The War of the Worlds*, but then, as the creature's head emerged briefly from the fog, he saw that it matched more closely another of Wells's favoured monsters: the giant squid.

And ranged around this beast, which seemed to suffer no discomfort from the lack of its natural element, were Garrick's dozen. Like straw dolls they were in size, and batted about just as easily by stray tentacles that caught them as they fled. If that wasn't enough to bring a smile to a Puritan's face (though these particular Puritans being swatted by a giant squid were probably not in a smiling mood), Riley would be damned if that wasn't Albert Garrick himself having the senses shaken out of him by the creature; being pulled in nice and close, he was.

Riley hunched down among the reeds and clutched the axe handle tightly in both hands.

This was not the time to rush in swinging. This was the time for watching and waiting. Perhaps this great beast would do his work for him.

Which doesn't make you any less of a murderer, said Riley's little voice. *You had the bad intention and that's what goes down in your ledger.*

Nevertheless, it was of some comfort to Riley that the creature seemed intent on rending Garrick limb from limb, and wouldn't that be a weight off the boy's mind? But that was not how it turned out. In spite of the odds, Garrick was more than a match for the giant squid and literally wore it down, sucking the juice right out of its skull, until both figures were obscured by the mist and Riley could make out nothing but shifting shapes in the shadow.

I ain't one jot surprised, he thought bitterly. *For if there is anything in this universe that can kill Albert Garrick, I ain't encountered it yet. Even the blooming wormhole gave him an easy ride. Some people get cat's eyes or animal parts and all Garrick gets is powers and comprehensions.*

There was a flash from within the mist, then a booming gunshot that sounded loud enough to be cannon fire and for a split second Garrick was illuminated as he flipped backwards into the lake.

Riley didn't even bother hoping.

If a giant blooming squid can't do the big job, then a barker ain't gonna manage it.

But perhaps all this chaos could work in his favour. Garrick saw himself in the role of hunter here, not hunted. And a smart fellow with a shiny axe in his hand might be able to turn that fact to his advantage.

And so, even though his heart pounded like the clappers of Big Ben and his hands shook so furiously that he almost dropped the axe, and for a full five minutes he underwent a fit of anxiety the like of which he had never known in spite of his travails, Riley determined to press on. He was on a mission now. All his life he had been hiding from Albert Garrick, which had ill served him to say the least. Now he must turn the tables on his old master.

Garrick felt the swamp water pour down his gullet and into his lungs, and his instinct was to cough but he fought it. The particles would attack the invading liquid, he was sure of it, as this was not the first time he had been submerged or partially so. Indeed, on one occasion when the world had known and feared him as the Red Glove, a pirate with a reputation to rival Blackbeard's, he had been caught away from his ship in a little cutter and blasted to Davy Jones's locker by a rival gang's cannonball. The pilot had died of course, and Nubs Lewis, a Taff with no fingers but a genius with explosives in spite of that, ended up dead too. Garrick had simply settled on to the seabed with the wreckage and then walked ashore, marvelling as the time particles fashioned some form of gill mechanism in his throat that enabled him to breathe.

He wondered what the particles would do now, when he was barely submerged and his lungs were filling with gloopy marsh mud. To his delight his organs convulsed and drove the liquid out through his mouth like the plume of spray from a whale's blowhole.

'Thar she blows,' he cried, then flapped his arms to come upright in the water. As he stood, something – a small pebble or the like – plopped from his person into the water, and with his magician's reflexes Garrick scooped the object out of the murk. He saw it was the bullet that had lodged in his brain barely a minute ago, and he marvelled that with all these repeated bashings and shootings he wasn't losing something of his intelligence, like a horse-kicked village idiot.

Perhaps I am, he thought. *For how would I know it?*

But he was not.

It is more powerful I am becoming and none can harm me.

But this was not true, and he knew it. The wormhole would have melted him like butter on a pan this time had it not been for the silver. For some reason the precious metal had the same effect on the wormhole as it had on vampires and werewolves.

And how did one kill a werewolf?

You shoot the shaggy blighter in the heart with a silver bullet, that was how.

If only . . . If only.

There was silver enough. But did the wormhole have a heart to shoot?

Perhaps I could summon the heart.

'Master Witchfinder,' said an anxious voice, and Garrick glanced up from his thoughts to see a bunch of so-called militiamen wading his way, concern writ large on their rustic faces. Concern, or perhaps it was fear. These were generally the expressions that greeted him. Never happiness. Perhaps gratitude from clients who had sought his particular services over the years, but the gratitude was tainted by greed, or base relief, or even revulsion for the assassin that they themselves had hired.

Not that Garrick felt sorry for himself. Not for a moment. He had striven for long decades to establish his fearsome reputation over and over again. Only once had he tried the *goodly man* life and it had not agreed with him, nor with those around him when his patience finally broke.

Garrick smiled at the memory. It was amazing really, how quickly monks could run in those ridiculous sandals.

'Do you yet live, master?' asked the lead idiot, as though Garrick were not standing there before him breathing. In all probability, what the dolt meant to ask was: *But how do you yet live?*

'I do, praise the Lord,' he said, 'for there is work to be done. One witch-born creature has been vanquished, but the witch herself remains and it is of the utmost importance, I say to you all now, that she be taken alive. And should one of you panic and loose a shot in her direction, loose so much as a nasty glare in her direction, then that person shall be deemed to be in collusion with the witch, for I want her unharmed. Is that understood?'

This was a confusing argument indeed for simple country folk to grasp. The Witchfinder appeared to be saying that if anyone harmed the witch they would be considered her confederate, which was not the usual run of things.

'Be you saying that the one who harms the witch is a friend of the witch?' asked the leading man.

'Yes, I *be* saying exactly that,' said Albert Garrick, mocking their old ways of speech. 'Exactly that dost I be saying. With mine own mouth from whenst came the words.'

The militiamen stood silently for a moment in the murk and mist like ancient pagan statues, water lapping gently at their thighs, afraid that more beasties would emerge from the water, but still more afraid to move before the Witchfinder gave the word.

Garrick let them suffer the chill for a few moments, so his words could penetrate. On no account must Chevron Savano be harmed, for she was the means he would use to finally rid himself of the wormhole.

Chevron Savano and her Timekey.

'Now, good men of Mandrake,' he said eventually, when their jaws had begun to knock together from the cold. 'Now we hunt.'

And hunt they did, throughout the day, late into the afternoon, with little to show for it but bone weariness and gnawing hunger. There were incidents that Albert Garrick would consider minor but which scared the wits out of his militiamen. A flock of tiny lizard-birds descended on them, pecking hands and faces with their tiny beaks. But the poor creatures were wormhole-stupid and easy prey for musket-shot and pike. Though the militiamen suffered no serious wounds, they were shaken to the core by this attack of devil birds, a notion that Garrick encouraged, for it strengthened their dependence on him.

The second attack came from the marsh water; this time it was no giant squid but an oversized toad, which seemed almost comical until it began to speak the King's English.

'All right, boys,' the toad said, a Scot by the sound of him. 'I was looking for the chipper and then, *bang*, I'm crawling out of some kind of a swamp.'

That was as far as the poor creature got before the lead militiaman cried, 'A talking toad!'

And another: 'A Scotch toad. Have at it!'

And they did have at it, with speed and brutality. The toad gave a good account of itself, notably with headbutts, but ultimately was skewered and rolled back into the water.

Garrick affected an anxious mood. 'The witch sends her minions. She would destroy us all. Forward, men, forward, though our bellies and the very elements are against us.'

So forward it was, through the fog that would not be banished, until the sun accepted defeat and sank into the marsh, or so it seemed, and the stars blinked their watery eyes through the gloom.

In spite of his great speech of a few hours earlier, it was Albert Garrick who tired first, for he had been awake for many hours now and had done battle with a giant creature. Even though the dark matter had repaired his form, his mind was weary and he thought he would lie himself down by a tree and perhaps sleep a half of the hour.

And thus, when a tree presented itself, Garrick ordered the men to continue their search and leave him to pray for their success. The militiamen were less than happy to move forward through the failing light without their leader, but who among them would question Albert Garrick? Not a one. Obediently they checked their loads and powder, finished whatever provisions they had, and plodded ever further into the vastness of the fens.

In fact, this tree that Garrick chose was the very one from which Riley had been spying on the band. From afar initially, but then ever closer as the group took an unexpected turn and seemed to head directly for him.

Have I been careless and eyeballed? Riley wondered. *Will those men deal as brutally with my person as they did with those other creatures?*

But they could not have seen him, he reasoned. The light was dim and his form was well hidden by foliage. Also was he not a master at the art of concealment? Perhaps Albert Garrick could find him if he was looking, but there had been no contact from the town, of that Riley was certain, so he concealed the blade of his axe beneath his cloak and hugged the branch on which he lay.

When Garrick lay down in the lee of the mighty tree and turned on his side, with a root as his pillow, Riley could not believe what he was seeing. For there, directly below him, all wrapped up in cloak and hat, with his head raised on a virtual chopping block, was the man he had come to slay.

On a platter, he is, Riley realized. *A chance like this will never come again.*

Riley knew he could have the man's head off in a flash.

I could be off and running with that head before Garrick's body has ceased its spasming.

That he was even considering such a ghoulish act caused his stomach to churn.

This would see me swing back in London, he thought. *And I would indeed deserve to dance the Newgate Jig.*

Riley gripped the axe's handle and it felt greasy in his fingers. *I must do it*, he thought. *I must sacrifice my soul for Chevie's life.*

But could he?

Could he feel the axe blade sink through flesh and bone, no matter that the bone was evil to its marrow? And could he then carry the severed head by the lank hair, with Garrick's eyes rolling at him, to a safe distance so he could set it alight and bury it?

Strangely it was Garrick's own voice that Riley heard in his head: *Go on, son. Do it. Make your bones. Lively now, opportunities the likes of this don't grow on trees. Ha ha.*

Garrick would not have passed up the opportunity to make one of his dark jokes. Gallows humour was his most favourite type.

I must strike, thought Riley, and the axe blade was strangely warm against his cheek. *I must.*

From a good distance came the report of a single gunshot, echoing flatly over the marsh.

Riley glanced in the direction of the shot, and then immediately down at Garrick, but the Witchfinder had not been disturbed, and the boy was almost disappointed that his chance was still open to him and now he must make a decision.

There is no decision. I have no choice.

And so, committed to action, Riley grasped a branch, swung himself down, making no more noise than a falling leaf, and landed square beside Garrick in the perfect position for the strike. Inch perfect he was and there would never until Judgement Day be a better opportunity.

You will be a blight on this planet no more, he thought, and raised the axe high.

The instrument was familiar in his hands, for had he not learned to throw every blade known to man as part of his training? And he knew the edge was sharp just by a look, for a starlight seemed attracted to it and collected in ruffles along the swirls left by a whetstone.

So no excuses.

Strike! he told himself. *Strike!*

Yet he hesitated. To cleave a man's head from his body, even when he was a monster like Garrick – this was a terrible act.

Strike! Damn you for a fool. Think on Chevie.

But he could not. The bad blood did not run through his veins and he could not murder a man in his sleep.

He is not a man.

Riley knew this and he still could not do it. He felt the flush of shame and anger rise in his cheeks.

'You best be to work, son,' said a voice over his head. 'I ain't going to lie there all night. Oh, bless me, I ain't lying there at all.'

Riley's shoulders slumped. A dupe. Of course. This whole time. He kicked Garrick's cloak and there was nothing in it but cloak.

The gunshot had given Garrick the moment he needed to

slip away and climb the tree, leaving Riley to stalk his wardrobe.

Riley looked up and there was his master, his stockinged feet dangling, astride the very same branch that had borne Riley moments earlier.

'I left the boots for effect,' Garrick said. 'You have lost your touch, Riley my boy. I spotted you an hour since. And now you are distracted by a gunshot like some wide-eyed punter. I feel shame for you, son.'

'I ain't your son,' said Riley, gripping the axe with new resolve.

'Too right, you ain't,' said Garrick. 'I brought you up to seize the moment and look at you, dithering like a child in a sweet shop. You ain't got the gumption, boy. You never did.'

Riley took a step back to give himself room to swing. 'Maybe, but what I do have is an axe.'

Garrick was not in the least bothered by this. 'Tell me, the Cat's Collar. How did you figure it out?' He winked. 'It was my own blasted vanity, wasn't it? That would be my downfall, if that were possible.'

Riley needled him. 'It is possible, though, ain't it? The wormhole will have you, Albert Garrick. And next time you ain't coming out.'

Garrick's eyes flashed but he recovered himself. 'I'm working on that, boy. I have the bones of an idea, as it were.'

Riley hefted the axe, figuring to brazen it out. He reckoned he was done and dusted but might as well go down swinging, as the pugilists of Covent Garden would say.

'I have a bang-up idea of my own, Albert Garrick,' he said belligerently.

Garrick moved suddenly, hoisting himself up on to the branch and squatting there like a monkey. 'So I see. Lop my head off, was it? Bury it some place far away.' He tilted his head. 'That might have worked. A pity you will never know.'

It struck Riley that he was the younger man, with a lethal weapon to boot, and still he felt outmatched and, if he was honest, doomed.

'Come on then, sir,' he challenged. 'Let's be about our business.'

Garrick smiled. 'At least you go down into the dirt with some spirit. I like it when they have spirit.'

With that comment, Garrick leaped high into the air and seemed to hang there suspended, lips drawn back in a vicious snarl, arms spread wide like the wings of a vulture.

And there he hung.

And did not descend.

Pinned to the sky, it seemed.

Riley could not understand it. *What is happening here? Garrick can fly?*

But if Riley was puzzled, then Albert Garrick was even more so.

'What devilment is this?' he said, and actually seemed comical in his amazement.

Albert Garrick.

Comical.

The words did not seem to fit together, and that impression

was fleeting, as Garrick fought the forced levitation, concentrating till a vein pulsed in his forehead and slobber dripped from his lips.

Comical no more.

Riley felt a tug on his own person like a gust of wind at his back and, although he was not lifted from the ground, he recognized the sensation. The attraction. And his eyes were drawn upward.

There, in the twilit sky, was a slash of copper light. A tear in the sky that might be a sunset-tinged cloud, but Riley knew that it was not, for it called to him the way no mere cloud ever could.

The wormhole is here. In this world.

This was terrifying. That science was no longer in control. Now the wormhole had come looking for them and there would be no need for dematerialization.

On the bright side, it wanted Garrick most of all.

But Albert Garrick would go nowhere easily. He grasped a branch and held on.

He's holding a branch, thought Riley. *And I have in my hands an axe for chopping wood*.

So the lad ran round to the other side of the tree, where Garrick could not reach him without releasing his hold, and hacked at the branch. It seemed less awful somehow than chopping a man's head from his body.

'Up you go, Garrick,' he cried with each swing. 'Up you go.'

Garrick howled and cursed him for a traitor for here above

him was the only thing he truly feared. It was not that the wormhole would kill him; it was that it would undo him. Which was worse somehow.

The branch was stout but the axe was sharp. The branch yielded with a splintering crack.

'No,' said Garrick. 'This ain't how Albert Garrick goes.'

But it seemed as though this *was* how the great scourge of Garrick was to quit the earth, reclaimed by the wormhole for the particles in his body. The last strip of bark peeled away from the branch, revealing lighter wood below. With a soft snap Albert Garrick was cut adrift and began his ascent up to the waiting rift.

'I will not!' he shouted. 'You shall not have me.'

Riley would have dearly loved to watch him go: to be sure this time, for once and for all, that Garrick was gone. However, just at that moment an explosion rose through the western trees; a great blooming flower of flame and black smoke, quickly followed by the roar of combustion with a strange noise like the clang of a blacksmith's hammer on a giant anvil.

That explosion has Chevron written all over it, thought Riley. *Or my name ain't Something Riley.*

So he took his eyes from Albert Garrick and ran hell-for-leather across the marsh in the direction of the explosion, praying that he would not be too late to save Chevie's life.

One quarter of the hour earlier, Chevie had been in no immediate danger of dying, presuming that one could not actually explode from frustration. She had a million questions in her head and could voice none of them, for she was under strict instructions from Special Agent Isles to act like a statue. Still and quiet.

Isles is probably out of his jurisdiction, she thought. *But he's still my superior officer.*

Her frustration came mainly from the fact that, as far as she knew, Riley was trussed up somewhere in that town, being subjected to whatever hellish torture Garrick had dreamed up for his witch-finding tests, and all she could do was sit here on a home-made sofa and grit her teeth.

And she had so many questions for Smart.

How can I get home?

Does my home exist any more?

Will I ever truly be myself again?

But all she could do was watch the professor flicker nervously by his desk, staring at his old-fashioned computer monitor. He was glowing on low wattage but with Chevie's photosensitive vision he shone brighter than the Las Vegas strip.

Isles seemed impervious to stress and had bunked down in a back room, apparently content to snore softly until someone shook him awake.

Eventually Chevie could take it no more.

'Do you have any motion sensors?' she whispered to Smart. 'Or cameras on the perimeter?'

Smart tried to smile and it seemed to hurt his face. 'We don't even have a perimeter, lassie. Agent Pointer is our advance-warning system.'

'So what are you watching on that screen?'

Smart invited her to see for herself. 'It's infrared. From one of Agent Isles's scopes. I found out that it picks up dark matter too. One of those accidental scientific discoveries you read about, like penicillin or radioactivity.'

Chevie looked at the screen. It was mostly dark except for a spooky red grin off centre.

'The rift?'

Smart nodded. 'The beginnings of it. Any time now it will open wide.'

'And then the end of the world, right?'

Smart's features relaxed into their habitual miserable expression. 'Yes, no, who knows? I can't say anything for certain any more. It might take months or years, or perhaps the rift will repair itself. But the anomalous energy has worn the inter-dimension's skin so thin that it would take a burst of dark matter to bolster it. More than I have.'

'Couldn't you take mine?'

Smart tried to stroke her face and Chevie felt pins and needles along her cheekbones.

'No, child. It might kill you and, besides, it would be nowhere near enough. No, I injured the inter-dimension and I shall heal it. I have a responsibility.'

The professor returned his attention to the screen, and was soon working on his responsibility. Chevie gave him two minutes to become completely absorbed, then backed away quietly.

I have a responsibility too, she thought. *The FBI brought Riley into this and now I have to get him out.*

It was more than responsibility she knew. More than duty. She tip-tapped the floor with the toe of her boot until she found the knot in the wood, and pressed it. A single board see-sawed, and Chevie thought, *If the pooch can squeeze through there, so can I. Just hold my breath is all.*

It was a tight squeeze, but she made it.

Almost before Chevie's feet touched ground, she realized that her plan had a few flaws.

She didn't know where the town was.

She was unarmed and undisguised.

She could really use a pair of sunglasses right now.

And also, in point of fact, she had no actual plan.

I'm an improviser, she thought. *That's always been my talent.*

Which would be just wonderful if she could *improvise* herself a map of this godforsaken swamp.

Luckily she did have cat's eyes, which she would freak out over for years at a later point when Riley was safe, but for now she simply appreciated being able to see in the dark.

It's a pity I can't climb trees.

Chevie would grudgingly admit that she had a tendency to act on instinct rather than information, but on this occasion it was pure emotion. So she picked a path from many and set off along it. Yesterday she would not have seen even one path, never mind several, but her cat's eyes noticed the slight bend in the grass stalks where they had been brushed more than once.

I am not even following my gut; I'm following my heart.

Which was pretty much at the top of the FBI not-to-do list, just below: *Don't shoot the agent in front of you in the butt.* In fact, if this had been a legitimate mission she would have been removed for emotional involvement. She could just imagine her old boss, Special Agent Witmeyer, yelling at her: *You're off this case, Savano. You got too close to the kid.*

But there was nothing about time-travelling mutations in the Fed handbook and she was nowhere near close enough to the kid.

Chevie tried to remember if this was the way Isles had brought her into the field office, but she had been pretty out of it at the time.

I remember a swamp, she thought. *And trees.*

That was a great help. You truly are a genius.

The word 'swamp' resonated with her.

Don't swamps have alligators in them?

Chevie was pretty sure there were no alligators in England.

Yeah, but I'm also pretty sure that humans don't have cat's eyes, and dogs can't talk.

And, speaking of talking dogs, Pointer appeared in front of her, poking his head through a line of scrub.

'Woof,' he said, or maybe it was 'Ruff'.

Because they had bonded and she didn't want to be impolite, Chevie tried to interpret the syllable.

'Yeah,' she said. 'Rough day all round.'

In response to this Pointer gave her the evil eye, which Chevie felt was unfair. 'Hey, how am I supposed to know? It just sounded like a bark to me. You need to enunciate, Agent.'

This seemed to annoy Pointer so much his hackles rose, his head dipped and he drew his lips back in a snarl.

'Pointer, dude. I don't have time for this. You gotta take me to the town, OK?'

Cue more snarling and hackling from Pointer.

'I know what Isles ordered me to do,' she said. 'But this is the perfect time. Garrick's out in the swamp. We can sneak into Mandrake and rescue Riley. In and out. Five minutes. We're gonna laugh about this tomorrow.'

Judging by the expression on Pointer's face, it did not seem like he would be laughing at anything any time soon. In fact, it seemed to Chevie that he was downright angry. His flanks were heaving like bellows and he moved forward from the bushes, revealing himself and the remarkably square white patch on his hindquarters.

I don't remember a white patch, thought Chevie, and then: *Oh, shoot. Wrong dog.*

If this wasn't Pointer, it had to be one of Garrick's dogs.

And he's looking at me like I'm a cat.

'Good boy,' she said. 'We can be friends, can't we? You wanna smell my hand?'

But it seemed obvious that this dog was done sniffing. Now was biting time. The animal barked, three short yips that Chevie just knew were signals to his handlers, and then he attacked.

Chevie was forced to do something she never thought she could: punch an animal right in the eye socket. There followed two howls of pain, one from the punched and another from the puncher.

Chevie stuffed her hand under her arm, thinking: *There's a whole lotta bone in a dog's head.*

The dog skittered off in a circle for another attack, but he never had to make it because a ring of burly men emerged from the wooded marsh with pikes and muskets.

'Be still, witch,' cried one. 'And bear the manacles.'

No thanks, pal, thought Chevie, and kicked the guy in the knee, which is not an obvious choice or an easy target, but if the kick is dead on then the pain caused is immense.

The man went down howling with agony and clutching his popped joint.

Chevie managed to deck another swarthy gent with a punch in the neck, which again would not be considered classy fighting, but there was nothing noble about the odds here, so Chevie didn't feel too bad about it.

What she did feel bad about was the sack, which was pulled down over her head by a third man and swiftly tied off at the ankles. And it doesn't matter how good a martial artist a person is, there is no kung-fu'ing your way out of a sturdy sack.

Dammit, she thought, toppling over. *Now Garrick has us both.*

Chevie realized that she should have listened to Isles and made like a statue.

The Isles in question was roused from slumber by a furious crackling in the antechamber, which he recognized as Professor Smart's signature *I'm excited* noise. And Professor Smart being excited was rarely a good thing, as in: *Look, everyone. I've found the way home.* Usually the prof was excited in an anxious way, as in: *Look, everyone. Doom and catastrophe are about to descend on us all.*

Isles rolled out of bed and padded into the main area. The ghost of Professor Smart was literally fizzing in front of his monitor.

'Hey, Prof,' whispered Isles. 'What's up?'

Smart did not take his eyes off the screen. 'Doom and catastrophe are about to descend on us all,' he said, as predicted.

'I thought so. And what is it this time?'

'The rift,' said Smart. 'It's wide open. Visible to all. I have destroyed the earth.'

Isles decided to take this seriously. 'Destroyed the earth? Seriously? I always thought that was, you know, Scottish hyperbole.'

Smart glowered, which he could do most effectively by speeding up his particles. 'There is a gate between two dimensions that were never meant to be joined. The other dimension, or more accurately –'

Isles was getting a little impatient. 'Inter-dimension. I know, Prof. Get on with it.'

'The inter-dimension is stuffed to the gills with giant beasties and dark energy. All of which are about to be poured on to this marshland.'

'That does not sound like hyperbole,' admitted Isles. 'Sounds like you were underplaying it, actually. Can't you do anything?'

'I can detonate the electromagnetic pulse and that might send the rift energy into recoil, but not for long. Perhaps twelve hours. No longer.'

Isles hurried round to look at the monitor, which was almost covered in swirling red tendrils. 'OK, good. Great. Let's do that. How many of these EMPs do you have?'

'One,' said Smart miserably. 'And we built it years ago. It

might not even work. I've been using the field to protect the office, so I don't get dematerialized altogether.'

'But what about you?'

'I'll be fine, probably. Anyway, we have no alternative.'

Isles did not like this plan, but there were no alternatives.

'OK, prof. Do it.'

The professor sent his fingers into the computer itself, re-arranging power flows and powering up the EMP built into the coils that wrapped the office.

As Smart worked, Isles muttered to himself. 'EMPs, dark matter. It's like some Saturday-morning cartoon. Like *Scooby-Doo*.' This reminded him of something. 'Where is Pointer anyway? He's been gone all day. I swear if he's off chasing rats again I will kick his tail.' This reminded him of something else. 'Hey, prof. Where's the girl?'

The professor was halfway into the monitor now, but he popped his head out to say, 'She went out. Through the floorboards, I think.'

Isles knelt. The see-saw floorboard was still see-sawed, and there was light coming from below.

He peeped down to see two hounds that were not Pointer clawing at the oak's trunk and a group of Puritan militiamen with lanterns clustered round the base of their treehouse.

'Egad!' said one. ''Tis the traitor, Isles.' Musket barrels swivelled Isles's way.

'This be the witch's lair,' said another voice from below. 'Grenadier!'

Grenadier! thought Isles. *Oh, crud!*

Then instinct took over from thought as a dozen musket

balls peppered the planking around the gap, two making it through and one grazing his shoulder.

Isles rolled away from the hole and almost immediately wished he had closed the gap first as an apple-sized metal sphere spun neatly through it and plonked on to the wood.

That grenadier has got a hell of an arm, thought Isles, scrambling away.

This thought was confirmed when two more grenades joined the first, rolling to form a deadly hissing cluster.

'We gotta go, Professor. Time's up.'

'One more second,' said Charles Smart. 'One more second.'

Five seconds later the entire field office went up in a roiling mushroom of flame and black smoke, which set the dogs running scared and the militiamen chortling, clapping and stamping their feet.

'Good throwing, sir,' said the captain to the pock-faced, lanky youth who had tossed the bombs. 'Good throwing indeed. The Witchfinder will shake our hands for good fellows after this day's work. The witch is ours and her familiars have gone to meet their maker. Or rather, their master.'

Inside the sack, Chevie bucked and elbowed, but she was as trapped as a salmon in a net and her struggles made the militiamen's chortles all the more hearty and their self-congratulation all the more sickening.

From his vantage point high above the fens, Albert Garrick saw the red rose of explosion bloom in the forest and heard the strange clang that accompanied it and almost immediately the rift released its grasp on him. Albert Garrick did not know how or why but he was glad nonetheless. He would dance with the devil himself if it meant escaping the wormhole.

Praise be, he thought, then plummeted the five full seconds to earth.

Garrick landed with a thump that shattered his collarbone and dislocated two of his vertebrae. While he lay on his twisted back feeling the pain lance through his body as the bones mended, he watched the rift recoil above him as though wounded.

Wounded but far from vanquished.

'How does one kill a werewolf?' he asked the stars, still mulling over his question of earlier that day. And when the stars did not answer he said, 'Put a silver bullet through its heart.'

Garrick smiled at the rift.

'Oh, my ancient enemy, I think you have shown me your heart,' he said.

12

DROP CHUTE

Riley ran like Lucifer himself was on his heels, which in a very real way he was – for when the mysterious explosion lit up the night sky Riley felt his own pace suddenly increase as the explosion's shock knocked out whatever beam of attraction the wormhole had thrown around him.

And, if I am freed, then so is Garrick.

But he could not stop to look, for there was no time to spare as, in Riley's experience, wherever there was riotous mayhem it was either Garrick or Chevie at the nub of it. Since Garrick was to the rear, hopefully incapacitated, then it must be Chevron who was close to this latest havoc.

Not too close, Chevie. Not too close.

For it would be heartbreaking to be almost in sight of the girl and then to lose her.

Riley had a sudden horrifying thought that almost halted his gallop.

Could I bear to see Chevie's dead form? Could I stand to feel her grow cold in my arms?

Riley increased his pace and weaved through the trees, feeling dread like an icy fist gripping his heart.

I will not allow that to happen.

So he ran on, praying to the Lord above that his feet, made careless by desperate haste, would not snag on a root. His bones would not heal like Garrick's. If he stumbled into a rut or a sinkhole while running at this peg, his ankle would snap like kindling and he would be forced to lie in the mud till Garrick toddled over to do the job he'd been hankering after.

Lady Luck smiled on Riley for once and allowed him to dodge disaster as he ran, virtually blind, over the treacherous ground and dodged between trunks that loomed from the mist like the masts of long-abandoned ghost ships. In Riley's mind the trees creaked and groaned as he flitted past.

Riley's luck ran out when he earned a ducking for himself in a shallow pool and he crawled out, covered with death stink and pond scum. The chill set his teeth chattering and weighed down his clothes, which was his primary concern.

Oftentimes I've smelled worse and shivered more and that will pass, he thought. *But tardiness could cost me everything.*

On he ran towards the flaming tree till it towered above him and its flames set steam rising from his clothes. The branches burned like a penny sparkler, and the trunk was blackened but as yet uncombusted.

Riley did not have to search far for the perpetrators of the fire. The militiamen were so jolly and boisterous that they might have been toasting muffins on the heat and setting up a sing-song. And, at their feet, a wriggling sack with Chevie's boots sticking out of the opening.

Chevie in a sack. And not for the first time.

Riley was consumed by a heady mixture of emotion. There

was fear in the mix, and rage too, which might have been manageable was the brew not topped off with love.

He made a sound that was somewhere between a death rattle and a growl, which fortunately was swallowed up by the fire's racket, and made ready to charge these scoundrels who would so ungallantly truss a young lady.

Riley had taken barely a step when two bear-like arms emerged from the shadows and wrapped him in an expert restraining hug. Perhaps if Riley had had the luxury of time he would have figured a way out of this grip, but even as he considered his options a voice whispered in his ear.

'Not now, kid. These guys have little training, but there are too many. We regroup and plan.'

Riley was lifted bodily and shifted backwards to the shadows of a nearby tree.

'You OK, kid?' said the deep voice. 'If I let you go, you ain't gonna blow our cover?'

Riley shook his head. He knew that term. Chevie had often talked about her cover.

When the hand left his face, Riley whispered, 'Fairbrother Isles. Is that you?'

'Yeah,' said the voice behind him. 'How did you know?'

'Blow our cover. That's federal talk and you are Fairbrother Isles. FBI. Obvious, ain't it?'

'Finally,' said Isles. 'Someone gets it. I knew it was a good code.'

The militia waited by the fire, reckoning it was an excellent beacon, until the Witchfinder limped through the mist. His almost perpetual scowl of office was wiped away by the sight of Chevie in her sack.

'See her wriggle,' said the captain. 'Quite the catch, Master Witchfinder.'

Garrick was delighted. 'Quite the catch indeed. Good, Captain. Your men have earned a place in heaven this night.'

The captain brought forward the young grenadier. 'This boy here, Master Garrick. A wonder, he is. Tossed his grenades up there while we were standing below. That takes nerve and skill.'

Garrick patted the young man's shoulder. 'It does indeed. I thank you, grenadier. You have served your country well. I will see you are rewarded.'

The militia's glow was not all due to the fire. This level of praise from Master Garrick was unprecedented. And the smiling? Garrick often smiled, it was true, though his expressions were tinged for the most part with wicked delight or irony. But here, egad, the man was grinning from ear to ear.

The grenadier was eager for further praise. 'Her confederates' bodies have not been recovered. Perhaps I could wait till the fire dies down and investigate the charred remains?'

'No,' said Garrick. 'The witch is the thing. We must return to Mandrake and fortify her position. There is silver to be collected.'

'Silver?' said the captain.

'Aye,' said Albert Garrick. 'The Lord's metal. Poison to witches and all demons. I need every goblet and coin in the town.'

The captain had quite the cache of silver goblets himself, which he enjoyed gazing into by firelight, so he could not help but ask, 'For what purpose, master?'

Garrick's smile shrank a little at the very idea that someone would dare to question him, but his humour was buoyant and so he answered.

'The gates of hell are open above our little town, Master Captain. I have fought them alone in the swamp with some success. But tomorrow they shall open wide like the jaws of a great beast and, when they do, I would send this witch home to her kin and after her a silver cannonball.' Garrick paused to savour the notion. 'We shall not simply vanquish hell. We shall destroy it.'

It was a stirring declaration and the captain thought it best not to ask more questions.

'Now we go!' said Garrick. 'Mandrake will be our stronghold.' He peered into the shadows. 'For the witch's familiar is hereabouts and he will undoubtedly attempt to liberate his mistress.'

The captain addressed the assembled men. 'Men of the militia. We march for Mandrake. Home by dawn, I say.'

The men formed into rough ranks and moved off, away from the fire's flickering light, and were soon lost in shadow and mist.

All Riley could do was to watch them go, hands tightly clenched by his sides. For all his running and jumping, he had achieved nothing and the frustration brought bitter tears to his eyes.

The fens. Huntingdonshire. 1647

For the first few years in the field office, Fairbrother Isles had had a niggling worry that they had no fallback position should it be needed. Most embassies had some kind of extraction protocol in the event of a siege, but all the Mandrake field office had was a tree trunk, which would be pretty easy to set fire to, should some hostile happen upon it. A jug of oil and some flint, and that would be it. So about five years ago in a fit of enthusiasm, which coincided exactly with the last time he had quit drinking, Isles had used his woodwork skills to put a bug-out plan in place. This plan consisted of hollowing out a drop chute through the tree trunk, which without power tools took him six months, and connecting the chute to a hole in the ground twelve feet away. The hole in the ground was initially supposed to be twenty feet away, but Agent Isles fell off the wagon. It wasn't exactly the White House's legendary escape tunnel, but it did get Fairbrother Isles out of the field office alive.

The sun rose to find Isles and Riley shook up and soot black-ened, and sharing a log outside Fallback Position 1, or, as Agent Isles had coded it after his favourite book: the Hobbit Hole.

He had almost finished his debrief when Pointer trotted into the clearing, a handgun dangling from his jaws. The dog dropped the weapon at Isles's feet and said, 'I guess the Hobbit Hole wasn't such a stupid idea after all, partner.'

Isles was delighted to see his partner and they high-fived, palm to paw.

'Hey, buddy. You're still breathing. Where the heck were you? I've been beside myself.'

'Take it easy, Mom,' said Pointer. 'I tangled with Rosa and had to go lie down. I fetched her gun, though. Five shots left.'

'They're the only ones we have,' said Isles ruefully. 'The rest went up in the fireworks. Along with the guns and most of my blades. All we have is a few vests, the walkies with one charge in them and the professor, who's gotta stay in bed from now on.'

Riley felt that he should have reacted strongly to a talking dog, but he could not. All he could do was grunt once and even chuckle a little, as if to say: *A talking dog. But of course.*

In medical terms Riley was on the verge of what would become known, after the First World War, as shell shock. After many more wars it would become known as post-traumatic stress disorder, or PTSD. Already his eyes were developing the thousand-yard stare.

Pointer had seen army buddies in the same state and knew the signs. He slapped Riley in the face with a forepaw.

'You're Riley, right? Snap out of it, kid. Your beloved is alive, OK? And she's got her marbles back, so don't you go losing yours.'

Only one word penetrated Riley's funk. *Beloved*.

'*Beloved?* Why would you say that?'

Pointer snorted. 'I can smell it off you, and her. You two guys got it bad, which is not good for the operation.'

'Did Chevron say something?'

It was Isles's turn to snort. 'She didn't have to. It was all

Riley this and *Riley that*. Not to mention the fact that she exposed our entire operation to go rescue you.'

The fog in Riley's head receded. 'She did? My dear Chevron put herself at risk for me? I cannot bear that.'

Pointer rolled his eyes. 'Oh man. We got a romantic on our hands. He's gonna be writing love songs next. Tell me he ain't got an acoustic guitar.'

A walkie-talkie on Isles's belt squawked and he unclipped it. 'Yeah, Prof. Pointer is back. Battered and bruised but still his charming self.'

Smart's voice was urgent at the other end. 'Good. Good. We must begin our preparations. My battery will only last so long. And I think I know what Albert Garrick intends to do. The misguided fool will be the death of all humanity.'

Riley straightened up. He knew from Isles's briefing that the voice belonged to Professor Charles Smart, although he might have recognized it anyway from their previous meeting, when Garrick had murdered him. But what really caught his attention was the phrase 'of all humanity'.

Chevie was part of humanity.

'Very well, gentlemen,' Riley said briskly. 'What must we do?'

BURN THE WITCH

Mandrake. Huntingdonshire. 1647

Chevie was tied with stout chains to an actual stake with a pyre built up round its base, thinking:

Stake?

Pyre?

No one even uses those words any more.

But it was not *any more*, she realized. It was *way back when*. And, in the way-back-when, things were a little different from how they would be in what Chevie thought of as *my day*.

Here guns fired one bullet at a time if the barrel didn't explode in the shooter's hand.

People locked prisoners in stocks and used words like 'thee' with a straight face.

And perhaps more seriously and relevant to her present situation: they burned witches at the stake without a whole lot of evidence that those being burned were witches in the first place.

Though, in her case, she *had* fallen from the sky and she *did* have cat's eyes, which was about a million times more evidence than Garrick usually needed. By all accounts the Witchfinder generally threw a bit of a wobbler, pointed at some unfortunate female, pronounced her a witch and that was the end of it as far as the good people of Mandrake were concerned. All a female had to do was look a bit different or have her own opinion.

Why am I surprised? she wondered. It wasn't as if things were any different *in her day*. Persecution still flourished all over the world and on a much grander scale.

Half the world's people are starving and the other half are trying to ethnic-cleanse each other.

But Garrick was taking it to a new level. He was done fooling around with witches and warlocks. If the whispers of his plans were correct, he was leapfrogging right over ethnic cleansing to global cleansing.

One of the guards had swaggered back and forth on the dais in front of her, saying how her witchcraft would be of little use against a cannonball of pure silver that would destroy hell itself.

Hell itself being Smart's inter-dimension.

So Garrick was planning to destroy the wormhole.

And as Riley might say: *That particular trick only works the once.*

Garrick was taking no chances with Chevie's security. The stake was ringed with militiamen with pikes and rifles, ready for any assault on the prisoner; silver rings and bracelets had been threaded along her restraints in case the wormhole got grabby; and the great Witchfinder himself restlessly patrolled the outer wall, possessed of a fidgety excitement that made him irritable one minute and gregarious the next, so that men stepped from his path, uncertain how he would react to their presence.

There are no women or girls outdoors, Chevie noticed. And it didn't take a genius to figure out why. Garrick could name any woman a witch at any moment and there were enough zealots in this town to make sure the accused were quickly under lock and key.

Overhead the rift was clearly visible in the sky, though it could easily be mistaken for a sunset-tinged wisp of cloud, unless a person watched it for a minute and realized that, though it undulated and yawned, it resisted the easterly wind and remained fixed over Mandrake.

The U-bend, thought Chevie. *The end of the world.*

It was difficult to take that notion seriously.

It's been done to death. I saw a dozen movies last year about the end of the world.

The rift was hazy scarlet around the edges but grew darker inside, with a slash of deep blue night at its centre, and on occasion it seemed as though something flashed across that dark patch. When that happened Chevie felt a yearning to be there, inside the wormhole and at one with the creatures, but she knew that this was just the quantum foam in her system acting like some kind of magnet.

Kind of the opposite of the silver cannonball Garrick intends to blast in there.

She squinted into the evening sky, thinking, *Which would*

be one helluva shot. That's gotta be a thousand feet, there's a brisk wind picking up, and the cannons around here aren't actually precision instruments.

Chevie was afraid, of course. Terrified really, and, though she tried hard not to be consumed by terror, sometimes it broke through her armour of bravado and manifested itself as violent spasms, which rattled her silver chains and shook the stake in its mount. Chevie did not want to give her tormentors the satisfaction of seeing her reduced to a shivering mess, but she was still an adolescent, after all, and the traumas had been building up inside her over the past series of adventures.

Strangely, though, the shakes did not consume her entirely and Chevie found that she was able to hold it together reasonably well most of the time, even though she was cold, hungry, dying of thirst and lashed to a stake for imminent burning.

I've been desensitized to life-or-death situations, she realized. *And I still believe that Riley will come to rescue me.*

After all, he had done it before against extremely steep odds.

'How now, miss. Does it hurt thee?' said a voice from below, and Chevie looked down to see the man Woulfe standing at the base of the pyre studying her.

'Does what hurt me?'

The mason seemed embarrassed to ask. 'The witch eyes. It would seem that they rightly belong in another skull. That of a mouser, say.'

'A mouser? Oh, cat. You mean cat?'

Woulfe nodded. 'Aye. Cat. Those are cat's eyes lodged in your sockets, miss, and I was idly wondering whether or not the mismatching of eyes with sockets was a cause for mortal agony?'

Listen to this guy, thought Chevie. *His patter is worse than Riley's.*

'No,' she said. 'The mismatching of sockets and eyes is not a cause for mortal agony. If you really want to know, I can actually see a lot better in the dark. Not that I need cat's eyes to see that water jug you're holding.'

Woulfe looked at the jug as if he'd just realized it was in his hand. 'Ah yes, I come bearing water, for even witches deserve mercy is the truth of it.'

'That we do,' said Chevie.

Woulfe took a step backwards. 'You would admit it? I thought perhaps you were simply an unfortunate abomination.'

'Take your pick,' said Chevie wearily. 'But leave the water.'

Woulfe came closer warily. 'So, witch or no. Which is it?'

Chevie met his eyes. 'It is whatever Garrick says. Ain't that so, Master Woulfe? I can't believe you people. This guy strolls in here and you hand him the keys to the city.'

'He battled the man-lizard!' objected Woulfe. 'And others besides. Monsters all. Master Garrick delivered us from evil and he aims to seal the gates of hell forever.'

Chevie chuckled bitterly. 'Yeah, because that's how you seal things: shoot silver cannonballs at them.'

Woulfe climbed the makeshift steps up the pyre until he was level with Chevie. There was no anger in his eyes, just pity and maybe a shadow of fear. Chevie got the feeling that he was not afraid of her.

'I am not a witch,' she told him. 'I just came here through the same tunnel as Garrick. He lost his complexion temporarily; I lost my eyes and got these ones. This time a few days ago I was as normal as . . . your daughter. She is your daughter, right? That cutie with the blonde hair? I saw her when they dragged me in here. Before Garrick scared all the women off the street.'

Woulfe lifted the spout of the jug to Chevie's lips and poured a glug. 'Yes. Elizabeth. Lizzie, as she is commonly known. There was some suspicion on her last year but it was unfounded, praise God.'

Chevie felt the cool water slide down her gullet. 'Thanks,' she said. 'I'm glad Lizzie isn't tied up here beside me. I bet she's a good kid.'

Woulfe smiled. 'A kid? Yes, a giddy goat betimes. Indeed, she has a mischievous spirit.'

'That's what my dad said about me. Well, what he actually said was that I was a pain in the butt, but he meant mischievous spirit.'

It flashed across Woulfe's features, the image of his daughter up here – which was of course Chevie's plan.

Hostage Psychology 101. *Plant the seed of doubt. Make the true believer believe the real truth.*

Maybe I can rescue myself, she thought, which was premature, for at that moment their budding conversation was cut short.

'See, master,' said a voice. 'He brings refreshment to the witch.'

It was Godfrey Cryer, the walking wounded, loath to miss the adventures. And there beside him was, of course, Albert Garrick.

'Have I not said it?' said Cryer, bobbing with excitement. 'Lizzie Woulfe is a witch, and now she enchants her father to give comfort to her fellow witch. They both must pay.'

Garrick, cleaned up and decked in a sombre buckled hat and finery, was in high spirits and actually patted Cryer's head. 'Now then, Constable. The only thing that good Master Woulfe is guilty of is human kindness.' He coughed into his fist, a sign that a quotable line was on the way. '*The quality of mercy is not strained . . .*'

Unfortunately for Garrick, he chose just about the only William Shakespeare line that Chevie had picked up in high school and so she could not help but complete it.

'*It droppeth as the gentle rain from heaven*, isn't that right, Master Witchfinder?'

Even Chevie's impudence could not dampen Garrick's spirit, as he was having himself a royal old time back here in the seventeenth century.

He wagged a finger at Chevie. 'Silver-tongued, you see, Constable? It is common among devils, witches and many travelling players.'

'And witchfinders,' Chevie added.

Garrick was enjoying the feisty exchange. 'My words droppeth from heaven, witch, while your vile utterings are whispered into your ear by the prince of darkness.'

Cryer thought it was time to stick his oar in. 'It will take more than water, Jeronimo Woulfe, to aid this witch.

More than water indeed.' And he giggled then, hunching with mirth, and seemed less a man and more a malicious goblin.

'Leave Master Mason be,' Garrick admonished his acolyte. 'Perhaps he is wheedling a confession from the witch. Betimes water will crack a stone more effectively than fire.'

Woulfe allowed Chevie one more draught, then stepped down from the pyre. 'This girl was deprived of a trial. Should she be deprived of sustenance too? And water itself?'

'Witch-lover!' spat Cryer. 'I have said it before. Once this matter is dealt with, we will come calling on you, Master Woulfe, and your pretty Elizabeth.'

This was too much. Woulfe hurled the jug at Cryer with some considerable force and it happened to clip the constable's injured shoulder, causing him to stumble backwards, cursing in a most ungodly fashion, which made Chevie smile for the first time in a while.

'What time is it, Mr Woulfe?' she crowed, which probably seemed like a straightforward question to anyone who had not been brought up playing the game in gym class.

Even Garrick laughed. All these matters were childish to him now. An entertaining distraction from the main event, which was not to say he was growing complacent. He had made that mistake once before and would not commit it again. There was no doubt in his mind that Riley would attempt some form of rescue, but for the life of him he could not imagine a way that the boy could thwart him on this occasion. After all, Garrick was virtually invulnerable now and soon even the creatures of the wormhole would bow before him.

Cryer held his shoulder gingerly; the fresh blood seeping

through his clothes spoke of a reopened wound. 'You will pay for that, Woulfe. You and that girl of yours.'

Jeronimo Woulfe was in no mood for the constable's threats. 'I ride to Huntingdon at first light. I will petition the council there for some assistance. The constable has gone mad, I will testify to it. He threatens good English women and all because he cannot get for himself a wife.'

Cryer's face was purple with rage. 'This is slander. This is heresy.'

Woulfe turned his anger on Garrick, past caring now. 'This is who speaks for you, Master Witchfinder? This buffoon? I have seen things, I grant you. Monsters and perhaps witches. But this zany halfwit would burn the wheat with the chaff. He will not rest until Mandrake is a town of men. Were your mother present, Master Witchfinder, he would accuse her.'

'I never would,' swore Cryer. 'Never.'

Chevie chimed in. 'He would, Garrick, and you know it. The man's a wack job.'

Albert Garrick patted the air, calming his audience. Enough was enough.

'Very well. Now, now, everyone. The gates to hell hover above us and that must be the priority. Let there be no discordance among us.'

'But, master,' objected Cryer. 'I bleed. My very blood issues forth.'

Garrick's character had never been that of placator and, though he was of buoyant mood, his patience for fools was limited.

'Constable!' he barked. 'Offer up your suffering. It is a small price to pay to witness the wonders that will happen here. The gates to hell itself shall be forever sealed, using this witch as our vessel.'

This was news to Chevie. 'Wait a minute. I thought I was being burned alive and you were firing a silver cannonball. That's what the goons said.'

And now Cryer ceased in his mewling, for he wished to observe the witch as she was told about the changes to the Witchfinder's great plan.

Garrick laced his fingers and strolled to the foot of the pyre until his long face was inches below Chevie's.

'Burned at the stake, aye, that was the initial sentence. However, much as I have always been a man of my word, there have arisen some new circumstances, and it is a fool who ignores the truth, so the sentence of burning has been commuted.'

'Praise God,' cried Jeronimo Woulfe. 'Good sense prevails, for I feel certain there is no evil in this poor wretch.'

Chevie did not waste a second on relief. If Garrick wasn't going to burn her, it was only because he'd thought of something worse. If there was a fate worse than being burned at the stake.

'What new circumstances?' she asked.

'Various,' said Garrick, teasing her.

'But there is a stay of execution, Master Witchfinder?' pressed Woulfe. 'Is that not the essence of it?'

Garrick steepled his fingers, one of his favourite stage poses. 'Of burning at the stake, yes. And of death? Who can say what will happen to a witch in the realm of hell? Perhaps her master can save her, perhaps not. My plan is to send the witch back from whence she came.'

Woulfe glanced towards the rift, which had grown visibly larger in the last minutes.

'Simply release her?'

Chevie doubted it.

'There is a little more to the strategy,' Garrick admitted, drawing it out.

'Please, Master Witchfinder. Won't you reveal your machinations? You are employed by the town council, after all.'

'Oh, we are far beyond cash and prizes, good Jeronimo. We are in the realm of souls now. Souls and their saving, I say to you. Every soul in England.'

Woulfe paled and his hands clenched by his sides, but to the mason's credit he asked again, 'Your strategy, Master Garrick, if you would?'

Then suddenly Garrick switched personas, from indulgent father-figure to absolute ruler. 'You would know my plans, Master Woulfe? You would share my burden? Have you the stomach for what needs to be done?'

'If it needs to be done, absolutely. Yes, my resolve is firm, Master Witchfinder.'

Garrick took three quick steps and suddenly he loomed over the mason, and it seemed to Woulfe that the air grew colder.

'Look to the heavens, good Jeronimo. What do you see?'

Woulfe's eyes flickered skyward and he could not help but

flinch, for the rift was growing larger and seemed closer, with sinister flickerings within. 'I see hell, Master Garrick. Hell being visited upon us here in Mandrake.'

'I would cut short that visit, Master Woulfe. I would snuff out the flames.'

Chevie had a point to make. 'You're gonna shut down hell, Garrick? Where are the sinners supposed to go? Vegas?'

'Indeed, Witchfinder,' said Woulfe. 'Where now must the freshly damned dwell?'

Garrick scowled, as this was a legitimate question that he had been hoping Woulfe would not happen upon. Bluster was his only response.

'You would prefer the sinners from ages past to inhabit our bodies?' he demanded. 'You would prefer your Elizabeth to succumb to the forces of evil?'

'Nay,' said Woulfe. 'Never.'

'Then the gates must be sealed.'

'And how then? By cannon-shot? Burn the witch, and fire the ordnance, is it?'

'That was indeed my plan, but I had misgivings. The entire strategy was entirely too fraught with uncertainty, in point of fact, and I was more than a little perturbed, but then my constable, godly Godfrey, happened upon a surer strategy.' Garrick graciously yielded the stage with a sweep of his arm. 'Enlighten the witch, Constable.'

Cryer was proud of his plan and delighted to share the details. 'As you command, master.' He elbowed past Woulfe and clambered along the base of the pyre until Chevie could smell his fetid breath.

'You are, witch, familiar with the tale of Troy?'

Chevie planned to ramp up the attitude and say something along the lines of: *Yeah, sure. Brad Pitt inside a horse? That Troy?*

But just at that moment she became overwhelmed by the entire situation. Funny how she had held it together reasonably well until the constable's breath hit her nose and tipped her over the cliff. Perhaps her subconscious had already figured out what Cryer's plan was.

'If you remember your classics, witch, the Greeks could not breach Troy's defences. Wave after wave of their finest warriors they sent crashing against the mighty walls, only to have them cut down by arrow and spear, until at last Odysseus had the notion to build a giant wooden horse with a band of soldiers inside, and through such chicanery the Greeks tricked their way inside the walls.'

Woulfe stepped up behind the constable. 'Please, Cryer, is there a need for such relish? Make your point. It is the very devil of a job to wring details from the pair of you. Might I remind you, that you are public servants both.'

Cryer, emboldened by the supernatural situation, actually pushed the mason roughly. 'I am a servant of man, Woulfe. The time for councils and governments is past. Judgement Day is upon us, I say to you, and we shall all be judged by our actions this night.'

'Enough!' shouted Woulfe. 'You posturing buffoon. Hell is bearing down on us, man. Speak plainly.'

It was plain in Cryer's eyes that he would dearly love to strike Jeronimo Woulfe, but he was a scarecrow of a man and Woulfe hefted stone for a livelihood, so he refrained, lest he earn himself a second shattered collarbone for his troubles. Instead he contented himself with taunting the mason.

'Jeronimo Woulfe would have me speak plain. Jeronimo Woulfe the great theologian.' Cryer pointed a finger at the yawning rift. 'Be that not plain enough for thee, man?'

Perhaps it was Cryer's tauntings that prompted Woulfe to blurt the most courageous statement of his life, or perhaps it was the series of veiled threats against his dear Elizabeth that drove him to it; in any event the words were soon hanging in the air, clearly audible to every soul inside the town walls.

'It be plain enough to me, Cryer, that when the gates to hell split open over Mandrake that Albert Garrick was the first one through it!'

Chevie held her breath, as she knew through bitter and often painful experience that Garrick could go either way when slapped with accusations: he could either be amused or gravely offended, and if he chose offence then brave Jeronimo Woulfe's days of bravery were over.

Cryer too looked at Garrick, but the magician-turned-witchfinder simply nodded at him as if to say: *Master Mason makes a good argument, and what say you to it?*

Cryer realized he was on his own, but also saw his chance to impress his worth on the Witchfinder. And so he drew himself up to his spindly height, ignored the blossom of blood on his shirt front, and rained down scorn on Jeronimo Woulfe.

'Indeed. Master Garrick was first to emerge from this rift and with a witch by the tail, if ye remember, and her familiar to boot. Risked his body and soul did Albert Garrick to deliver us all. For the devil must be conquered, sir. Conquered, I say. And this is our very purpose here on this night.'

'So you say,' said Woulfe. 'So you persist in saying.'

' *And the gates to hell shall be sealed with silver,*' said Cryer. 'You are familiar with this line, I presume, a God-fearing man like yourself?'

With a nod, Woulfe allowed that he was.

'And so the master planned to fire shot made from silver at the gates, but then, says I, this is a tricky shot and the metal is soft and so may not either survive the barrel or pierce the gates' revulsion to it, and these were sound points, for Master Garrick conceded them all. "So what is the alternative, good Constable?" says he to me. And says I directly to him, "Why, master, the Trojan Horse. We conceal that which is undesirable inside that which is not."'

Woulfe was somewhat puzzled. 'Are you saying that your plan is to conceal the silver that you have collected about this girl's person?'

'No,' said Cryer. 'Not about. Within. Inside. The precious metal is melted and down her gullet it goes, and at that exact second we activate the infernal device round her neck and summon the rift. It will snatch her away.'

'And she will die by unspeakable cruelty,' objected Woulfe, pale with the horror of these details.

'The Devil's Brew, as the method is known, has been relied upon by the Church for centuries,' said Cryer. 'And, when the witch ascends, the gates will close forever and all England shall hear of Albert Garrick and Constable Cryer.'

Chevie had known fear in her life, and loss and unspeakable

sadness, and love too more than once, but here now, listening to this casual description of her torture and death, she gave Garrick the satisfaction he craved by hanging her head and lapsing into quiet sobs.

The yellow slash of a smile spread across Albert Garrick's jaw, and he patted Cryer's good shoulder with some affection.

'Well said, my man. Nicely said.' And it seemed as though Cryer's head might explode with pride.

Then the moment for satisfaction was past and Garrick turned once more to business and his secret dread of failure.

'Double the guard on the witch!' he commanded. 'And have the silversmith make his preparations. I want every man, woman and child with eyes in their heads on the battlements scouring the fens. No one is permitted entry, not even Cromwell himself.'

And, without bothering to wait for a sign of compliance, Garrick strode to the wall, his cloak swirling about him like a shadow.

Not this time, Riley my son, he thought. *This time things go my way. This time and forever more.*

14

TRASH TALK

On the south side of the town, three hundred feet from the wall and in the third line of trees, the canopy of a large elm held a small covered platform that was technically known as a satellite observation post. It had also become, over the past few years, a sleep shack for Special Agent Fender Rhodes Isles when he was a bit too grogged to make it back to the field office but did not fancy a night in the stocks. Isles reasoned that it was his duty to sleep in the shack rather than trudge back across the fens to the field office: firstly because he would possibly drown in the lake; and secondly because his senses were usually too dulled to be certain that no one was following him.

But now the satellite observation post was actually being used as a satellite observation post.

Riley, lying flat on his stomach, wiped a smudge of Agent Isles's pungent home-made camouflage paint from his eyelid and peered towards Mandrake.

Isles lay beside him like a beached killer whale beside a minnow. A beached whale with his face painted in olive and black stripes.

'You notice anything, kid?' asked the federal agent.

'I notice that these boards reek of beer,' said Riley. 'They smell almost as rank as this make-up.'

'Yeah, OK. I get it. Maybe I gotta cut back on the booze. But let's stick to the matter at hand, whaddya say?'

Riley glanced up at him. 'This matter is very much at hand, Agent Isles. We're going into the town presently and I need to know you ain't going to heave all over me at the first fence.'

Isles sulked for a moment, then said, 'Don't worry about me, kid. We got plenty else to worry about. Look.' He pointed and Riley saw that the town walls were lined with people, all staring out into the blackness, waiting for a rescue attempt, no doubt. Every second soul held a torch so that the entire wall of Mandrake's Groan was lit up like Piccadilly Circus.

'Garrick is waiting for us,' said Riley, drawing his cloak between him and the planking, as it seemed the frost was rising. 'He wishes us to make a try for Chevie.'

Isles huffed. 'Well, I ain't gonna disappoint him. We got an agent in there still breathing and we Feds don't leave our brothers or sisters in the lurch.'

Riley reached into Isles's equipment bag and withdrew futuristic optics. A double telescope with green lenses and complicated dials. He screwed it to his eyes and exclaimed.

'Spanking night-vision goggles, Agent. Clear as a July picnic it is.' For of course Riley had been to the twenty-first century and witnessed all manner of marvels.

'Yeah, those are a nice set. Came through the inter-dimension without a scratch. Seems like binoculars ain't got a subconscious to mess them up. I did have a copy of *The Hobbit* in my bag when I jumped and it ended up as a tiny dragon. Flew off into the night coughing sparks. I ain't seen it since. Even the professor can't explain that one.'

Riley scanned the townsfolk on the wall. 'Seems like Garrick has every able-bodied person on watch. Whatever he's planning to do, he ain't leaving a thing to chance. I don't see a way in, Agent. He knows all my tricks of misdirection, smoke and mirrors and whatnot. Ain't nothing going to work with the Great Lombardi as was.'

Isles slapped a small wooden chest beside him on the plat-form. The chest hummed gently and seemed to rock in objection to being thumped.

'Don't worry, Riley. We got our secret weapon here. Some-thing very sneaky up our sleeves. There's no way your guy Garrick can see this coming.'

Riley was not much comforted. 'There's not much of a range on that weapon. Barely arm's length, and that's a deal closer to Albert Garrick than I like to get.'

Isles did not offer any further reassurances. The odds were against them and there was no point in sugar-coating it. The entire enterprise was a hair's breadth away from being a suicide mission, unless the professor's weapon actually worked. In spite of his show of confidence in the contents of the wooden chest, Isles had little faith in any weapon that he could not understand. You take a gun or a knife, then it's pretty clear what's going on, mechanically, as it were: point the thin end at the bad guy. But this magic chest? Isles had no clue how it was supposed to operate and the only reason he was putting any faith in it was because the prof had assured him it would work, and if there was anyone who had a handle on all this inter-dimension malarkey it was Charles Smart.

I wish the prof was taking point on this, Isles thought.

But that wasn't possible. The professor was pure quantum energy and, if the wormhole got even a sniff of him, then it would hoover him up before he could say, *It's not a wormhole; it's an inter-dimension* (as he often did).

Inter-dimension. That name is never going to catch on, thought Isles.

Suddenly Pointer was at the foot of the tree, and neither Isles nor Riley, who could both be pretty sneaky individuals when the situation called for it, had heard the smallest sound to herald his arrival.

'Hey,' whispered the dog. 'Are you guys up there?'

Isles whistled their theme tune softly and in seconds the dog had scaled the trunk and wriggled between the two humans.

'I think you have a bit of goat in you, partner,' said Isles. 'The way you can climb trees like that.'

Pointer scratched his mud-coated nose with one paw. 'Do you want the intel? Or do you want to insult me some more?'

'What did you learn, Agent?' asked Riley impatiently.

'You see that, Fender?' said Pointer. 'The kid called me *Agent*. Maybe you could do that once in a while.'

'Apologize to Mister Pointer,' said Riley. 'The sun has set and we are none the wiser.'

'Yeah, OK,' said Isles. 'I'm sorry, partner. Can you fill us in now?'

'I can,' said Pointer. 'But only because time is of the essence and not because I thought for a second that your apology was sincere.'

'Chevie yet lives?' asked Riley. This was after all the most vital piece of information.

'Alive and kicking,' said Pointer, but he frowned as he said it.

'And yet?' prompted Riley.

'Well, she ain't exactly swimming in gravy, know what I mean? She ain't exactly quaffing champagne with the president.'

Isles took the binoculars and trained them on the wall, searching for a gap in the line. 'Yeah, we kinda guessed that, Donnie. What is she doing exactly?'

'She's hanging in there, either crying or trying not to cry. Mostly keeping it together, to give her credit.'

'On the stake?' asked Riley. 'Where they will burn her?'

Pointer wiggled closer to them for warmth. 'Oh no. They ain't burning her. That's off the cards.'

Riley felt as though he might sink through the cracks in the planking from sheer relief. 'Thank heaven. Thank providence. And thank you, Agent Pointer. That is surely the most excellent of news.'

'Don't thank me, kid. They ain't burning her. It's much worse than that.'

'Worse?' said Riley, thinking perhaps the dog was toying with him, but then he remembered that Albert Garrick was involved and knew that if there was a worse fate than being burned alive then he would be the devil to find it. 'Tell me, Agent. I beg you.'

Pointer took a deep breath. 'I crept in through a drain, which is why I might be a bit on the stinky side – but, hey, I gotta hide my aura or whatever it is Garrick can see. You know, if we ever get that creep in custody, I'm gonna be asking some tough questions.'

'I don't think custody is an option with this guy,' said Isles. 'It's us or him, the way I see it. And by *us* I mean the rest of the planet.'

'But what of Chevron?' Riley insisted. 'What news?'

'So, in I go,' continued Pointer, 'all stealthy. I'm like a goddamn ghost, if I say so myself. And I creep towards the square, which I can find in my sleep since that's where they restrain good old town drunk Fairbrother Isles when he's had a few tankards.'

'I have always appreciated the concern,' said Isles drily.

'So Chevie is up there on the stake thing – pole or whatever. And they got her surrounded. Every man jack in the militia is in the ring, all armed up the wazoo with pistols and pikes. But these guys look shook. All jittery and anxious, like something is up. So I trot in for a pet, which I am prepared to tolerate in the name of information. And I hear this kid in an old Roundhead helmet talking about the Devil's Brew and how this is the plan for Chevie.'

'So not burning?'

'They got that on standby apparently, but the primary weapon is this Devil's Brew. The kid is talking about it and he's shaking, like big time. His sword is rattling in his belt. It's un-Christian, he says, to pour molten silver down a girl's gullet even if she is a witch.'

These words, spoken so casually, may well have signalled the end of Riley's world. *Pour molten silver down a girl's gullet.*

He could not stand it. He would not. And in that second all fear vanished from Riley's mind and was replaced by a hard determination rare in one so young. He would rescue Chevie, and if he could not rescue her he would ensure that she never drank the Devil's Brew.

It was unbearable, the very notion, and Riley's body acted almost independently of his mind, tensing to rise. Indeed, he would have risen and leaped from the platform, and possibly sprained one or both ankles and been of no use to man, woman or beast, had not Isles placed a large flat hand on his back.

'Dial it down, kid. We gotta consider this development.'

'Development, says you?' spluttered Riley. 'A development, is it? That devil plans to pour molten silver down the neck of my . . .'

And even now he could not say it.

Say what?

Beloved, was that it?

Perhaps. He knew they could be happy. The tunnel had shown him a vision of happiness and it had been so clear that he wanted to cry.

Isles patted his back and the huge hand felt like a shovel. 'I know, kid. You guys are sweet on each other. Even a mutt like Pointer can see that. But I gotta check in with the professor. See what he makes of this Devil's Brew thing.'

Riley held himself still with some difficulty while Isles fished a radio from his duffel and keyed the *talk* button.

'Prof,' he said, 'you there? We got some intel. Sounds medieval but there could be some science to it.'

Smart's voice came out of a crackling wash. 'Right here, Agent. What has Agent Pointer learned?'

'Garrick has changed his plan. No more silver cannonballs. Now it's molten silver inside the girl.'

The radio crackled while Smart pondered, then he said, 'This Garrick is more than a mere Luddite. He has calculated, perhaps correctly, that the rift would reject silver, even at those speeds, so he means to cloak it using Chevron's own body. No doubt he plans to activate the Timekey at the moment before death, hoping that the combination of key and foam in Chevie's own DNA will flummox the interdimension's natural aversion to silver. This plan is much better thought out than the last one. All credit to Mister Garrick.'

'All credit to Garrick,' said Riley. 'By all means, let us heap praise upon the devil who would first cleanse the world and then rule the ruins.'

Smart sighed and through the small speaker the noise set Riley's teeth on edge.

'I was merely making an observation, Riley. The man is a formidable adversary and will at the least be the death of one of us and at the most be the death of us all.'

'So what should we do, Prof?' asked Isles. 'Back to base, you reckon? I think the plan needs a bit of a rethink.'

Smart's reply was sharp and immediate. 'No. The plan is sound. All that has changed is the manner of Miss Savano's planned execution. We must still assume that Garrick will execute his plan at the darkest point of the night when the solar radiation is at its weakest, and the draw of the inter-dimension is strong enough to overcome its repulsion to the silver inside Chevie's person. If his plan succeeds, then this world is going to be a lonely place. It's possible that Agent Pointer would survive, and myself, but you will die, Fairbrother, and Riley too, and the world will be overrun by abominations.'

'Thanks for that,' grunted Pointer, scratching the planking with his claws. 'So Pointer is an abomination now.'

'So we go in?' said Isles.

'As soon as possible,' confirmed Smart. 'I hate to say it, but the entire team is expendable in this instance. Everything depends on saving Agent Savano.'

Riley shrugged off Isles's hand. 'At last we are in agreement.'

Isles switched off the communicator. 'A lot of interference for such a short distance. I guess it would work better if the professor actually needed a radio at his end.' He pocketed the device. 'I guess we're going in. How's our breach point looking?'

Pointer's low growl could have been a chuckle. 'How's it looking, Fender? It's looking like a latrine, because that's more or less what it is, and I can guarantee you ain't gonna like it. Neither of you.'

'This is not the moment for levity surely,' objected Riley, who felt that the canine agent needed to apply himself to the task with a touch more gravitas.

'Oh, it ain't his fault, kid,' said Isles. 'That's the dog genes.'

'It's true,' said Pointer. 'The big questions don't mean a lot to me any more. Dying, the afterlife and faith don't even make the needle flicker. It all takes a back seat to beef and sunshine.'

Beef and sunshine, thought Riley. *What a luxury to think about those everyday things. Abominations and inter-dimensions, that's what I get to think about.*

And something that was not yet love but might be one day.

The promise of love.

The good folk of Mandrake's Groan kept their eyes peeled, motivated by a fear of witches and witch-born abominations, but also by terror of the Witchfinder, who strode along the rough battlements, shaking any shoulders that drooped, and issuing dire warnings to anyone who might be considering resting their eyes for even the briefest moment. It was uncanny how he seemed to be everywhere at once, propping up the weary and the distracted with a prod of his icy fingers.

In fairness to the townsfolk, though, they were amateurs in the surveillance game and, what's more, amateurs from the past, relatively speaking. Even with Albert Garrick encouraging their vigilance, they were no match for an ex-army sniper from the twentieth century who was extremely determined to gain entry. When it was taken into account that the others in the sniper's party were a hunting hound and a young magician whose business it was to make himself invisible, it seemed as though the advantage was with the interlopers. Although it was the sort of advantage a troop of mice might enjoy when creeping into a bear's den.

There was abundant cover to be had in the scrubland and

Isles made full use of it, inching forward with mind-numbing slowness that tore Riley's nerves to shreds and had him on the verge of rising to his feet and running full tilt for the town wall, but he did not: to doom himself would be to doom Chevie and, if Smart was correct in his calculations, the entire world of man along with them. So they crept forward, concealed by camouflage sheets, the underside of which Isles had coated with lead-based paint. Smart assured them that this would flummox Garrick's second sight and also somewhat lessen the draw of the rift on the quantum foam in their systems, as would the silver plates in their modified Kevlar vests. Pointer had no sheet or vest, but he was glad of the silver torque concealed beneath the shabby-looking leather collar round his neck.

The topography was on their side, and of course the lack of natural light. And so Isles led the way in, following a path that he had, like many TV chefs, prepared earlier, in case exactly such an incursion proved necessary. In all honesty, he had only made preparations like this out of sheer boredom, but he was ex-special forces and a federal agent and had, once upon a time, been a Boy Scout, so being prepared was in his DNA.

This particular route, one of three that he could have chosen, followed a hidden gully that snaked towards the town walls from the woods. Pointer jokingly referred to this route as the *beer path*, as its meanderings were a little like Isles's own when he had tied a load on. The gully was invisible from the wall, hidden by low ridges and scrub, and once the gully ran out there was a hotchpotch of thickets that Isles had surreptitiously planted over the years to provide cover should he need it. From the watch's vantage point, there was nothing noteworthy about the bushes' placement, nothing too regular or symmetrical, but for a camouflaged soldier who specialized in special reconnaissance missions these thickets were his own personal lines of cover, measured exactly to his stride and reach so that Isles could find concealment blindfolded. He was, in effect, invisible, and if Isles was worried about the boy behind him showing up in anyone's vision he needn't have been. Riley had spent years in enforced training, learning the secrets of concealment in even the tightest spaces.

But he'd had one suggestion to add. *Garrick knows all the secrets we know, and he will expect a distraction. That's the cornerstone of stage magic. Make the audience look the other way.*

So they had decided to give Albert Garrick the distraction he expected.

Garrick was overseeing the Devil's Brew preparations when he heard the voice. Actually the entire town heard the voice.

'Hey, Garrick. Albert Garrick, you phony! Come on out here and face me. Mano a mano.'

Garrick half turned from the sweating silversmith, who was at that moment pouring a bucket of appropriated silver coins into a hissing smelter. The entire wealth of Mandrake was being melted down for cannon-shot and the molten execution. Garrick was loath to leave the silversmith because this work was important. It was vital to the success of his fledgling plan.

To change the world. To truly be a magician. A warlock.

'Who calls my name?' he snarled over his shoulder, knowing that Cryer would be there or thereabouts.

Cryer's response was not immediate, for a boy had jumped from the wall's ladder and was now whispering in the constable's ear.

'Constable, I would have you answer promptly.'

'Y-yes, Master Witchfinder. The boy says . . . Well, he says it is a hound, sir. A dog, he says. Perhaps the child is bewitched.'

Garrick's mouth twitched in what might have been a smile. 'A dog, eh? A hound, says the lad.'

'Yes,' said Cryer, wincing, his shoulders hunched as if expecting harsh words or possibly a contemptuous blow.

But Garrick only rubbed his sharp chin.

There was a hound with the squid, he thought. *An FBI dog. So – as Riley's hero detective might have said – the game is afoot.*

Garrick treated the silversmith to a lingering and serious gaze, which impressed upon him the importance of this work, and then strode to the ladder.

'Well, then, Master Constable. Let us see what this dog has to say for himself.'

The walls of Mandrake's Groan were carefully engineered to withstand raids from casual bandits but not serious incursions from army regiments or the like. This would only mark Mandrake as worth taking, of strategic value, as it were, and the council was eager for the town to be overlooked and bypassed, especially by generals seeking warehouses stuffed with grain to feed their armies and stables packed flank to flank with fine mounts to bear their cavalry. So the council had hired an engineer from a fine firm in London and after a week of pacing and sketching Master Quill had declared that the walls should be of plain unlimed stone hewn from the local quarry, unlike the houses, which were of the famous Anglian brick. These walls should be precisely twelve feet high, which was too high for a man on horseback to clamber over but not high enough to offer any serious resistance to cannon, and there should be gates at the four points of a cross, which should satisfy the Church but not anger the Parliament.

However, Mandrake's council had never bargained on witchfinders or abominations. Though judging by the terrifying aspect of the fiery rift now yawning above them, the height of the walls would make no difference whatsoever. Walls would be little hindrance to flying witches and their demons.

A final further reminder, as if one were needed, that all was utterly changed in the humdrum world of East Anglia was now a hunting dog, possibly a pointer, though larger than the usual variety, gambolling a distance from the wall and calling for the Witchfinder, and none too respectfully either.

Pointer threw back his head and howled. He was planning to show these old-timey, superstitious, sack-wearing jug-heads how trash-talking should be done. After all, if a guy had to blow his cover, he might as well blow it big.

Which was how Donnie Pointer dealt with his dog-shaped predicament. He thought of himself as being in deep cover.

Not any more, he thought. *Not after tonight*.

In the red spectral light from the rift, Pointer saw Garrick's tall figure appear on the battlements and he felt his hackles rise.

This guy is bad news. The worst. And it will be my pleasure to toy with him a little.

'Hey, Garrick,' he called. 'Hey, Master Witchfinder. How's the big plan going? You all up to schedule on destroying the world?'

Garrick's fingers gripped the stone crenellations and he scowled into the red-tinged moonlight. This talking dog was an unexpected complication. Riley he had expected, even the bludger Isles, but a prancing pointer was a distraction for everyone. And should he, Albert Garrick, lower himself to converse with a mere hound?

Garrick looked up and down the wall at the rows of torchlit faces looking to him for a response of some kind.

For leadership, he realized. Though these expectations could be at times tiresome, on this occasion he felt that these people's almost tangible terror of him was augmented by – what could it be now? – reverence.

Yes, Alby, old fellow, he thought smugly. *These idiots do indeed revere you. You have become holy to them.*

He laughed. *And they ain't seen nothing yet. Wait till I split the rift.*

The townsfolk were surprised now, for Garrick had laughed aloud and this did not seem appropriate with such a threat looming large above them.

'See what the devil is reduced to!' he cried, which explained his mirth to the bystanders. 'A hound from hell.'

His voice carried across the scrub to the giddy animal.

'Hey, I ain't no hound. You're the mutt around here,' said Pointer, following this declaration with two barks, which undermined his argument somewhat, before adding, 'But you're right about me being from hell.'

'Aha!' said Garrick, triumphant. 'He admits it. A confession.'

'Yeah, I'm from hell all right. Hell's Kitchen, New York, New York. So good they named it twice. Where are you from, Witchfinder? Stupidsville?'

To the watchers on the wall these words were little more than gibberish, except for the word 'hell', which they understood only too well.

Garrick's nostrils flared as they detected the smoke from the silversmith's smelter and he grew bored with this game. 'Pah!' he said. 'Again the creature confesses. It is an abomination. Shoot it.'

This was the command the men of the watch had been awaiting, and a dozen long-barrel muskets were set in their notches on the wall and cocked. To pierce the hide of a witch's familiar would guarantee a man's immortality as regards his very soul and indeed his reputation in the taverns hereabouts.

'Fire!' ordered Garrick, and the muskets roared, spitting flames, lead and long unfurling plumes of grey smoke.

Pointer did not duck or prance but instead stood still defiantly, watching as the musket balls dropped to the earth before his paws, sparking against stones or burrowing wormholes in the soft clay.

'Hah!' he crowed. 'Did you ever hear the word "ballistics",

morons? Those old muskets you got there don't have the range to hit me. What you need is a cannon.'

'I would not waste a cannonball on you, hound,' said Garrick through clenched teeth, and such were his powers of projection that Pointer could clearly hear him.

'I tell you what, Garrick,' called Pointer. 'I'm gonna stand still with my eyes closed for a whole minute. I can't say any fairer than that. Surely one of you crack shots on that wall has got a rifle with a bit of range. Easy shot.'

The dog drew himself up straight and stood stock-still, mocking every man jack on the wall, but could not contain himself for the whole minute. After ten seconds he opened one eye.

'What? No one is taking the shot? Well, then, you gotta come out here, Garrick. Let's duke it out. Why don't you suck the juice right outta my brain like you did with my friend Rosa? You try to grab my skull and I try to bite your face off and we'll see who wins. I am calling you out, Witchfinder. This is a formal challenge.'

Garrick's mood darkened; he knew from centuries' experience that this was a dangerous time for him strategy-wise, as he tended to become deeply offended by the slightest slight and abandon his plans in favour of direct and usually violent action, a behaviour pattern that had cost him an entire platoon when he was a colonel for the British army at Alexandria.

You do not respond to taunts well, Alby, he thought to himself. *You knows this. So don't let yourself see red.*

The dog was prancing again, his dark body rippling with muscle and red light from the rift above.

'I'm waiting, Garrick. Let's see those magic hands at work. You can take me, can't you?' Pointer was so excited that he interrupted his own trash-talking for a series of yelps and barks, then wrestled control of his doggy side. 'Are you gonna stand there in front of all those true believers and take abuse from a dog?'

Garrick heard the squeak of leather, the clank of metal and the hiss of coarse cloth as every person on the wall turned to peek at him, waiting for his reaction.

What you need to do, Alby, he told himself, *is take control of this situation. Play it over the top, but inside stay controlled.*

And so Garrick lashed out at the man to his left, not caring who it was, particularly as it was simply a show of authority. The man tumbled backwards into the compound itself.

'Can you fools not see?' Albert Garrick roared. 'Have we learned nothing from Bonaparte?'

Cryer, to his right, had the temerity to ask, 'And who is that, master? Some class of a Frenchman perhaps?'

Garrick raged on. 'That is not important. We have serious business to attend to and the witch summons her familiar as a distraction. Can you not see it? Is it not blindingly obvious?'

Garrick stopped speaking. His mouth still moved but no sound issued forth.

A distraction.

One of the basic tenets of stage magic. *Distract the audience. Make them look where you wish them to look, so they will not see the trick.*

Riley's distracting them all with this sideshow freak.

222

How could he have been so stupid?

While they were standing there mooning at a blasted hound, the real trick was happening on the other side of the stage, as it were.

The far gate.

Cryer pawed his shoulder. 'Master, should I send forth some men? A handful to deal with that abomination. I am happy to lead them myself.'

'No!' cried Garrick, truly enraged now and fearful that he may have already missed a trick. 'The opposite wall. Move the entire watch. I want all eyes on the opposite side of the wall. Now. With utmost haste.'

Garrick turned with great speed, his cloak rising with the twirl, and leaped from the wall. Though he heard his ankle snap on landing, he raced through the town, ignoring the excruciating pain, for he knew the bone would heal momentarily. Behind him he heard the bustle of men doing his bidding. Smaller free-roaming livestock scattered before him, as well as children; the womenfolk shrank back towards the nearest shadows, terrified that they might be accused.

Garrick lurched onward, and it occurred to him that the bone might set crooked and he would limp for the rest of his days, but still he would not pause. The boy had dealt him the oldest trick card in the deck and Garrick himself had picked it up like a gulpy mark on his first trip to the big city.

'Riley!' Garrick cried as he ran, forcing his pain into those two syllables. 'Riley!' He swore to himself that if he had been foiled again by the boy then he would rain hell-on-earth down on this town.

Garrick approached the town square and the ring of guards drew themselves up almost on tiptoes at his coming. There was Chevie in the centre, still secured to the stake.

Or was she?

For was that not another trick in the illusionist's arsenal? Deception.

He expected to see Chevron Savano and therefore that is what he saw. Further investigation was needed. Albert Garrick barged through the circle of guards. Spitting venom and growling he was. More animal than human he seemed, with his bent-over lurch and his long fingers grazing the dirt. Up the pyre he scrambled, his injured ankle prodded by kindling. Even though Chevie was right there in front of his face, tethered before him, he did not believe it till his nose was an inch from her own, and then he jerked himself backwards as the Timekey under her clothing suddenly beeped softly, waking from electronic slumber.

He had forgotten about the key.

For him to be taken by the wormhole now could mean anything. He certainly would be master of nothing in the quantum sea. Garrick did not know if he could survive its caress again. So far its gifts to him had been of great benefit, but on the next trip surely Lady Time would redress the balance and curse him in some manner or other. The wormhole's claws would scrabble into his mind and strip away his powers and perhaps even his humanity.

Here on earth, however, with my feet on the ground, I am the master.

For all his grandiose thoughts, Garrick was skittish with

the Timekey in his environs. He descended quickly from his perch on the pyre to solid ground, and as he backed away the Timekey burbled and calmed, returning once more to its sleeping state.

Garrick sat on a log nearby and set to tugging off his boot, each tug causing great discomfort to his injured ankle. When the boot came free, his foot dangled and the bones grated sickeningly.

One more debit to your account, Riley my son, he thought, then gripped his foot in both hands and wrenched it into an approximation of its proper position. The agony was an excruciation and a reminder of his own vulnerability.

Garrick cocked his head, listening for the hiss-crackle of the quantum foam healing his wounds, as it had done for centuries. The healing had just completed when Cryer arrived, breathless from running.

'Master Garrick, the wall is guarded. The witch's minions are nowhere in sight.'

Tugging on his high boot again, Garrick addressed Cryer. 'The witch's familiar is coming. Make no mistake, Constable. Tell the men to remain vigilant. This is the night for which God created us both, good Master Godfrey. This very night. And the wrath of our Lord is in my hands and I shall bring it down on any man who turns from his post. On any man who so much as blinks for too long. I have grappled with this familiar before, and he is more dangerous than his witch.' Garrick rotated his foot and aside from minor twinges the healing was satisfactory. 'Now go. Patrol the wall.'

'Yes, master. And what of you?'

Garrick stood and took some experimental paces, grunting with satisfaction.

'I shall stay here, with the witch in my direct vision. Neither devilment nor diversions shall distract me. I shall neither eat nor drink till the gates of hell are closed for all eternity.'

Cryer's eyes were bright. 'Please, master, let me remain at your side. I am worthy. I am ready for any duty.'

At that moment Garrick decided Cryer would be the one to activate the Timekey when the time came. The man would be happy to give his life – for when the wormhole took Chevron Savano it would surely take Cryer too, and neither would survive the journey.

Garrick smiled a duplicitous smile that Cryer took for fondness but which was actually self-congratulatory, for soon Garrick would have his empire and Godfrey Cryer, through his own sacrifice, would make it come to pass.

'Good Master Constable,' he said, 'pass the word to the watch and then return directly to me and stay by my side this night until we may rid the world of witches forever.'

And off Cryer trotted, all eagerness and joy. Delighted he was to be chosen as the Witchfinder's right hand.

I sacrifice my most loyal servant, thought Garrick as he watched him go, and wondered whether there was ever a time when this would have plucked at the strings of his conscience.

Perhaps there had been such a time, he concluded. Once, long ago from his perspective. When he had been a boy.

Ah, but then I was merely a child.

Garrick remembered a lesson from 1 Corinthians that ran:

When I was a child, I spake as a child, I understood as a child, I thought as a child; but when I became a man, I put away childish things.

Albert Garrick turned to Chevie and spoke softly to her so that none of the watchmen might overhear.

'I have put away childish things,' he said, then glanced upward at the descending rift. 'And very soon now, Miss Savano, I shall put away all children. Including your good self and the brat Riley.'

If Chevie heard, she made no sign.

Outside the wall, Pointer watched the men leave their posts in a mad rush for the other side of the town.

'That was too easy,' he said, grinning. 'Garrick is a soft touch. He wouldn't last five minutes in New York.'

There was a slight rustle in the undergrowth beside him and an arm extended, seemingly from the earth, and patted his head. 'Good job, partner,' said a small shrub.

But of course the shrub had not spoken. The voice belonged to Fairbrother Isles, who'd been lying there for the entire jibing match, concealed underneath his camo-sheet.

Pointer ducked away from the petting hand. 'Quit it, Fender. Yeah, but it was a good job. Too good. I was looking forward to a real slanging session like we used to have on the basketball courts. Remember?'

'Yeah, sure I remember. Isles and Pointer: the best two-on-two team in the Bureau. We retired champs, partner.'

'Isles and Pointer?' said the dog. 'It was Pointer and Isles, the way I remember it.'

Riley poked his head out from under his own sheet. 'Agents. Please.'

'Sorry,' said Pointer. 'Dog genes. OK, let's move it out.'

Pointer led the way, sniffing the ground like a minesweeper, guiding Isles and Riley towards the wall, which now had only one guard left to watch over that approach, thanks to Riley's double bluff.

Garrick will sniff out a distraction, he had told the federal agents earlier. *But not a second one, as that don't work in the theatre, because it sets the eyes looking where you didn't want them to look in the first place.*

And it had worked. The moment Garrick sniffed trickery, he was off to the far wall as though his boots were on fire, but it would not take him long to suspect a ruse and so they must breach the compound while they had the chance.

When they were ten feet from the wall, Pointer ran ahead and set his forepaws scrabbling at the stone, howling and barking at the guard above, and while the man was fumbling with the load for his musket Isles and Riley rolled the last stretch to the base of the wall itself. It would have been relatively easy to scale, but difficult to conceal their silhouettes from anyone in the town casting even a casual glance in their direction, so instead Isles elected to take them through his bolthole.

I had Pointer dig this for me one time when the town was evacuated during a plague scare, he had explained back in the field office. *He wasn't too happy about using what could be classed as canine talents, but I convinced him that in this situation having paws and claws were boons to the mission. Then he got all snippy cos he thought I said 'bones'. It's exhausting. You have no idea, kid.*

Nevertheless, the secret tunnel had eventually been excavated and here they were, with the blue night deepening all around and a bloody gash in the sky overhead, squatting in a blind spot at the foot of Mandrake's wall, making ready to enter the town, where a small militia and a powerful magician waited for them.

And their only weapons?

A mysterious chest.

One flash-bang from Riley's cape, which might or might not work after the swamp ducking.

One standard-issue 1980s Fed revolver, Isles's beloved whittling knife and a bulletproof vest apiece.

'Remember, kid,' Isles whispered now, 'these are innocent civilians. So no killing.'

'Except Garrick,' insisted Riley.

'Yeah, well, obviously Garrick. And if you wound that guy Cryer I won't lose any sleep over it.'

'So Garrick and Cryer.'

'Anyone else, leg shots only.'

Isles reached his fingers into a crack in the wall and lifted out an entire block of stone as though it were made of paper, which it wasn't. The false stone was actually moulded from first-aid-kit plaster of Paris, which had been carefully painted to match the wall.

'I would say that *leg shots* do count as wounds, Agent,' Riley said.

'Theoretically yes, but chances are you won't hit anything anyway, so don't worry about it.'

Agent Isles went first into the black hole, nudging the small chest in front of him. He was a big man and it was a small hole, but he wiggled his way through and popped a second plug on the far side. When through, he clicked his fingers once as a signal for Riley to follow. Riley did so with all speed, using the method they had discussed. Feet first he went, taking hold of the false block and manoeuvring it roughly across the hole, shutting out the stars on himself. Groundwater soaked his clothes, and he could hear the click and snick of beetles and insects as he wiggled through. A great fear overtook him at the persistent idea that this wall would collapse in on him, although Isles had assured him this would not happen as he had travelled this way a hundred times without misadventure.

But this ain't no normal day, thought Riley. *Everything that never happened before is happening this night*.

Then Isles had him by the ankles and was dragging him through the oppressive darkness.

'You OK, kid?' whispered the federal agent.

'No need to worry on my account,' replied Riley, though the shake in his voice belied the words. 'I am ready and able to do my part.'

'You sure?' asked Isles. 'Your face is about as pale as a full moon.'

Riley sat up, brushing the remains of a squashed beetle from the flap of his cloak. 'There is no alternative, Agent. Chevie hangs upon a stake ready for the cruellest of executions. So let us away and no more talk about it.'

Isles punched his shoulder gently. 'All right, kid. You got your bearings?'

Riley looked around. They were behind the jail shack, exactly as Agent Isles had shown him on the scale model. To be more precise, they were behind the pigpen's water trough, which was fed by the occasional bucket when times were dry. If the bumping, snorting pigs noticed their presence, then they paid them no mind, accustomed no doubt to Isles popping in at irregular intervals. The odour was not as rank as one unfamiliar with porkers might assume, which was not to say that it was pleasant. Much worse was the noise: a constant honking and screeching that would drive a person clear out of his gourd should he be forced to endure it for long periods at short range. Smell or no, Riley would be glad to be out of this cacophony and on to the next stage of the mission.

'And you know what to do?' Isles continued.

Riley nodded. 'I got it in my noggin, Agent. Bluff and bluster is all we need.'

'Yeah, and a smile from Lady Luck.' Isles sighed. 'You know, kid, this isn't how I saw my life going. I thought maybe a pretty girl. A couple of kids. Promotion. All that stuff. But here I am in a pigsty about to take on some kind of quantum magician.'

'The Forever Man,' said Riley. 'Or so he calls himself.'

'The Forever Man. That's quite a title.' Isles shook his head. 'There ain't no way we're coming out of this unscathed. You know that, don't you?'

'I do right enough,' said Riley. 'But Chevie is waiting. And we two have a history of rescuing one another.'

'You, kid, would make a good junior agent,' said Isles.

'And you, Agent Isles,' said Riley, 'would make for a terrible magician's assistant, as it would be the devil of a job fitting a lummox like you in a box for to be sawn in half.'

It was perhaps unwise for the pair to be chatting, however low their voices, for the men of Mandrake's militia were on high alert, with ears pricked for anything out of the ordinary, so far as anything could be considered ordinary on this day of days when hell itself would be forever banished, or so they thought. Either Riley or Isles may have spoken loudly enough to be heard over the pigs' raucous bashings and snufflings, for a voice suddenly came from the left of the piggery. A smug nasal voice that said the following: 'How now and by Jupiter. Egad and zounds. See what wallows with the pigs, Ben. Aren't we the fine fellows altogether to be bringing home the bacon?'

Isles and Riley had been spotted by two fellows of the militia sent to patrol the shadowy spots. The one who had spoken was small of stature and big of mouth, clothed in a Roundhead three-barred helmet and breastplate, while his partner was a rotund gent in faded Royalist finery, which proved that a man could not be fussy with regards to his uniform in these hard times. Both men held muskets that were primed and pointed directly at Isles and Riley. At such close range it was unlikely that either would miss their target.

The small man spoke again. 'Raise yourselves up now, my fine fellows. And let us all march peaceably to the square. And best beware, devils. Good Master Ben here can shoot the bobtail off a rabbit at a hundred paces, so he won't have no trouble with your carcass, Isles. And this here musket saw me through the war without a single misfire nor wide shot. So go easy and it will go easy, as it were.'

Isles whispered to Riley, 'Listen to this guy. He talks too much.'

Which was a touch ironic, since *talking too much* was what had landed them in dire straits in the first place.

Riley's only reply was a curt nod. And the nod communicated to Isles that his young companion was ready to do what needed to be done.

The man Ben spoke next, and it was immediately apparent that he was the more taciturn of the pair.

'Stand or I fire,' he said.

The interlopers stood, mud and dung dripping from their clothing.

'Raise your mitts in the aspect of surrender,' ordered the Roundhead.

'I like Ben,' said Fairbrother Isles.

'Very well,' said Riley. 'Then perhaps you should introduce yourself.'

Isles clenched his fists. 'Yeah, perhaps I should.'

'Silence!' ordered Roundhead. 'I do not like your tone. It is not appropriately fearful for such a situation.'

'Aye,' said Ben. 'Usually we gets tears and begging and suchlike.'

Isles spoke seriously to Riley. 'Remember what I said. No killing innocent civilians, even if these two are technically not innocent and in the militia to boot, so not civilians either.'

'I understand, Agent,' said Riley. 'But I trust they can be knocked from consciousness.'

'Oh yes,' said Isles. 'Absolutely.'

With that Riley's hand flickered downward and there was a bright flash and a puff of smoke. When it cleared the two prisoners were prisoners no more; they had disappeared.

'Ye gods,' said Roundhead, blinking the glare from his eyes.

Ben said nothing as he was already unconscious.

15

OLAF THE BOAR

For all intents and purposes the town of Mandrake's Groan in the county of Huntingdonshire was now the centre of the universe. If the inter-dimension's various creatures were to be deposited on earth, it would only be a matter of time before the world's energy was depleted and the quantum foam would attach itself to stardust and be carried to other planets, and the entire galaxy would soon be just as barren as twentieth-century scientists believed it to be.

This catastrophic collision of dimensions had occurred on one previous occasion, when the sophisticated minds of Atlantis had succeeded in opening a pinhole to the inter-dimension. However, the hole proved more than large enough to admit a flood of omnivorous worms that succeeded in devouring every living thing on the island before turning their attention to the island itself, gnawing it to the very stump of its volcanic toadstool and destroying its civilization in all but the mustiest books of legend.

Garrick knew that the results of his meddling with the rift would be disastrous for humanity, and for the wormhole too, but then its power would be greatly diluted and it would no longer have a claim on his body or soul.

King Albert, he thought. *Or Emperor Albert.*

In a way he would transcend all titles, for there would be none to be his equal besides God himself.

And why, Alby, why do you do this? Why not simply take your revenge on the boy and his FBI friend?

Because the wormhole would have him eventually, unless he could eviscerate it first. Now was the time when it was weak and vulnerable, its belly sagging like the gut of a rotten fish. Then, when it took the girl, the silver in her gullet would rupture it entirely.

And never again shall it have dominion over Albert Garrick. In fact, Albert Garrick shall have dominion over the world.

The wormhole was the only thing in existence that Albert Garrick feared; the rest was mere pettiness. There were small victories and irritations, but always with the wormhole tugging at his person, waiting for the chance to snatch him. And, though Garrick was strong, he thought that were he to enter that quantum ocean once again it would penetrate his very soul.

And change me accordingly.

Garrick had the awareness to know that the creature that resided in his soul as a result of his life's work was truly an abomination. On that last tumble with Riley and Miss Chevron in the wormhole he had been given a glimpse of his own twisted soul: a cold-blooded leprous creature, which slithered in the dirt where it belonged. All scales and hissing, it was. All milky eyes and boils. It made him shudder to think of him, Albert Garrick, becoming that thing.

'Never shall it take Albert Garrick,' he said now. 'This I vow.'

Garrick felt a sudden tugging at his innards and a faraway roar in his ears, which reminded him of conch shells at the seaside, and he felt himself levitate from the flagstone on which he sat. He knew that soon the rift would have grown so large and its force would be so strong that he would be sucked up entirely, weighed down by silver though he was.

Now is your time, Alby, he realized. *The moment has come.*

He stood to face the people of Mandrake.

This is the greatest role you shall ever play, Albert Garrick, he thought. *Saviour of the world.*

Chevie drooped weakly from the stake, supported only by her bonds. She had always been a fighter, but now it seemed that all her gumption had been drained out of her by the notion of the terrible Devil's Brew, which she would shortly be force-fed. Chevie knew that she was going to die that night. She knew it because she could see no way out – after all, Garrick was invulnerable as far as she could tell – but also she knew it because her life was flashing before her eyes. And that was the sign, wasn't it? Just before you die all the major events in your life clamour to make themselves seen. And so, in her state of mental and physical exhaustion, dehydration and extreme hunger, Chevie's life played out in her mind's eye like the trailer for a movie that could have been really good but blew it with a sad ending.

Chevie was surprised to find that she could remember her mother's beautiful brown face in perfect detail.

'Mom,' she whispered, and the word was like dust in her dry mouth. 'Mom.'

Her mother had been killed by a black bear in La Verne. Big joke, right? A Native American killed at a campsite by a bear. And then her father was lost to her in a motorcycle accident.

Losing one parent is unfortunate, but losing two is just careless.

A tough guy in her first foster home had thrown that in her face at dinner and she in return had thrown her dinner in his face, which was poetic justice at least, but still got Chevie moved along to the next home.

After that first move came a series of foster homes where she had never seemed to fit in or make a meaningful connection. Sure, there had been a couple of friends along the way, but Chevie saw now, in a flash of self-awareness that would have made her school counsellor proud, that she was afraid to make good friends because she couldn't stand to lose someone else. Chevie hadn't felt truly at home until the FBI had recruited her for their juvenile consultant programme and she had got to work out her aggression on firing ranges and assault courses. She had reckoned that it was OK to bond with other consultants on a professional level. She had even dated one guy a couple of times. There wasn't much of a spark, but at least Chevie felt she was inching towards a time when she would be able to hold down a real relationship.

Then came the WARP programme, and Riley. In spite of all the other seismic events that had shaken her life to the core since then, it was Riley who shone the brightest in her mind, because the wormhole had connected them somehow. They both knew that a shared happiness could be theirs.

And now Garrick was about to snatch that away from them, and probably devastate the planet in the process.

Chevie's daydream was interrupted by the clink of her silver chains as the wormhole drew closer and tried to literally draw her into the sky.

The time has come, she realized, feeling the links cut into her shoulders. *Garrick's moment is here and my time is up.*

And she wished two contradictory wishes simultaneously. The first was:

Riley, my only true friend. Come and deliver me from this evil.

And the contradiction:

Riley, my sweet boy. Get away, far away from here. Or he will kill you too.

And Chevie could not honestly tell which wish she would prefer to come true.

Garrick settled his cloak round his shoulders and patted the silver at his neck, wrists and belt, as he did habitually dozens of times each day to ensure the protective jewelleries had not somehow been magicked away. The cold touch of the metal comforted him in a way that nothing on earth had for a long while.

Tomorrow, he told himself, *I will have no need of silver.*

He stood in the square of Mandrake's Groan with the residents ranged before him, the zealots to the front, their eyes red with eagerness and the reflected crimson of the quantum rift, which they believed to be the gates of hell. The sensible stood back, close to the walls of their modest houses or shop fronts. The children of course were eager to be in the square itself – they would be poking the witch with sticks if given leave – but their mothers held them close and tight enough to stifle their breath, for there was not one woman in this place who was not in mortal fear of the Witchfinder and his accusations. And who would dare challenge him with the gates to hell yawning overhead?

Who indeed would dare accuse me? thought Garrick. *Except perhaps Miss Savano, but conveniently she is a witch and has no right to speak here.*

Garrick waved a dismissive hand at the militiamen who guarded Chevie.

'Move ye back. All must bear witness to the events of this day.'

The men moved aside so that Garrick was visible to all. Even the jail and almshouse had disgorged their residents on to the main street so that all could behold the Witchfinder's glorious achievement.

Garrick had adopted his speechifying pose: legs manfully apart and hands on hips, when Jeronimo Woulfe stepped forward.

'Master Witchfinder, I feel it most imprudent to gather for ceremonies when danger hovers above. We must be gone from this place and seek refuge to the south.' This suggestion sent murmurs rippling through the good folk of Mandrake. After all, it was a fool indeed who courted the devil's wrath.

But Woulfe was not finished. He had some imagery up his

240

sleeve. 'At this moment, good Master Garrick, we are as ants in a boar pit waiting for the boar to fall on our poor heads. Tell me why we should not at least remove the womenfolk and children?'

It was an easy argument for Garrick to refute. 'Refuge, you say? To the south, says you, Master Woulfe? Be my guest, says I, but know this: the fens are crawling with abominations and they converge on this town where their mistress is held captive. Anyone setting a single toe outside the border of Mandrake's wall will surely be consumed or, worse, infected.' Here Garrick's tone became threatening. 'And any person suspected of infection must of course be tried.'

Almost as one, the townsfolk reared back and a tumult of shrieks and terrified roars issued forth from the crowd.

For a moment Garrick was impressed by his own powers of oration, then he apprehended that the horror was directed not at him but rather above.

The rift, he realized. *Something has issued forth*.

Garrick whirled, his cloak whipping round with the speed of the turning and his silver-buckled hat toppling from his head, and he saw descending a formation of dark flecks that clung together initially, then ranged apart and grew larger as they fell.

Diverse creatures, he thought, squinting for details.

The rift belched forth another flock of creatures, one large enough to be distinguished as a tusked boar of mammoth proportions.

Jeronimo Woulfe is to blame for that, thought Garrick, *with his talk of boars*.

The creatures separated, most being sucked immediately back inside the rift like minnows dragged along with the undertow, but a few seemed to be on course for the town itself, including the giant boar.

Garrick pointed a rigid finger at it. 'Now what say you, Jeronimo Woulfe? Are you for leaving now? By all means, take your family and go. Or stay by my side and watch your Witchfinder defend the faithful.'

He then turned to the militia. 'Form a ring round the witch and, no matter what manner of creature drops from the sky, be certain that nothing gets close to the girl, or you will answer to me for it.'

Garrick had no choice but to deal with what the wormhole threw at him. However, he would not allow Riley to take advantage of his distraction.

Garrick was in two minds about the descending creatures. He had little time for these distractions, with the rift growing in power, but to defeat this monster in full view of everyone would be the ultimate proof of his own strength.

Down came the boar, howling all the way, its proportions that of a fully grown elephant, a fact only Garrick and Chevie would appreciate, and with horrifying swiftness it crashed into the chapel, sending masonry and lumber flying and spinning. For a moment all hoped that the creature was dead but Garrick knew better. He could see its aura shrugging away the impact, and he set off running in its direction before the creature could regain its senses.

Off went every musket, and the watch and the militia

peppered the dazed beast with their lead shot, but the projectiles bounced like pebbles from its hide.

'Desist! In the name of God!' shouted Garrick to the men as he ran. 'Do you wish to hamper my efforts?'

The shaggy boar rose, masonry dropping in chunks from its coarse hair, and Garrick could see through the creature to the man it used to be. It was there standing like a ghost inside its host: a hugely muscled warrior in a full-face helmet, wielding an axe.

A Viking, or the like. Olaf was his name. I feel it.

'Olaf,' he called. 'Steady now.'

The boar was in no mood for *Steady now*. He kicked his hooves free of the rubble and attacked, his thundering run shaking the very ground, and Garrick thought, *This will be a sight for the cheap seats. This ain't one bit boring.*

The boar opened its maw and roared, '*Jag kommer att doda dig!*'

Which Garrick rightly interpreted as a crazed death threat and not an invitation for tea with the queen. He steeled himself for the impact, knowing it was going to smart quite a lot before his quantum foam fizzed and rushed to make him whole.

I will endeavour to grasp the tusks, he resolved. *And then suck this savage dry, just as I did with the giant squid. And there won't be a soul in this town who will dare speak of quitting the place.*

Garrick laughed then for, even in a life as extraordinary as his, to fight giant squids and boars was undeniably a distraction from the humdrum day-to-day dreariness of existence.

For him nothing else existed but the moment. He was child-like in his investment in the now. Immortal he may well have been, but Albert Garrick was no lover of physical excruciation and would appreciate a few less broken bones or ruptured organs on this outing.

Olaf the boar charged and the folk of Mandrake howled and fled his path, all except the brave, stupid or petrified. Jeronimo Woulfe gathered his lovely Lizzie under one arm and his dear wife, Anne, under the other and shepherded them inside his house, then took down the musket above the mantel, which he had vowed never to use again unless his ladies were in peril.

And they were in dire peril now.

Woulfe's musket was long barrelled and rifled, and Pointer was fortunate that Woulfe did not have it with him while on the wall. It had the range to put a leaden ball in his haunch, and Woulfe had an eye for shooting too, having served his time in the militia. He'd never had occasion to wound a man, but he had once knocked the helmet from a renegade Roundhead who'd tried to scale the wall. And he *had* been aiming for the helmet.

'Dearest wife and treasured daughter,' he said to his family, 'stay ye both inside our home and see to your prayers. I will defend the door to my last breath.'

Good Anna clung to her husband. 'Jeronimo. Stay with us, in the name of heaven, for surely this is Judgement Day and God will spare the faithful.'

The mason's face was uncommonly hard and his eyes slits

of flint. 'This be not God's doing, I do think. There are other forces at work here.'

The house trembled as the giant boar thundered past, shaking their walls with his mighty blunderings.

'Oh, will you stay with us, Father?' begged Lizzie, who loved her father dearly and would not see him outdoors with these creatures, though in her heart she feared the Witchfinder more than the beasts from hell.

Woulfe pulled away from his wife gently. 'Lock the door,' he said. 'Admit no one but me.' He paused to make sure he was understood. 'No one. Church nor state. For I believe everything is not what it seems on this weird night.'

And with that Woulfe was gone into Mandrake's thoroughfare, firmly pulling the door behind him. His wife and daughter wept bitter tears at the idea that never again would they feel his loving embrace, for surely no mere man could survive the madness of the open air.

Albert Garrick snarled at Olaf in response to the boar's own snarl; Garrick planted his boots solidly in the earth, all the better to meet the creature's charge. The thoroughfare vibrated with each drumroll of his enormous hooves. Garrick was possibly the only man alive who would not quake with fear at being run down by such a creature.

Truth be told, he felt a little giddy at the prospect of the coming tussle. In the case of the giant squid there had been little time for preparations or decisions, but now he had several moments before impact and really he didn't have time for these shenanigans. His place was by the silversmith, who would doubtless bolt given half the chance.

As it happened, what seemed inevitable turned out to be avoidable, as another shape fell howling from the sky, landing square on the Viking boar, the impact instantaneously excavating a crater in Mandrake's main thoroughfare. Mud and shale flew in great jetting plumes into the sky.

Both are dead surely, thought Garrick, even as all around him wailed and shrieked.

He stepped forward and peeked into the pit. The boar was dazed but recovering, and there was also a humanoid figure of massive proportions, clad only in a loincloth and a strange crystal helmet, laying about the boar with a short sword made of the same transparent crystal.

Garrick stared at the man, using his gift of *rift sight* to divine what class of creature this thing was. He discovered, to his shock, that the giant man had come through the wormhole unchanged from some other reality.

One such as him could challenge my reign, he realized, and resolved on the spot to put his own plan into motion there and then.

No more time for dallying.

Garrick turned from the otherworldly conflict to the men of the watch on the walls. 'Cannon!' he roared. 'Destroy these abominations.'

Here now was something the men understood in this day of confusions. Unprecedented it might be to fire shot into the town, and yet it seemed the sensible, even prudent, option to pursue.

Only two of the guns, the north and the south, had lines of sight along the main street, the east and west guns being obscured by the remains of the chapel and a row of dwellings. But north and south were primed on well-greased carriages and it took a matter of seconds for the small crews to swivel their guns, captains shouting encouragement, but even then they looked once more to the Witchfinder for confirmation of his command.

'Fire, damn your eyes,' said Garrick, running down the thoroughfare towards the town square. 'Fire.'

The chief gunners made their final adjustments, then ordered their sparks to set embers to the touch holes, and seconds later the smooth-bore cannons spewed forth dragon's breath and their deadly projectiles, which could hardly fail to miss their targets at such short range, unless the bombardiers be total duffers, which they were not, both having served with the Parliament forces in the civil war. The recoil, however, proved more powerful than anticipated and the north cannon reversed off the wall entirely into the fens, while the south crushed the life from an unfortunate powder monkey who had forgotten to step aside.

The cannonballs sped faster than eyes could follow and threw up a further spume of mud from the crater, but on this occasion there was blood and bone in the spume, and crystal too. The dust and smoke dissipated with the echoes of cannon fire, but the particles did not. They hung suspended in the air: large sections of trunk and limb, mingled with eyeballs and rows of teeth – all that was left of the deci- mated combatants. And the people of Mandrake watched, for how could they not, so horrible and unprecedented was the sight?

Even Albert Garrick could not help but raise an eyebrow, but his bemusement turned to resolve once the lumps of bone and gristle ceased hovering and instead sped to the mouth of the rift, which loomed large now, fiery lips crackling. Garrick felt his own person rise so that his heels barely scuffed the earth as he ran.

She would have me now if not for the silver.

The moment had come for his ploy.

Mandrake was spared more attacks by the wormhole's inhalation of those creatures, but the residents were more than willing to do whatever Garrick ordered at this point, for was it not clear that their town was under attack from hell itself? And all because of this witch.

Garrick mounted the stone dais in the town square, keeping towards the edge and away from Chevie in case her Timekey activated and sucked him to his doom. Already he could see its electronic lights twinkling and he knew that she must drink the molten silver now before the wormhole ripped her right out of the chains.

'Silversmith!' he roared, beckoning with his crab-leg fingers. 'Now is your moment. Bring the Devil's Brew!'

The silversmith, Master Baldwin Sherry, felt his stomach churn with even more acidic violence than it had when the creatures fell from the sky. He had always believed his trade an honourable one and occasionally sacred. Now, though the Witchfinder had told him what he must do, and though he believed the rightness of it, he hated this perversion of his art and wished cravenly that the blacksmith could have taken his place at the smelter. But silver was a delicate metal and must be handled properly, and Mandrake's blacksmith could barely nail on a horseshoe without hobbling the poor beast, so it was Baldwin Sherry's duty to God and county to force down his misgivings and prepare the so-named Devil's Brew as commanded. He swabbed his glistening scalp with a work rag and tilted the smelter on its trundle to check the viscosity.

The crucible sat atop a small furnace, which had been moved in its entirety from Sherry's workshop, and the fire burned bright – or *merrily*, as the silversmith generally thought of it. But not today. He imagined that after today he might never think of the furnace flames as *merry* ever again. In fact, he might even go so far as to seek out a new profession. It occurred to him that as a thatcher or the like he might have less occasion to be called upon to execute witches.

All that remained was for Sherry to carry the heated crucible, using long-handled tongs of his own construction, and pour the molten silver down the witch's throat. The crucible was in the shape of a squat vase but would serve perfectly to pour silver into the girl's mouth, as though made for the job. Baldwin Sherry had heard that once upon a time there were moulds made specifically for this job. Not moulds really, but *containers*, as it were, but he had never foreseen the need for one.

The silversmith peered again into the crucible and saw a shining bubble pop. Previously that sight had never failed to cheer him and remind him of his good fortune in these harsh times; now, however, all he saw in the pot was hissing death.

Sherry felt almost stupefied by the gleaming molten silver.

Could he do this deed?

Should he?

Sherry felt his forearms break out in goose pimples in spite of the long leather gloves that covered them, and he turned to find Master Garrick's eyes upon him, the Witchfinder's veins clear in his milk-white face.

'Bring the silver,' said Garrick in a voice of cold thunder that would not stand for hesitation, never mind defiance. 'This witch has a mighty thirst.'

Heaven help me, thought Sherry, and said, 'It is almost there, Master Witchfinder. One minute more and the brew will be ready for pouring.'

Albert Garrick had orchestrated some feats in his days as the Great Lombardi. And though most tricks were simple when you stripped back the layers and got right down to the nub, as it were, some required delicate timing or wires, pulleys, smoke and mirrors, contortion, escapism and showmanship to sell them successfully to Johnny Punter. But, no matter how well thought out his plans, there was often the blasted unexpected intrusion, which Garrick referred to as *earthly intervention*, which could set his stratagems toppling like dominoes. A sharp-eyed punter perhaps, or a competitor catcalling in the stalls, or some other interference that could set the trick on its ear.

And here he was smack bang in the middle of the most

complicated illusion he had ever attempted. He'd set himself up as some fashion of holy man and convinced good people to murder a mere girl and all the while cobbled together a plot to save himself from the wormhole, which he had sold to the bumpkins as the gates of hell.

It was a pity that Riley was not here to witness this latest and final trick, a great pity indeed, but very soon there would be nowhere on earth for Riley to survive. If indeed he survived at all, which Garrick fervently hoped he would, due to the quantum foam in his bones.

Perhaps he will live on as some form of twisted ghoul, Garrick thought maliciously. *Then I may keep him on a leash as a pet. He can be my familiar.*

This notion almost made him laugh aloud, but that would be unseemly at this moment, and he would not allow any unprofessionalism in his performance.

After all, what does a man have if not his art?

He glanced up and saw the rift loom overhead, casting its crimson light laced with orange sparks like dancing fairies. And he could feel the same sparks dancing in his own self and knew that, silver or not, the wormhole would have him at any moment.

It wants me too, thought Garrick. *I can feel it. But you shall not have Albert Garrick, you damned creature. Albert Garrick shall put an end to you. Whatever the cost to mankind.*

'Now, Master Sherry,' he called to the silversmith, while the townsfolk watched, stunned into silence by the recent battle of god-like creatures and the crater in their thoroughfare. 'Ready the brew. Master Cryer, at your post.'

Godfrey Cryer stood at Chevie's side, his hand poised by the Timekey, its lights blinking agitatedly now, waiting for activation.

'I am at the ready, master,' he said with a shake in his voice, which was due not to any anxiety but to zealousness, convinced as he was that the name of Godfrey Cryer was on the verge of immortalization. By this hour on the morrow his name would be on as many lips as Cromwell's own.

'Excellent, Constable,' said Garrick. 'Apply the tongs.'

Cryer was happy to oblige. The tongs in question were a pair of square-bit tongs, which were usually employed to grip horseshoes while the smith hammered them, but on this occasion they would be used to force apart the witch's teeth while the silversmith did his pouring. There was a part of Cryer's being that quailed at performing such a barbaric act on a mere strip of a girl, but this part was small and timid and easily subjugated by his righteousness and vanity.

And so he said, 'Yes, master. The tongs, at once.'

As he lifted the heavy implement, which would surely crack the witch's teeth, if not her jaw also, there were cries of shock and horror from the townsfolk who watched from their windows or doors. Even if there had been revolution in the square, the militia was easily a match for anyone who might decide to take issue with the proceedings. Cryer had instructed no fewer than three of the surliest soldiers to keep a direct eye on Jeronimo Woulfe, who had always and ever been the biggest splinter in Cryer's thumb.

Cryer raised the heavy tongs, testing their action by opening and closing the flat flanges before the witch's face.

'Confess,' he hissed. 'Confess, witch, and at least heaven will claim you.'

Chevie knew that there was no point in trying to reason with this moron, but try she did.

'Not heaven, Cryer,' she said. 'You are bringing hell down on us all.'

Her words made no impression on the constable, as she had known they would not. 'A witch to the end,' he said, pressing the tongs to her lips.

'Ready the silver, smith,' he called to Baldwin Sherry.

Sherry peered into the crucible, watching the last lumps of cutlery dissolve and the level of silver rise. As the smith worked, Garrick addressed the crowd, which was not congregated before the stage as was normal but scattered behind walls or piles of goods, as though there was any escaping what was about to happen.

'Now, good people of Mandrake's Groan, bear witness to what happens here today. The greatest feat ever performed will take place before your disbelieving eyes. This ain't no common feat of magic, no trickery, no mere illusion. I, Albert Garrick, will change the world forever, here and now. And the name of this common-as-muck town will be scorched for evermore into the scrolls of history. So bring forth your children and your womenfolk and bear witness to the miracle of Albert Garrick.'

Slowly they came, shuffling out from houses and shops, taverns and even the almshouse. It was obvious that these good people did not wish to witness any miracles today, especially ones that involved giant slashes of fire in the sky and pouring molten silver down the gullets of young women, witches or no.

With them came Fairbrother Isles, stumbling forward as a militiaman prodded him with the barrel of his musket.

'I have him,' called the man, voice muffled through the face guard of his Roundhead helmet. 'I have Isles, but not the familiar.' They came forward, closer to the dais. 'In with the pigs he was. Can you believe it, master?'

Garrick squinted at the pair. There was no aura about the FBI agent, as the wormhole had not changed him, but it was Isles right enough, carrying a small chest, his face bloodied and beaten, eyes downcast, and the fellow behind him all swagger and cocksure.

A pity not to have Riley, he thought. *But the pot's half full, as it were*.

Still, prudence at all times.

'Search the African,' he commanded. 'And bring that chest to me.'

The helmeted militiaman gave Isles a hefty boot to the rear end, sending him stumbling forward.

Another command from Garrick: 'Watch the shadows. The familiar will be drawn to his mistress in these final moments. So ready your pikes.'

Four men of the militia pounced on Isles, pinning him firmly to the ground. He was a gent of considerable heft and it took the full weight of the four to hold him down. A further two were needed to tear the chest from his hands.

Isles howled when they took the box. 'Noooo! No, you

fools! That chest is the only chance for any of us. Don't let him touch it. Don't touch it, Garrick, you animal.'

The rift pulsed overhead. Ever lower. A sound like the pounding of the surf against a cliff face emanated from its raw scar of a mouth.

Silver, thought Garrick. *Rift. Chest. Organize yourself, Alby. Juggle those balls.*

'Bring it here,' he ordered. 'Bring the chest.' Then to Sherry: 'And, you, be about your business. Pour the brew.'

'No!' repeated Isles, dust puffing from the corner of his mouth. 'No. He will kill us all.'

'Bring it to me!' shouted Garrick, and then to Cryer, 'Prise open the witch's mouth.'

The militiaman who had captured Isles held back and bided his time, waiting for the perfect moment when all the crises would overlap.

The silversmith then lifted the crucible by its handles and walked slowly towards Chevie, careful not to spill a drop.

'Good,' said Garrick. 'Good.'

That was under way, now for this chest.

The box was deposited at Garrick's feet and even as he bent towards the simple clasp it occurred to him that there was no reason to open it.

And no reason not to.

But why take the risk when he was so close to banishing forever the hated tunnel?

Why indeed?

So he stayed there in a curious crooked posture,

considering, until finally he decided. *Destroy the wormhole and then consider the chest*.

The Witchfinder was moving his fingers back from the clasp when suddenly he was under attack.

'You shall not open that box, demon,' said Riley, for of course it was he behind the Roundhead faceplate and he would have emerged from hiding sooner had not fiddling with his armour taken time. In his hand was a large revolver, not of this age, which commenced spitting bullets at Garrick. Four bullets he fired and each one struck home, catching Garrick in the shoulders, chest and knee.

The pain was excruciating and Garrick howled with rage and annoyance as he sank to the ground, wounded but not mortally so. Barely a trickle of blood issued from each wound and he had grown so powerful now that the pain faded within seconds.

'Why do you persist in interfering, boy?' he said, seething with rage. 'After all I have done. I might have let you live.'

Riley, though, was not looking at Garrick but at Chevie.

'I am sorry, Chevie,' he said simply, and pointed the gun at her.

Chevie nodded. He had saved the last bullet for her and she was glad of it. A quick death at least.

But it was not to be, for Riley was felled by a gunshot that knocked him on his side and set his own gun skittering out of reach.

'I am sorry, Chevie,' he said, blood leaking from his mouth. 'Forgive me.'

'Riley!' screamed Chevie, vainly struggling against her silver bonds. 'Riley!'

'Hah!' said Cryer, waving the tongs in the air as though they were a trophy. 'The familiar is vanquished.'

Chevie swung her head towards Cryer, attempting to butt or bite him, but the constable dropped the tongs and moved to help his master.

'Witchfinder,' he said, kneeling at Garrick's side. 'Praise God, you are alive.'

One of the bullets had worked its way up Garrick's oesophagus and he spat it out. 'I have divine protection,' he said, grateful for the quantum foam that had already healed his innards. 'Our mission continues. See to it, Master Constable.'

'Of course,' said Cryer. 'But the chest. Surely we must see what the familiar was attempting to hide.' And his fingers reached out towards the clasp.

Time froze for Garrick then, and he saw it all. Riley on the ground before him, gaze intense, eyes on the chest. Blood in his mouth, yes, but what better lad to concoct himself a blood pellet? And the shot that felled him? Who had made such a shot? Was not every load spent on the boar creature? Garrick himself had taught Riley to make squibs. A trick, then. But why? So that he might spare his beloved a cruel death? But that could have been done from a distance and with the first shot, rather than waste four precious rounds on Garrick, who could not die. And, if a fellow did not want a chest opened by another fellow, why lay it at the feet of that other fellow?

Unless it be a trap of some sort. A parcel of dodgy goods.
Dodgy goods sold by the death of the pedlar.

Garrick attempted to lunge at Cryer, to kill him if need be in order to stop him from opening the chest, but he was not properly healed and air still whistled through his punctured chest. His breath felt etherized and he could see his hands before him moving as though through molasses.

Cryer, the bone-headed fool, had the clasp flipped in a trice and, says he, all triumphant: 'Now we shall see what manner of witchcraft –'

Then he stopped, for his face was lit by a golden glow and his expression was all puzzlement. 'I don't . . .' he said, and then again: 'I don't.'

Garrick's face drew level with the constable's and every ounce of his good sense could not stop him from peering into the wooden box to see what it was that so perplexed Cryer – though it would not take much to puzzle such a dolt.

Inside the box was something that Garrick could never have imagined.

In the lid was a bisected coil of copper wire and a battery. And in the chest itself the rest of the coil, which had broken its connection as soon as Cryer had flipped the lid.

Also inside the box there was a ghost.

16

DARK MATTER

Squashed and transparent atop the lower copper wires was a ghost, and the ghost spoke to Garrick.

'Albert Garrick, you killed my son.'

Garrick's instinct was bemusement, but this faded when the ghost darted from the chest and into Garrick himself. It was inside him, like a butterfly fluttering inside his ribcage.

'Master?' he heard Cryer say, as though rousing him from sleep. 'Master?'

But Garrick was beyond rational response. He rose and backed away, slapping at his chest, then punching his own head as the ghost invaded his brain. He felt as though he were in the tunnel once more, or rather the tunnel were inside him.

Bees, he thought. *I am as a swarm of bees*.

'Begone! Begone!' he cried, which made for perplexing viewing: a man of stature punching his own head and crying *Begone*. The ghost had moved with such flashing speed that none but Garrick had seen it, and so to others he seemed no more than the common horse-kicked zany.

Inside Garrick's spasming frame, the spirit of Charles Smart worked quickly. Even though the silver protected Garrick from inter-dimensional traction for the moment, it was possible that he might realize what was happening to him and marshal his quantum antibodies to reject the visitor. Smart expanded until he occupied every atom of Garrick's being and then he sucked, inhaling and absorbing the quantum foam, which squatted like a parasite on the strands of Garrick's DNA. To the outside world it seemed as though the Witchfinder were performing some class of demented Irish jig as he skipped and pirouetted around the stake to which Chevie was tethered.

Charles Smart's labours inside Garrick did not last long; the moment he had absorbed all the Witchfinder's particles into himself, he surrendered entirely to the inter-dimension's pull, which was too powerful to be dissipated by mere silver. The spirit of Professor Charles Smart left Garrick's body and sped upward. And, where Smart had once been orange, now he glowed bright gold. Brighter than the summer sun, as many of Mandrake's men would swear in the Huntings over the years. Like a golden missile Smart flew, and there was no fear in him, for in his mind he was putting right what he had put wrong in another time and in a different state, when he had been of unsound mind and solid matter.

Now he was pure quantum foam, or *dark matter* as scientists would eventually come to know it. With Garrick's quota of this exotic matter inside him, the professor had calculated that he was now composed of just enough energy to seal the rift. Or more accurately to *heal* it. For was he not the one who had injured the being in the first instance when he had poked holes in it with his accursed portals and emptied out all that incompatible energy?

But now, Charles Smart, you old duffer, you can make things right.

As he whizzed towards the yawning rift, Smart's final thought before he spread himself nano-wafer thin was that he wished he had been able to punish Albert Garrick more comprehensively for taking the life of his dear son. But he felt certain Riley would take care of that.

From the ground the healing process took the form of a sunburst explosion in the heart of the rift, which spread outward along the rent, sealing the edges with flurries of golden sparks. There was an accompanying sound that was like nothing ever heard on earth and so each person who heard it found it similar to something from their own experience. Some heard the pounding of rain on a canvas sail, while others heard the crackle of an enormous bonfire, and one small child even heard the soothing voice of her departed grandfather saying, 'There, there, my sweet Sue. There, there.'

Regardless of the differences in what the folk of Mandrake heard, what they saw was totally uniform. The golden shape that had flown into the air was spreading its balm across the gates of hell and wiping them from the night sky. Wherever the golden particles touched the fiery gates, they seemed to cancel each other out, leaving only the true and proper stars in their wake. The process was so wonderful that again people would come to differ in their opinions of how long it actually took.

Nevertheless, it was clear to all that the great rift in the sky had disappeared and the town was safe. Indeed, it could be said that the entire world had been saved. A collective sigh rose from the lips of the good people of Mandrake and any last stragglers left indoors rushed outside to marvel at a night sky that was as it had been for always and ever. The sigh became a cheer, which was strange to hear from the mouths of Puritans, but such was the level of relief and communal elation.

Mandrake was saved.

But who had saved it?

Riley spared barely a glance for the aerial wonders and picked himself up from the ground. He spat the remains of the blood capsule to the dirt, stooped to retrieve his revolver and charged ahead towards the still-bound Chevie, whose eyes darted from earth to sky with bewilderment. Something important had happened, of this much she was certain, but it was not clear whether or not she had been saved. The silversmith still bore his deadly crucible and Albert Garrick still drew breath, and it was a matter of course that if Garrick lived then he was intent on killing someone.

'Riley!' she called, straining against her bonds, sawing her shoulders back and forth until her torso gained some play. 'Riley!'

There was a new tone in her voice that Riley had not heard before; it was obvious to him that she wished him both to save her and to take the utmost care, for she could not bear to lose him.

Chevie feels as I do.

Perhaps he should take to referring to her as Miss Chevron, in the more formal manner of a suitor.

But later for all that. Now for liberating Chevie.

Riley thought as he ran: Garrick was always the most dangerous man in any situation, but at the moment he was on his knees, stricken senseless by Charles Smart's sacrifice.

Agent Isles had tried to talk the professor out of the idea, which he had called *the dumbest crock of stupid I've ever laid ears on.*

But the revenant of Charles Smart had not entertained debate: *Did you think the box was simply my bed, Fairbrother? I need to get close to Garrick without him seeing my aura. I am completely composed of dark matter and, with Garrick's to augment my own, it might just be enough to seal the rift.*

Isles had been close to tears. 'But you'll die, Prof. You will straight up die.'

In response, Smart had winked a sparkling wink. 'Yes, Fender my boy. But I will live again, and so will my son and so will Agent Pointer. As an upstanding man.'

And that was it.

Slam dunk.

No arguing with that one, and now Riley was dealing with the aftermath of Smart's ambush. It had been the boy's dearest wish that the spiritual intrusion would stop Garrick's heart outright, but apparently there was life in the old dog yet.

There were militiamen too to be dealt with, and watchmen, but Riley's sense was that these persons were rudderless without Garrick or Cryer to screech at them.

Cryer?

That cur would be at his most dangerous now that his power was slipping through his fingers.

Where was the scoundrel?

Riley saw that the constable had wrestled the crucible from the silversmith, who'd had a change of heart about murdering a girl no matter what the colour of her eyes, what with the gates of hell being clearly shut and all. And now Cryer was lurching towards the pyre, eager to finish his master's business.

One bullet left in my weapon, thought Riley. *And given a choice I'd spend it on Garrick.*

But there was no choice. As Garrick himself had often said: *Needs must, and life or death are needs indeed.* Which Riley had always found a bit of a corkscrew to repeat.

And so Riley, a crack shot since the age of twelve for the old bullet trick, stopped dead in his run and took careful aim. He was certain he could nail the jar at this distance and not make a murderer of himself, especially with such a sweet barker as this FBI pistol. All a chap had to do was aim a tad low and the bullet would fly true as Cupid's arrow to where it was intended.

He fired and the bullet pierced the mould, but, given that the crucible could withstand molten silver, it did not shatter as an ordinary urn might; instead it merely sprung a leak, forcing Cryer to hold the jar at arm's length but still the constable continued towards Chevie.

Riley cursed the man and vowed to tear the crucible from

his hands, but he had ground to cover and Garrick was rousing from his stupor and taking stock of the recent happenings.

Garrick's first glance was towards the sky and he saw that the rift had disappeared, which pleased him greatly, for with it had disappeared the wormhole's attraction for his person.

I am safe, he thought. *Albert Garrick has survived yet another dastardly attempt to destroy him.*

Garrick's second glance was at Riley. The boy was *mounting an offensive*, as he might have said in his army days in far-off Afghanistan. And he'd be damned if the boy was not charging his way.

A third glance, over his shoulder, confirmed to Albert Garrick what he had instantly suspected. Chevron Savano yet drew breath and here came her horseless cavalry riding in to save her.

If Garrick's first objective had been to banish the wormhole, which had somehow been achieved, had not his second been to murder the maid in front of her dearest friend?

And beloved now, if I am not mistaken. How much the sweeter?

Riley almost made it past Garrick to the pyre itself. He was a hair's breadth from success and probably would have succeeded had he been a shade lighter on his feet, which he would have been were it not for the heavy breastplate weighing him down. But, as it was, he was a shade heavier and that gave Garrick the second he needed to lunge sideways and snag Riley's boot heel with his fingers. It was not the firmest of touches but it was plenty to send the lad flailing on to the dais, with only the faceplate of his helmet saving his nose from flattening. Down he went with an *oof* and Garrick was after him, not yet the full shilling but recovering fast. He staggered to his feet just long enough to take two steps and fall on top of Riley, pinning the lad with his full weight.

'Do not trouble yourself with trickiness,' he said into the boy's ear. 'For was it not Albert Garrick who drummed those tricks into your noggin, son?'

Riley beat the stone dais with his fists. He was so close: the pyre was within reach. Could the fates be so cruel as to allow him this far and no further?

'Do your duty, Constable!' Garrick called to Cryer. 'Pour the Devil's Brew.'

Cryer did not require the telling. He was climbing the wooden steps to the top of the pyre, bringing himself level with Chevie's head. On any other day a match between these two would barely have been any competition at all, but now Chevie was bound from chest to toe, with none of her martial arts training at her disposal.

However, in spite of the direness of her straits and the whirlwind of worldly and, indeed, otherworldly events that had battered her emotions, Chevie felt a sudden resurgence in her natural energy. For the first time since exiting the wormhole near this very spot, the fugue and nausea that had dogged her suddenly evaporated and she found herself focused and motivated.

Riley was down. He needed help. And looky-looky who was coming at her with a jug of molten metal.

I guess if I can't play by the Queensberry Rules then I'll have to fight dirty, she thought. In the pause when Godfrey Cryer was considering how he would accomplish a two-man job on his lonesome, Chevie used every inch of the wiggle room she had struggled so hard for and every pound of force she could muster to headbutt Cryer on the bridge of his nose, snapping the bone and sending the constable stumbling backwards down to the dais, where he bashed his crown on the flagstones. So, two injuries — neither critical — but the crucible took a series of unfortunate bounces and dumped its remaining contents on the constable's face. And Cryer might have survived even that injury had not his mouth been gaping to cry out in pain.

Chevie winced and turned her face away as the silver melted the constable's flesh. His cry never made it past his throat, for the silver forced it back down. Godfrey Cryer expired without making a sound, apart from the hiss of steam jetting from his nostrils and ears.

Garrick watched this turn of events with a sense of disbelief and a twinge of amusement.

'Your young lady don't go easy,' he said to Riley, who struggled vainly underneath him. 'I'll say that for her. But nevertheless I have publicly proclaimed she is a witch and at the very least she must burn. At the very least, says I.'

Fairbrother Isles was used to being restrained and the men of the militia were more than accustomed to restraining him, for was not this the same Fairbrother Isles who threw a drunken fit once every full moon or so and built up a rage against the entire world such that nothing would calm him but a night in the stocks? Was this not that same individual who had been wrestled and booted and knocked about like a true dunderhead?

Yes, it was.

But then, also, it was not.

That Fairbrother Isles had been trying to drink his way out of depression born of centuries' worth of displacement, and in reality had never put up much resistance when the militiamen manhandled him into the jail or the stocks, unless they got a little free with their clubs and then Isles would throw in a jab to the kidneys or an elbow to the groin that seemed at the time like a lucky connection, but which were actually signs that his combat training was still lurking below the fuzzy, drunken surface.

This Fairbrother Isles, on the other hand, had full access to his combat training and his mind was crystal clear and focused. His primary mission had been achieved, i.e. to get the professor close enough to do his science thing. That being accomplished, Isles saw no earthly reason that he should lie placidly beneath these militia guys like some kind of bearskin rug, and so he gathered his arms and legs underneath him and exploded upward, scattering militiamen like bowling pins.

Secondary mission: locate and secure the release of FBI comrade Chevron Savano, currently being restrained by chains to a stake, having been accused of witchcraft.

I swear, thought Fairbrother, *there surely never was a time zone crazier than this one.*

Chevie was at his two o'clock, and Isles looked that way just in time to see her deliver the mother of all headbutts to that creep Cryer.

Ouch, he thought, and then he spotted some movement in his peripherals that told him he had better get his focus back on his own fight, for the militiamen had apparently not learned their lesson and were back for more.

'How now, good Master Isles,' said their captain, a potato-headed farmhand with the teeth of a man who liked a punch-up but let his guard down often. 'Know your place now, man. It's only home you're going, to the stocks for the night. Think yourself fortunate I don't throw in a flogging.'

Isles did not engage in conversation, nor did he vow dramatically that he would never be flogged again. He simply took the militiamen apart as a mechanic might take apart an old engine.

Isles wasn't as quick as he might have been a decade ago, but he knew more about incapacitating a human than almost anyone alive. The militiamen quickly realized that Isles was possessed by some kind of demon and the smartest thing to do would be to shoot him or run away. Since virtually every man jack in Mandrake's militia and watch had shot their musket balls into the giant boar, they were only left with pikes and swords and, as they quickly discovered, jabbing a blade towards Fairbrother Isles was tantamount to offering him the weapon on a velvet cushion, for no sooner was the pike or sword thrust forward than it was spun round and making the journey back. Isles did not kill anyone, but he striped a few shoulders and pierced a few buttocks, which was all it took to scatter the militia.

There were two likely lads with primed weapons who stood their ground, twin sons of Bartleby Primly, the richest merchant in Mandrake, who'd wanted his boys toughened up by serving with the militia but who'd also decided to flaunt his wealth a little by doubling up on their weapons. So, whereas your average militia member was lucky to have a musket younger than his own self, the Primly boys were armed not just with long-barrelled muskets but with French screw-barrel pistols, which their father had purchased in London at immense expense. These extraordinary pistols had three revolving chambers, each fitted with its own striker and sprint, or simply put: three shots per load.

Randall Primly had discharged his musket at the boar creature but had completely forgotten the screw-barrel, as had his brother Henry. Randall, though, now he remembered and called urgently to his twin: 'The Frenchies!'

'Egad, yes!' said Henry, and both boys drew their triple-shot weapons.

At this particular point, Isles was beating a militiaman with the flat of his own blade and knew nothing about the screw-barrel pistols until the first shot took him in the stomach and the second in the upper chest. He grunted twice but did not bleed, for he wore his FBI Kevlar, which had no trouble with seventeenth-century weapons of that calibre, but he still felt each strike like a hammer blow and was sent staggering backwards, his vision blurred and his legs turned to rubber.

Encouraged, the Primly boys advanced, firing again. One slug would have pierced Isles's kidney, and a second succeeded in worming its way between a strap and armhole, giving him a nasty flesh wound along his fifth rib. Big as he was, Isles went down as though struck by cannon-shot and lay winded on the thoroughfare, flailing helplessly.

Henry's third shot went wide of Isles's head, but Randall hesitated to fire his final lead ball.

'See here, brother. Hardly a drop of blood. His clothing is armoured perhaps.'

Henry discarded his own pistol, which had grown hot. 'Perhaps,' he agreed. 'But his head is not armoured.'

'No, indeed, brother,' said Randall, taking careful aim.

Just in the split second that the trigger was pulled, a brown blur streaked from the shadows and threw itself between Isles and the bullet. Pointer – for of course it was Isles's partner come in the nick of time to save his old friend – took a nasty graze to the ridge of bone above his left eye and spun away, whining in pain. The dog came to rest beside Fairbrother Isles, blood running back over his ears.

Isles turned himself over with some gargantuan effort and held his partner's head.

'Donnie, Donnie. What did you do, man? You took a bullet for me.'

Pointer's brown eyes focused on Isles with some effort. 'Well, you know. We're partners, buddy. It wasn't like I had a choice.'

Then the dog whined and the tension drained out of him, which was a sensation Isles had felt too often from wounded men he'd held in his arms over the years.

'Don't die, you stupid dog,' he said desperately, pulling Pointer close. 'You're all I got left. Don't die.'

Pointer licked Isles's face. 'I ain't dying, moron. It's a flesh wound. Concussion at worst. So I ain't dying but . . .' The hound's eyes lost their focus. 'But I think I'm going.'

And then those doggy eyes closed, and Isles was left wondering what his friend had meant by that final statement. He would find out soon enough, but first he needed to have a little heart-to-heart with the Primly twins.

'What kinda man,' he said, almost growling, 'what kinda man shoots a dog?'

But he was talking to himself. The twins heard about two syllables of that voice and made a simultaneous decision, as twins often do, to run away as fast as their legs would carry them.

Twenty feet away Albert Garrick shifted position, pinioning Riley beneath him with the palm and fingers of one hand cradling the boy's head, forcing it into the dirt, and one knee pressed hard into a nerve cluster on Riley's spine. This hold would do, he decided, while he figured an on-the-hoof strategy.

Kill the girl and Riley is the general thing, he thought. *Ideally the girl burns and Riley watches. But I do seem to be operating on my lonesome on account of the militia cowards fleeing. With the African down and the girl in chains, it is one on one. Man on boy. Perhaps it was always going to come down to this.*

Garrick turned Riley's head to make sure the boy could hear him. 'Do you remember your training, son? Do you remember our snatch-the-book game?'

Riley was in no mood for the remembering of games. 'Get off me, devil!' he shouted. 'Get away from Chevie.'

Garrick pressed harder with his knee. 'This is important, boy. This could save her life. Do you remember that little game?'

Riley nodded curtly. He did remember. When they had dwelled in the Orient Theatre, books had been Riley's only joy in life, as they transported him from the hell of being apprenticed to Albert Garrick. And, as a way to torture him further, Garrick would take whatever novel he happened to be favouring that week and place it on a small table on stage.

You can have your precious book, my son, he used to say. *All you need to do is come through me.*

So Riley, thus motivated, would charge his master over and over in an attempt to lose himself once more in the worlds of the penny dreadfuls or Sherlock Holmes. Initially Garrick rebuffed him almost casually, but with practice Riley's attempts became more skilful and sly, until eventually one day he did make it past his master, only to find nothing on the table. The book had been magically spirited away from where it was supposed to be. How Garrick had laughed at that. How his eyes had teared with merriment.

'That's all it is,' said Garrick now. 'A little game of snatch-the-book. And the title of this little book is *My Beloved Burns*.'

With that, Garrick punched Riley full in the ear, stunning and disorientating the boy.

'Better be nimble, son,' said Garrick, and suddenly his weight was gone from Riley's back.

17

SNATCH-THE-BOOK

Garrick strode briskly across the square towards the nearest oil lamp and lifted it down from its hook. In spite of all the falterings in this day, it seemed as though events would end on a positive note.

The witch and her familiar are dead. Hell has been banished. All hail the conquering Witchfinder.

But he was getting ahead of himself. The witch lived and the boy lived and they had overcome towering odds before.

So buck up, Alby, and do your celebrating after the show.

Half a dozen paces took him to the foot of the pyre, where he held the oil lamp aloft and projected his voice along Mandrake's thoroughfare. 'The gate of hell has been closed and to lock it forever all that needs doing is to burn the witch.'

If Garrick had been expecting a rousing cheer in reaction to his proclamation, then he was disappointed. The people of Mandrake had seen too many horrors and were dismayed at the thought of another. Yet none had the temerity to question Albert Garrick after all he had done.

To hell with all of you, thought Garrick. *After all, this is chiefly for my own amusement.*

And he hurled the lamp into the kindling at the base of the pyre.

'Burn, witch!' he said. 'Burn.'

Riley got to his feet and staggered like an ale-sot. His ears rang like cathedral bells and there was a hot rod of pain in his jaw. He chose his hands to focus on and stared at them until the knuckles and nails were clear in his vision. When the ringing in his ears faded somewhat, the first sound he heard was the dry crackle of flames.

Snatch-the-book, he thought.

Riley steadied himself. When his feet would obey their orders, he turned to find Albert Garrick limbering up for a set-to, and behind him Chevie still tied to the stake, where she seemed to have been forever.

'Come on, boy,' said Garrick, cracking his knuckles as though he were about to attempt a tricky concerto, and not burn an innocent lass. 'Let's be having some sport. You don't have all night.'

Riley, goaded and terrified, rushed into the battle like a rank amateur, hoping against hope that he could bowl the magician over and then . . .

And then what? Open those chains with your teeth?

But what choice did he have?

So Riley blundered in and Garrick swatted him aside simple as pie without hardly seeming to move.

'That was so stupid,' said Garrick. 'I expected a ruse, but it was just stupidity. I taught you better than that.'

Riley turned himself round, cursing his own foolishness.

Chevie would not be saved by blunderings. He must play it smart.

The flames took hold now in the kindling, spreading throughout the entire base of the pyre and reaching fiery fingers into the larger logs, which had been doused with oil and were eager to receive them.

Too quick, thought Riley. *Too quick*.

He attacked again, this time sliding in low, hoping for an upward strike against the inside of Garrick's thigh or knee, but his former master sidestepped like a matador, then, grasping Riley's collar, used the boy's own momentum to roll him back the way he had come.

'Slow, Riley son. You are oh so slow. And the flames are oh so quick.'

It was true. Riley knew that it would take him several minutes to fully shake off the blow to his head and by then it would be too late.

He appealed to the townsfolk for help.

'Will no one stop this madman?' he asked. 'Do we burn maidens in England now? Is that how far we have sunk?'

But there was no help forthcoming. The townsfolk dropped their eyes and turned their backs. Garrick had these people cowed and none would stand firm against him.

And there was Fairbrother Isles flat on his back beside his man-dog partner, Pointer, a pool of blood gathering around them, black in the lamplight. So no help from that quarter.

Or perhaps there might be, for Isles was rummaging in his pocket.

'Kid,' he said, and that was all. However, from his pocket

he drew forth something that flashed silver, and tossed it towards Riley.

A knife. Fairbrother's beloved whittling blade, with which he had built most of the field office; both Riley and Garrick recognized what class of implement was twinkling through the air at the same instant.

Now it was a race, for Riley would surely catch the blade and throw it at his target, which would be Garrick's heart. Garrick knew this; he himself had taught Riley to aim for the heart in such a situation. He also knew that Riley could hit a bullseye blindfolded from twenty paces with any sharp implement a person cared to mention, and, though the blade could not kill Garrick as far as he knew, it could certainly grant the boy a few moments' advantage to free his young lady friend, and this Garrick could not permit. So his part in the race was to move his heart to the right of where it currently was before the blade reached that point.

Riley caught the blade, and in one fluid movement turned and flung forward his hand, dropping to one knee as he had been taught. But there was no *thunk* of blade on bone nor *squelch* of knife through organ – and Garrick reckoned himself safe for the moment.

'Too slow again,' he gloated. 'You've forgotten your lessons, son.'

Not this one, Riley might have said, or: *I remembered the knife palm you forced me to practise all those years*.

But there was no time for banter, as the flames were rising and Chevie's face was a mask of terror. Riley could not stand to watch the fire burn her feet and calves, so he simply threw

Isles's knife, which he had not previously thrown but simply concealed in his palm. This time his target was not on the balls of his feet ready for the dodge but leaned to one side and woefully off balance.

Blast, thought Garrick. *I hate stabbings.*

He had been stabbed many times in his long life and it seemed as though each one hurt more keenly than the last. Although they had healed in mere seconds, Garrick swore he felt the diverse pains whenever the night was cold.

Today, however, he had barely the time to grit his teeth before the blade buried itself deep in his shoulder. Garrick had to admit the boy's aim was true — which was to his own credit, of course — before that particular sharp pain of a knife wound blasted like a white light through his brain and he could not hold in a yelp of pain, which he felt sure must have given Riley some satisfaction.

But still Garrick would not yield. He plucked the knife from his own shoulder, refusing through sheer willpower to sink to the ground. The pain was debilitating, certainly, but it would be brief and this game could still be played.

But the pain persisted and blood flowed from the wound. Garrick felt himself light-headed.

'What?' he said. 'What is this?'

Riley moved left and right, searching for a way past. 'Ain't you figured it out, Garrick? Didn't you feel that spirit inside you?'

Garrick knew that it must be true, for the wound was not healing. That spirit had stripped the wormhole right out of him.

'But . . .' he said. 'But I am the Forever Man.'

'Forever is over,' said Riley, and readied himself to commence his run.

For he had formulated a desperate plan in those last few seconds: even if Garrick lay down like a lamb, there was still no earthly way to extinguish the fire and save Chevie in time. He could not *snatch the book* unless he could use Garrick's old trick and magic the book away from where it was supposed to be.

But Garrick was not about to lie down and die, for, in fact, he was not mortally wounded and what he lacked in energy he made up for in hate.

'No!' he shouted, brandishing the blade. 'None shall tell me when my time is over. Perhaps I ain't immortal no more, but I am still Witchfinder here and I will burn who I please and none will dispute my orders. I would build a bonfire for every man, woman and child in Mandrake and they would trot into the flames on my orders. I am the master here and no parliament, king or god shall say any different.'

At those words, Riley despaired. Even now, with the blood pumping from his wound, Albert Garrick thwarted him.

I was wrong. Garrick cannot be killed. He is the Forever Man.

But then a small round hole appeared in Garrick's forehead and it was followed by the report of a musket. In the middle of the thoroughfare stood Jeronimo Woulfe with his rifled musket. He lowered the smoking gun and spoke a single word: 'Enough.'

Albert Garrick was dead.

★

Riley saw Garrick sink to his knees and he could not fathom what had happened or whether perhaps it was a ruse. At any rate he knew that it didn't matter much, as he could feel the heat of the bonfire on his own face and could not even imagine the agony Chevie was feeling with the flames at her knees.

I must go now and there are no two ways about it. Life for us both or death for the two.

Of course he was afraid, as his plan was at best foolhardy and at worst a dolt's errand, but Riley's fear was that he would not be able to end Chevie's suffering.

Garrick was now on his knees, slumped with his life's blood pouring out of him, useless to man or beast.

Perhaps not quite useless, thought Riley, and he began to run directly towards the pyre.

From behind he heard someone, probably Fairbrother Isles, shout, 'No, kid. It's too late. There's nothing you can do.'

The devil there isn't, thought Riley. *The wormhole is not yet open*.

His expression grim, he used Garrick's shoulder as a vaulting stool and launched himself through the flames directly towards Chevron Savano.

Chevie was going through changes, of this much she was certain. Something momentous was happening to her, but she wasn't quite sure what it was.

And now I will be burned alive before I will ever know.

Her mind refused to settle on this notion and slid off it whenever possible, distracting her with the fantastic array of events that were unfolding all around her. With her feline vision she saw everything more clearly than a human ever could.

She saw the great boar fall from the sky and the huge humanoid grapple with it, and she knew somehow that the giant man was not of this earth.

She saw the cannon fire decimate the battling pair and she grieved for them both briefly, for they were but flies in the wormhole's ointment, as she had been.

Then came Isles with his magnetic box, prodded into the square by Riley, and she knew it was him even by his walk and could not believe Garrick did not.

She saw Cryer, of course, as he had attempted to pour the molten metal down her throat, and she had seen him die, though she wished she had not.

Then there was the final showdown between Riley and Garrick, which had been coming for hundreds of years, and which was finished by another man's hand.

And yet, although Garrick was surely dead now, the flames rose about her ankles, and she tried to no avail to activate the Timekey by pressing it against her bonds, and the pain was so great that it seemed to fill the entire world, and yet . . .

And yet something had changed.

And now Chevie knew what.

She regained something of her senses just in time to see Riley fly towards her through the smoke and flames, his eyes fixed on hers, and she wanted to tell him:

Oh, Riley. There isn't any need.

Riley crashed into Chevie, knocking the breath from both of them, and the stake swayed but did not break, as Riley had expected.

They were face-to-face for one moment, eyes locked and feelings clear, and then Riley felt the seat of his pants go up in smoke and decided that he did not want to be broiled in Roundhead armour. So he kissed Chevie hard on the lips and with a press of his thumb activated the Timekey round her neck.

The pair was instantly surrounded by a swarm of orange sparks. As the sparks swirled around them, Riley and Chevie shrank but kept their proportions, until they were small enough to fit into the heart of the Timekey, which duly sucked them in, then dematerialized itself in a fizzle of orange bubbles.

When the fire burned itself out, there was nothing left but the charred stump of wood and some soot-coated chains. Of the so-called witch and her familiar there was no sign.

18

DOG DOG

As the sun rose over Mandrake the next day, the townsfolk drifted to the blackened pyre, skirting the massive crater where many had seen with their own eyes the titans do battle until Mandrake's cannon crews had valiantly sent them back to wherever they had come from. People stood in small clusters, whispering their disbelief and confusion at the events of the previous evening. Eventually the reasoning spread that the Witchfinder had in some mysterious fashion succeeded in his efforts to banish his nemesis and her familiar but the struggle had driven him dangerously mad, and that Jeronimo Woulfe's bullet had been a mercy for Albert Garrick and the entire town.

That same Jeronimo Woulfe found Fairbrother Isles away from public view. In his old haunt, the jail hut, he was seated on the floor with his broad back to the wall, holding his elbow tight to his side on account of the Primly boy's gunshot. He had a large hunting hound lying docilely in his lap while he bandaged the animal's head, and Woulfe, who had always been a dog man, as they say, was mightily impressed that a man would tend to his hound's wounds before his own.

'Good Master Isles,' said Woulfe. 'How fares the hound?'

Isles looked up from his work and there were tears in his eyes. 'He's a dog. Just a dog dog. He said he was going but I didn't get it till he woke up. Just a dog.'

This was puzzling talk, but the man had been wounded, so perhaps he was a little dazed.

'Yes. Just a dog. And are the injuries serious, do you think?'

Isles secured the bandage with an unusual glue-backed paper. 'No, a flesh wound is all. But the scalp is a bleeder, you know? And Pointer, he bleeds more than most anyway. He jabbed himself with a staple once. I swear it bled for three days.'

These statements were as perplexing as the first had been, and Woulfe suspected that perhaps Isles had taken a drop of strong spirits to calm his nerves.

'He took that bullet for me,' continued Isles. 'Put himself in harm's way, the stupid lug. Now he's one hundred per cent dog and I gotta live with that. Talk about selfish.' Then Isles hugged the animal close, and the dog nuzzled into him and licked his face, like a normal dog would. 'Good boy, Pointer,' said Isles. 'Everything's gonna be OK. We're partners forever, right?'

Woulfe was touched. 'And you, Master Isles? Would you accompany me to my house? My wife is a most excellent nurse.'

Isles remembered his own injury and winced. 'You think she'd come down here, Jerry? I'm a little weak at the knees right now. And, anyways, I imagine I'm gonna be locked up for quite a while after this night's work.'

Woulfe smiled at *Jerry*, a diminutive of Jeronimo, which his wife had begun to use in the privacy of their home.

'There will be no imprisonment for you, good Master Isles.

Not if I have any say in the matter. We all saw what the supposed Witchfinder brought down upon our town. Every man heard his threats. If you are to be locked away, then so am I.' Woulfe's face was as stony as the gargoyles he laboured on. 'And I am not about to be locked away, Master Isles.'

Isles nodded. 'Yeah, you got the stuff. I pity the constable who messes with you right now, Jerry.'

A thought struck Jeronimo Woulfe. 'As a matter of fact, Master Isles, Mandrake is in dire need of a constable at this time.'

Isles almost laughed.

Damn, he thought. *They want me to be sheriff.*

And it actually did come to pass that Fairbrother Isles became constable of Mandrake's Groan, mostly due to the fact that Jeronimo Woulfe insisted upon it, on the condition that Isles forsook alcohol from the day he was sworn in and that he train the militia in the weird methods of combat he'd used to render most of them useless. These matters were agreed upon and Fairbrother Isles duly became the first African law official in all England, a fact which met with some resistance from certain sections of the community. But these were the same people who passed their days feverishly questing for matters to object to and they were largely ignored or, as Isles himself put it in memory of the little-mourned constable: *de-cried*.

In fact, Isles's appointment proved most fortuitous for the town. He schooled the militia in the arts of close combat, the use of natural camouflage and siege warfare, thus creating a fighting unit the like of which had never been seen and would not be seen again for centuries to come. It was under Isles's command that Mandrake survived the second civil war, in spite of raids from Parliamentarians, Royalists and organized brigands, all of which amounted to the same thing essentially.

Almost always at Isles's side was his faithful hound, Pointer. When not at his master's flank, he was ranging ahead checking for hostiles, and people swore the hound had more intelligence about him than any other dog and perhaps some humans.

Both dog and master lived long lives. In the hound's case, far beyond the span of a normal dog, and when they died it was within a week of each other. When Pointer's extraordinary longevity eventually came to an end, it was said that Constable Isles died of a broken heart.

Fairbrother Isles's final request was that he be buried beside his beloved pet, but not in the same coffin – as he put it in his strange manner of speaking: *That would be plain weird, and also if Donnie gets the power of speech back in the afterlife then I'm gonna have to listen to his griping for all eternity*.

The request was honoured. And, in memory of the pair's service to East Anglia, the militia's name was changed to the Fair Brothers and a man who proved himself most worthy to lead was said to be *on point*.

The town stocks continued to be called the Fairbrothers, though, for that was how the constable himself had referred to them all his life – *as a reminder*.

SURFER CHICKS
ROLLING IN CALI

Riley woke up in the wormhole, which was unusual. Maybe 'unusual' is the wrong word, because nothing is usual about the wormhole when you are not part of the wormhole. No two trips are the same. No destination is guaranteed; there will definitely be changes to the schedule; and things are apt to arrive in a different condition from how they left the station. Sometimes in a different state altogether. Solids become liquids, liquids become gases and monkeys become men. If Charles Darwin had travelled through the inter-dimension once or twice, his theory of evolution might have upset the Creationists a lot more than it already did.

So while nothing could be fairly called unusual when everything was unusual, what Riley found noteworthy was that he seemed to be sitting on the stage of the Orient Theatre with Chevie perched beside him. He was clad in full show get-up, complete with top hat and cloak, while Chevie was wearing her FBI jumpsuit — and neither of them seemed to be on fire, which was a huge relief.

Riley knew he was in the wormhole and not, in fact, in

nineteenth-century London because Chevie had made a few mistakes in her vision of it. Still, it wasn't bad for someone who'd only been in the Orient a couple of times.

Chevie spotted him glancing around. 'OK, smart guy, where did I go wrong?'

Riley pointed at the balcony. 'There are only four rows up top, and we ain't got no golden cherubs as far as I remember it.'

Chevie sighed. 'There's no pleasing some people.'

'Not too shabby, though, Miss Chevron. Not too shabby.'

'Oh, it's Miss Chevron now, is it? Very formal all of a sudden.'

Riley blushed. 'I'm guessing you know why. Being as we're communicating through our minds and whatnot.'

Chevie blushed herself, which was a first. 'I do know, Riley, but there's no need to go all *Your Majesty* this and *Your Highness* that. Just plain Chevie will do. That's how surfer chicks roll in Cali.'

Surfer chicks rolling in Cali?

Probably FBI code, Riley reckoned.

'Fair enough. Chevie it is. How about *Miss* Chevie? A compromise?'

'So long as I don't have to call you Master Riley.'

'No. I ain't no *Master* nothing.'

'This is true. What you are is the Great Savano.'

Riley scratched his head. 'I dunno about that. I got a few tricks up my sleeve, I suppose.'

Chevie swung one knee on to the stage so she could face him. 'You came through fire for me, Riley. We kissed in the flames. A girl doesn't forget something like that.'

'We save each other, Chevie. And I'm still behind in those ledgers,' said Riley. 'It's four–two by my count.'

'Five–two,' said Chevie. 'Not that anyone's keeping score.'

Riley took a deep breath. 'I saw us, Miss Chevie. The last time we came through. I saw us together. I felt we could be happy. I don't care about your cat's eyes, if that's what you're worried about. And, after all we've been through, the two years between us don't seem so much.'

'No,' admitted Chevie. 'What's two years to a couple of time travellers? A drop in the ocean.'

'So we can be together, you think? A courting couple, as they say?'

Chevie frowned. A bead of sweat ran down her cheek and the Orient's balcony shimmered and disappeared.

'It's not that simple.'

'What could be simpler?' protested Riley. 'It's the simplest question of all. And the oldest.'

'Things are different now. I'm different. Look at me, creating bubbles in the wormhole just so we can talk. This isn't easy, you know, and I don't know how long I can hold it.'

'You've got what Garrick had,' Riley realized.

'Yeah, except more so. I was a blank slate the last time I went in, so the wormhole filled me with quantum foam. I understand the beast.'

'It is a great pity you didn't happen upon this knowledge earlier in proceedings,' said Riley. 'You could have saved us both some bother.'

'Yeah, tell me about it, but between nearly dying and

289

getting eye injections, and, oh, being burned alive, I didn't have too much time for navel-gazing.'

'Navel-gazing being introspection, I am guessing.'

Chevie nodded. 'Riley, I'm different now. There are things I can do.'

'What things?' demanded Riley. 'I should be told.'

'Important things,' said Chevie. 'I can send you to where you need to be. Where you've always wanted to be. And I can fix what I never could.'

'Those ain't answers,' protested Riley. 'Those are riddles.'

More of the theatre disappeared and Chevie began to shake. The stalls vanished one by one and were replaced by an ocean of grey fibres.

'I could take your hand and see where the wormhole sets us down,' said Chevie. 'I would love to do that, but after a while it would eat away at me that I could have saved someone, and I didn't.'

Riley knew then that Chevie was talking about her own father. How could he argue with that?

'The wormhole will try to take you, Riley, so be strong. Tell it where you want to go. I will shield you from the worst.'

Riley was barely listening. 'So the great Chevron–Savano romance is over? That's it, then?'

There were tears in Chevie's eyes as she cupped Riley's face.

'Not quite it,' she said, and kissed him for the second time.

Malibu. California. 2008

The old lady wore sunglasses.

Never took them off in public. A bouncer teased her about it once in a Route 66 casino.

Hey, grandma, what's with the shades? You a vampire?

The old lady did some kind of kung-jitsu hocus-pocus on the guy and his partner. Stretched both of them out on the craps table. And she didn't have to take the shades off to do it either. Nobody asked her about the glasses to her face after that, but they talked plenty behind her back.

I mean, the old gal's gotta be eighty, right? She took out Gary and Ted like they were two sacks of trash. And did you see all that silver? Goddamn rings and bangles. The old dame jingles and jangles like a sack of spoons.

That was how it had been for Chevie these past few decades, for the old woman was she. Six months in a place; a year, tops. Then she lost her temper, pushed someone's face in and had to move on. She stayed in California near the coast, keeping an eye on herself, her younger self, trying to figure out how to stop her dad's bike exploding without actually causing the explosion. Her first thought had been to stick a blade in the gas tank on the morning of the accident, but what if he didn't notice the leak and got gasoline on the pipes? Then she considered busting her dad's leg in a bar fight. A mercy break. But one of the problems with that was that she knew enough about the time stream to realize that it often shook out the kinks, and the Harley road crash would come back round in a couple of months. The other problem was that he was her dad. And breaking your dad's leg was never going to

291

be a walk in the park, especially not for the hobbled parent. Not to mention the fact that the wrong shard of bone could slice the wrong artery and she would have to watch her own father bleed out in front of her eyes.

The idea to hang around just to change a life had come from Garrick. Albert Garrick. The magician who was death.

He sure is dead now, Chevie often reassured herself.

Garrick had stayed around for practically two hundred and fifty years just to kill his apprentice. Whereas Chevie's plan had been to emerge at the beginning of the twenty-first century and save her dad, but she did not have Garrick's core of hatred to sustain her in the inter-dimension and was forced to exit one century early. Then she had survived two prisons, three armies, a marriage and a hippy commune just to save her dad.

If only I could have saved Mom. But how do you fix cancer?

Chevie never had any kids, though. Probably just as well. No fun having an immortal parent with cat's eyes, right? Something else she hadn't been able to fix.

No. Immortal was the wrong word.

She was growing older, but slowly. A gift from the wormhole. Chevie had ridden it out for as long as she could in there, but she was like a sugar cube in a vat of coffee and eventually she had to get out or stay forever. That had been over a hundred years ago.

Now the day had come . . . maybe. Chevie couldn't be a hundred per cent sure of the day, but she had it down to a month, and this was the month. And so every day of the month she had dragged her slowly ageing carcass up through the Malibu hills, along the road that snaked past the ten-million-dollar estates and further up past the old frontier houses and round the back of the Savano cottage, where she sat on a stump and wondered why she was so uncertain all of a sudden, when she had been dead set on her knife-in-the-gas-tank plan for the last couple of decades.

She sat and drank from a flask of iced coffee and wondered what the hell she was going to do. Would she really leave it until the last minute to act, until her pop threw his leg over the motorcycle?

Pop? I could pop him one, I suppose. Maybe my subconscious is giving me a solution.

Not much of one. Sure, she had taken out those two meat-heads in the casino but they were dough balls. Her dad was faster than a rattlesnake even with a few beers sloshing around in his stomach, which he would not have at this time of the morning.

Sugar in the gas tank?

No.

Cut the brake lines?

Hell, no.

Chevie wished Riley were sitting on the stump beside her. The boy magician would have had a plan. She had gone to find Riley in London before the First World War and found him alive and well, living over the Orient Theatre with a wife and daughter (in matching yellow dresses on that particular day) and working as a stage magician. Riley had looked so happy pulling daisies from behind his little girl's ears that Chevie could not make herself intrude.

That should have been me in that yellow dress. That could have been us.

But it wouldn't be right to drag Riley into her world again.

After all, she could feel the time tunnel calling her and she knew how volatile her connection to this world was. Only the silver that adorned her fingers and limbs kept her form stable, and even then she could feel herself fade if she happened to cross a ley line or if there was an electrical storm flashing on the horizon. More than once she had awoken to find orange sparks circling her like quantum vultures.

No. The kid deserves a life. The best thing you can do for him is to steer clear.

She still thought about Riley in the present tense. Maybe she would see him again. The classifications *past* and *future* were not as concrete to her now as they had been once.

I have never loved anyone else, she realized, and then, with more than a dash of self-pity: *I have never been loved by anyone else.*

She felt a sudden jealousy again towards that young woman in the yellow dress.

'You dead, old lady?' said a voice.

Chevie bristled. She was an old lady, and older than she looked, but somehow she had managed to hold on to her rebellious teenage attitude.

'Not yet, I ain't,' she said, turning on the tree stump to find a young girl studying her from behind a hacked fringe.

Hacked, thought Chevie, *because I cut my own hair.*

It took a second for her to realize what was going on.

I am being glared at by myself. I am meeting a younger me. This is exactly what all those time-travel movies warned me never to do.

She did not need to ask what Little Chevie was doing here. This had been her favourite spot to sit and watch her dad work on his motorcycle.

'That's my stump,' said the girl, pointing at it with a hunting knife that seemed like a battle sword in her ten-year-old hand.

'You're not supposed to have that knife.'

Little Chevie responded quick as a flash. 'You're not supposed to sit on my stump, grandma. My name's on it. I carved it there with this knife I'm not supposed to have.'

At that moment, for the first time in her long life, Chevie understood that maybe it was a little annoying to try to hold a conversation with a smart alec.

'This stump is nature, kid. And you can't own nature. That's what we believe, right?'

'We?' said Little Chevie. 'What do you mean *we*?'

'Shawnee,' said Chevie. 'We. The tribe.'

Little Chevie twirled the knife in a reckless fashion, which made Old Chevie wonder how she had made it to adulthood with all her fingers attached to her hands.

'You're tribe?' Little Chevie said doubtfully. 'You don't look tribe.'

It was a fair comment. The silver had lightened Chevie's skin a few shades. She was not exactly Garrick pale, but in a couple of decades she would be.

'Yeah, well, I'm tribe all right. Take my word for it.'

Little Chevie raised the eyebrow of scorn and Old Chevie

couldn't blame her. Some old lady turns up on her stump trying to claim some kind of kinship. What kid wouldn't be suspicious?

She had to earn this young brave's trust and, as Little Chevie folded her arms across her skinny chest, time-travelling Old Chevie thought she saw a way in.

'I can prove it,' she said. 'That I am who I say I am.'

Little Chevie's other eyebrow shot up. 'Yeah? Grown-ups prove stuff every day. Lies mostly.'

Chevie remembered how anti-establishment she had been at ten years old, a common trait among Native Americans, and wondered how she had ever come to work for the federal government.

Old Chevie pointed at the fake tattoo drawn in Sharpie on Little Chevie's biceps.

'I like your mark,' she said.

'Don't talk about my mark,' snapped the kid. 'You don't know anything about it.'

'I know it's a chevron and you are named for it,' said Old Chevie. 'I know your father bears the same mark and so have all the Savano men back to the Shawnee wars, where your ancestor William Savano fought the Long Knives with Tecumseh at Moraviantown. For every officer he killed in battle, William daubed a chevron on his arm in blood, as this was the sergeant's symbol. He was a fearsome warrior. So, in memory of William, the Savanos have worn the symbol. And you intend to honour William, just as they did.'

Little Chevie must have been amazed to hear her own patter

recited verbatim back to her, but she didn't show it. Instead her scowl softened ever so slightly.

'How do you know this, grandma?'

Chevie stretched the neck of her T-shirt, baring her shoulder to reveal the same mark ingrained in her skin.

'That's how I know.'

Little Chevie was genuinely impressed now and prodded the mark with her forefinger. 'Wow. It's right in there. How did that happen? A burn or something?'

Chevie covered her mark. 'No. It's a part of me, of who I am. I am the spirit warrior of the Savanos.'

She almost winced, so outrageous was this line of bull, but Little Chevie was going for it.

'I didn't know we had a spirit warrior. What is a spirit warrior?'

Chevie nearly felt bad about manipulating a child, but the stakes were high and the little version of her was tough and would get over it.

'Well, a smart kid like you will have heard of spirit animals?'

'Yeah, I've heard of those.'

'And you've always felt close to cats, right?'

'How do you know that?'

Chevie realized that the truth about how she knew that was way weirder than the lie she was about to spin.

I know that because I remember our little cat, Tinder, and how much we loved him, you and I.

'I know that because the spirit warriors are part animal,'

said Old Chevie, and with that she pulled off her sunglasses to reveal the tawny cat's eyes beneath.

If she was expecting Little Chevie to be shocked or frightened, then she was disappointed.

'Wow,' the kid said again. 'That is cool. Cat's eyes. Can I touch them?'

'No, you can't touch them. What kind of question is that?'

'Yeah, well, maybe I can't touch them because they're really contact lenses.'

Chevie sighed. This was exhausting. 'OK, kid. Come as close as you like, but zero touching, got it?'

Little Chevie nodded, but dialled up her scowl again, to show how unsatisfied she was with this compromise.

And so they drew close, the two Chevies, separated by mere inches and yet centuries, gazing deep into each other's eyes. Old Chevie could have cried at the innocence and hope she saw in her younger self. So much pain had already been endured and there was so much more to go.

But not if I can help it.

'We need to talk, kid,' she said.

'Oh my God, those eyes are real,' blurted Little Chevie. 'You've come to recruit me, that's it, isn't it? I'm gonna be a spirit warrior. Cool.'

Chevie held the child's stare. 'Not so fast, kid. You gotta prove yourself first.'

'Yeah, and how do I prove myself to an old grandma like you? Climb a tree? Open a soda can?'

Old Chevie was feeling less guilty by the second about the whole spirit-warrior thing.

'You prove it by saving your father. He's in deadly danger.'

Chevie saw something glint in the corner of her cat's eye and realized Little Chevie had raised her knife.

'Danger from who? You, grandma?'

'No, not me, kid. Haven't you been paying attention? I bear the mark. I am tribe.'

The knife was slowly lowered. 'Yeah, OK. We're on the same side, right?'

Chevie blinked and moved a few inches back from the kid's intense stare.

'That's right. I see what is to come with my cat's eyes. And I see your father on his motorcycle this afternoon in a terrible accident.'

'I hate that motorcycle!' said Little Chevie vehemently.

Old Chevie was surprised to remember that this was true. She had somehow made the motorcycle a symbol of her dad's sense of freedom, but now she recalled that she had always feared the bike would take him away from her, leaving her alone entirely.

'I am gonna stick this knife into his tank,' vowed Little Chevie. And the older version did not doubt that this plucky kid would find the strength to do it.

Hey, she thought. *I like myself.*

'No!' she said hurriedly. 'Too obvious. You gotta be under the radar. Something stealthy.'

'Why don't you do it? Give Dad the whole weird-eyes thing?'

This was a fair question.

'This is a test, kid. I'm giving you a task, like Hercules or one of those guys. You do this and you're in the spirit warriors.'

Little Chevie tapped the blade's tip with her index finger. 'Stealthy, huh?'

'Yeah. You think you can manage that?'

Little Chevie thought some more. 'I could tell Dad about this dream I've been having.'

'Which dream is that?'

The blade's reflection twinkled in Chevie's eyes, or maybe the twinkle was all her own. 'The one where my mom who has passed to the spirit world comes to me and warns me about that motorcycle. Every night she comes and says if he doesn't sell the bike then there will be a tragic accident.'

'And he'll be killed?'

Little Chevie grinned a crafty grin. 'No, *he* won't be killed. *I* will.'

The older version returned a similar grin. 'You, my young friend, were born to be a spirit warrior.'

'Really? You're not just blowing smoke?'

Chevie felt herself relax. This kid would manipulate her dad until he had no idea which way was up. Using a vision of his departed wife to save his daughter? That was some kind of demented genius.

'No, kid. No smoke signals of any kind.'

Little Chevie frowned. 'Was that a Native American joke?'

'No. I was trying to bond. Spirit-warrior stuff.'

'Oh, OK.'

'You better get inside. Dad . . . your dad . . . will be making his run soon and you can't let that happen.'

Little Chevie tutted, which was not a sound made very often in real life. And the delicate noise made Old Chevie feel a little sorry for her father.

He has no idea.

'That will not be happening,' said Little Chevie. 'Not today, or any other day for that matter. Take my word for it, grandma. That motorcycle is history.'

Chevie believed it. She had been quite some piece of work in her day.

I still am, she thought, remembering the two bouncers she had KO'd the week before.

A voice floated through the trees. 'Chevron? Hey, baby. I'm gonna take a run down for some groceries. Hold the fort, OK?'

Old Chevie peered through the trees and saw her own dear daddy squinting into the forest. Her breath caught in her throat and she felt her eyes well up.

'I better go,' said Little Chevie, then made a sad face. 'How do I look?'

'Haunted,' said the older version. 'Haunted and terrified.'

'Perfect,' said the kid, and then she was off and running, dodging round the oak trunks.

Chevie watched the kid and saw she had worked herself into semi-hysteria by the time she reached the cottage, and she knew in her heart that her father was safe.

What will the consequences of that be? If Dad lives, I never go to London, never meet Riley.

But she didn't know, and nobody did. Charles Smart had never managed to unravel the wormhole; if he couldn't do it, then what hope was there for lesser brains?

It's all butterfly effects and paradoxes with these guys, she thought. *All shooting in the dark.*

She had met Riley and nothing could change that. She had lived a long and most eventful life.

And I have scars and aches to prove it.

Chevie stayed where she was on the stump for another couple of hours, mostly to make sure her dad didn't set so much as a finger on the motorcycle's throttle, but also to give her aching muscles time to recover from the climb up here.

I am tired, she realized. *So tired of fighting the tunnel.*

It followed her everywhere, the magic, never more than a layer of quicksilver away, singing its siren song to her, and now as her father stayed inside the cottage she felt the lure of this timeline slip away from her.

What would happen? she wondered. *If I just let go. If I let the sparks take me.*

No sooner was the question in her mind than Chevron Savano began stripping off the eleven pounds of silver that adorned her person. Off came the Santa Monica hippy bracelets and the Arabic name chain she had bought in a Moroccan medina and the etched earrings from Kenya and the Scottish circlet and the Kundan toe rings and the five Claddagh rings. And even the silver filling that she had worked loose with her tongue over the years was dislodged with a toothpick and spat into the scrub.

Chevie felt instantly lighter, and not just physically.

I have done all I needed to do. More than most will ever do. It's time to go.

She did not know where she wanted to go, or, more specifically, when.

Surprise me, she beamed out to her old friend the wormhole, and though she had evaded its folds and meanders for almost a hundred years she could remember its embrace as though it had been this morning, before her first espresso of the day.

Chevie stayed where she was until dusk, snacking on cashew nuts from a pouch she carried everywhere. She was extremely gratified to see a pick-up truck pull up to the front of the cottage around seven and load up her father's beloved motorcycle.

Hah! I was quite an operator. Riley would be proud.

She half expected something earth-shattering to happen then. Some kind of quantum rip or brain detonation, but there was nothing. Not a single wrinkle in time. She still remembered Riley and Garrick and all they had been through.

'Yep,' she said softly. 'Time to go.'

Down she trudged, taking care on the uneven terrain. A pity to snap a bone after all this time. A few centuries of fractured femur would be zero fun whatsoever.

Don't even think about it, she warned herself. *Don't think about anything.*

Because she knew now, with the quantum foam flowing through her neural pathways, that the wormhole was an emotional construct just as much as a physical one. It would heed her wishes, even her subconscious ones, and take her where it thought she wanted to go.

Jeez, how's an old lady supposed to catch a break?

And so Chevie tried to clear her mind as she had learned to do all those years ago on the commune. She tried to simply *be*.

The quantum tunnel came for her as she navigated the stepped path down to the Pacific Coast Highway. The orange sparks cycloned above her head, then settled on her like a fairy cloak, and though Chevie tried to think of nothing, nothing at all, a single word drifted behind her eyes just as she disappeared into the ether.

And the word was:

Riley . . .

Epilogue

THE INTER-DIMENSION

Chevie kissed Riley and he felt himself dissolve.

No! he thought. *I will not accept this.*

'Chevie!' Riley called, and again: 'Chevie!'

But the second shout was infected by a spiral of orange sparks that followed the curl of the sound wave, spiralling into the collapsing version of the Orient Theatre.

Riley felt like Old Testament Jonah as the mouth of the whale shut him off from all he knew and loved. Though he had not loved the wormhole or the seventeenth century, he had at least loved being with his dearest Chevron Savano, whom he now felt he would never see again. The only girl he had ever kissed and it had made his heart glow as brightly as the Trinity Buoy Wharf lighthouse.

To never see Chevie again seemed intolerable after all he had endured.

Never? Does that word hold any meaning in my topsy-turvy life?

A life that could very well be about to end.

Nothing was certain in the wormhole. Even though Riley had only a cursory knowledge of the science at work here, relatively speaking he knew almost as much as any being who would ever live, apart from Chevie herself. Riley knew that he could not be certain of anything from this moment on.

Welcome, the foam whispered to Riley as it closed round his atoms, phase-shifting as he watched. *Welcome home*.

Riley fought it as he would the effect of Garrick's ether-soaked rags.

No. This ain't my home. I don't belong here.

The wormhole wanted him, it was true, but it was as a cat wants a mouse to toy with. It would bat him between its quantum paws for aeons before ejecting him into the world, utterly changed and out of his time.

No, thought Riley. *It don't have to be that way. All I need to do is hold fast to myself and Chevie will put me where I need to be.*

Riley punched at the cloying foam with fists that were barely more than imaginary.

Release me, you darn time stream. I ain't ready to be absorbed.

But the quantum tunnel would not relinquish him just yet as it had spare parts it wished to give him. A set of wasp wings that would sprout nicely on his back, and the tail of a lizard, which would graft just dandy on to his rear end.

Riley, though, fought all the tunnel's advances, thinking: *I am Riley. I am Riley, I am. Human boy and that is the size of it and the whole of me.*

He thrashed mentally and cleared a space to his own time – and not only that but to his own moment, to the one golden synchronicity when all possibilities coalesced like the irregular wooden wedges of a jigsaw.

I see a light, so I do, thought the last neurons of Riley's conscious mind. He did not see a light in reality, as he could not *see* anything. His senses were more remembered than experienced, and even then the memory was fading as the wormhole coaxed his elemental side to the surface, drawing it up like a hungry trout to the bait, tempting him back to a primordial state.

But Riley was made of sterner stuff and he turned his mind from the tunnel and concentrated on the *light*, which he was determined to perceive and strive towards.

The wormhole offered him eternal peace and answers to all the questions of the universe. It wiped his brow and draped him with love.

No, thought Riley. *You ain't having me. My brother is not murdered and yet lives.*

Tom lives, thought Riley, bearing down on it and making the words his mantra. *Tom lives.*

As he projected those words, it seemed to him that the entirety of his surroundings, which he could never have described, sighed a little and whispered, *Very well, then, human child. Tom lives. So be it.*

The light drew closer and grew till it filled what was once again his vision, and Riley thought he could see faces beyond. Rows and rows of upturned faces, their mouths round with wonder as something occurred, something to slacken their jaws and bug their eyes.

Something magical, thought Riley. *And what is magical if not myself?*

Orient Theatre. Holborn. London. 1899

Truth be told, the punters and puntresses crammed like so many dollied-up sardines into the circle and stalls of the Orient Theatre were not expecting much of a show for a single penny. What could a penny buy these days? A couple of pigeons pulled from a hat mayhap, or a flash-bang or two? Not much more surely. Nothing of any quality. Especially since it was common knowledge that a mere strip of a lad was wearing the cloak. The Great Savano, he might call himself and good luck to him, but he was a boy making his way and no doubt there would be stumbling and fumbling along the path. Speaking of paths, it was the footpath outside that bore the advertisement.

COME ONE, COME ALL, AND WITNESS

THE SPECTACULAR DEBUT OF

THE GREAT SAVANO.

RAISED BY THE NOBLE AMERICAN INDIANS.

PRIVY TO ALL THEIR MAGICKS.

EVERY NIGHT FOR THIS WEEK ONLY.

EIGHT O'CLOCK SHARP.

Was a tomahawk too much to hope for? For a single penny, probably yes.

The boy was late. *Eight o'clock sharp*, the chalk advertisement had promised, and was it not now fifteen minutes past the hour? Unrest was growing. Bustles were rustled and feet stamped, and growing nervous in the front row was young Bob Winkle, Riley's chief bottle-washer, boot-polisher and investigator. It was he who had picked up the Ginger Tom trail in Newgate and was now gloomily aware that he had been fed a sack of lies.

And me a clever boots. And me a survivor of the rookery. It's shame I have brought on the Winkle name.

He knew that the Newgate tip had been bogus because one of his rookery snouts had come in with the real gin not an hour after Riley had set his course for Newgate.

That weren't no Ginger Tom in the Gate, Bob thought. *For I have that geezer beside me now.*

His snout had brought not only the news but the gent himself into the bargain, who had been nervous as a kitten at the thought of meeting his long-lost kin. And you only had to take one look at this gent's mush to see that he and Riley shared a mother.

Spitting image. Two bottles on a shelf.

And wasn't it a small world, as they say, for Tom Riley had been working not a stone's throw away as a stoker in Saint Pancras. He'd been a doddle to find once the railway track had been followed.

Sobbed like a baby, the man did, when he got the news. Fell to his actual knees in the rail yard. In fact, Bob was getting a little embarrassed by the continuing snuffle.

But I loves me little brothers too, right enough, he reasoned. *So perhaps Tom Riley is entitled.*

Now, though, wasn't Riley missing? And there were rumours of some commotion in Newgate this very morning. Something about magic and a poleaxed attorney, and Bob had a cramp in his gut from fretting over his boss and pal.

Come back to us, Riley. Come back.

★

Then something truly extraordinary happened, something the reports of which would spread across the country like wildfire until the number who claimed to have seen it would swell to the thousands, in spite of the fact that the cramped theatre could barely accommodate two hundred souls. Though the accounts were exaggerated, for they could not realistically be so, they would ensure that the Great Savano's reputation was solidly stamped in the register of great stage illusionists.

A hole opened in the air, ridged with a milky ring of sparks, and it was immediately obvious to the Orient's patrons that this was more than a mere workaday hole from which such things as sewage or bilge would spill. They witnessed the stars that lived inside this hole, and as it grew to the dimensions of a whale's maw it was clear that other things lived there too. Things that were multi-tentacled and vari-tusked flashed across the space within, and many gave thanks that they did not make it their business to investigate without. A noise emanated from this otherworldly aperture, which some veterans would later describe as the sound of a battlefield's entire complement of cannons, and others would swear sounded exactly like the drone of countless foghorns during a pea-souper.

Panic would surely have ensued had not a figure appeared in the hole and transfixed the audience with its radiance. Humanoid in shape but composed entirely of swarming orange sparks, as though a man were being held aloft by golden bees.

Bob was the first to twig.

Nah, he thought. *We ain't got the budget*.

But his instincts proved correct and the figure solidified.

'It's a man!' shouted a drunken swell a bit off his turf. 'It's the Great Savano!'

If this was the Great Savano, then he was indeed *great* and, as the figure took on more of a real aspect, it was clear that he wore the high-collared cape of a magician and his face, though young, burned bright with intelligence and triumph.

'Savano!' said another, and commenced a-clapping. 'Savano!'

The assembly took up the chant and the clap, some with trepidation, but this changed to genuine rapture when the illusionist closed the terrifying hole with a snatch of his fist, hung for a moment in the air, then dropped neatly into the glow of the footlights. Orange sparks trailed him down and gathered at his feet as though awaiting the illusionist's command.

In the audience Bob was on his feet with the rest of them.

Go on, boss! he thought. *Tie a ribbon on it!*

And Riley did, bowing low and sweeping the folds of his cape before him like the wings of a great black swan, dispelling the last of the quantum sparks.

'The Great Savano,' he said, and his voice carried to the rafters in spite of the tumult.

It seemed as though the applause would never end, and some claimed to have heard it clear across the river.

Though he had travelled through the centuries, to Riley the journey had seemed almost instantaneous and, though he was glad to be home and grateful to be fully human, as far as he could tell, his joy would not have extended to theatrical flourishes had it not been for three persons his keen eyes spotted among the audience members.

There, beside faithful Bob, a red-headed man sporting his own serious brow and high cheekbones.

Tom! he thought – no, he *knew*. This time there was no doubt and his senses, amplified by the wormhole (a gift that would serve him well throughout his long career), heard his brother's voice cry, 'Redmond! Redmond! Is it you, brother?'

Redmond, thought Riley, and the name fitted him more snugly than a baker's apron; he felt the rightness of it and remembered how his mother had told him he would carry the name of her Wexford clan as his own Christian name.

Redmond Riley, he thought, and felt himself whole at last.

There was another who Riley saw, standing in the wings and seeming as surprised to be there herself as she was to see him. It was his own dear Chevie, dressed out of character in a sunflower-yellow dress, woven bonnet, with silver on her neck and wrists, her clear brown eyes returned to her. Somewhere in his bones, which were still tingling with quantum magic, Riley knew that this day would be the first of many happy ones, and so he dropped to the boards he would tread so often over the years, bowed low, cast his glance sideways to his Native American princess and said:

'The Great Savano at your service.'